Isak Dinesen Reading Søren Kierkegaard
On Christianity, Seduction, Gender, and Repetition

LEGENDA

LEGENDA is the Modern Humanities Research Association's book imprint for new research in the Humanities. Founded in 1995 by Malcolm Bowie and others within the University of Oxford, Legenda has always been a collaborative publishing enterprise, directly governed by scholars. The Modern Humanities Research Association (MHRA) joined this collaboration in 1998, became half-owner in 2004, in partnership with Maney Publishing and then Routledge, and has since 2016 been sole owner. Titles range from medieval texts to contemporary cinema and form a widely comparative view of the modern humanities, including works on Arabic, Catalan, English, French, German, Greek, Italian, Portuguese, Russian, Spanish, and Yiddish literature. Editorial boards and committees of more than 60 leading academic specialists work in collaboration with bodies such as the Society for French Studies, the British Comparative Literature Association and the Association of Hispanists of Great Britain & Ireland.

The MHRA encourages and promotes advanced study and research in the field of the modern humanities, especially modern European languages and literature, including English, and also cinema. It aims to break down the barriers between scholars working in different disciplines and to maintain the unity of humanistic scholarship. The Association fulfils this purpose through the publication of journals, bibliographies, monographs, critical editions, and the MHRA Style Guide, and by making grants in support of research. Membership is open to all who work in the Humanities, whether independent or in a University post, and the participation of younger colleagues entering the field is especially welcomed.

ALSO PUBLISHED BY THE ASSOCIATION

Critical Texts
Tudor and Stuart Translations • *New Translations* • *European Translations*
MHRA Library of Medieval Welsh Literature

MHRA Bibliographies
Publications of the Modern Humanities Research Association

The Annual Bibliography of English Language & Literature
Austrian Studies
Modern Language Review
Portuguese Studies
The Slavonic and East European Review
Working Papers in the Humanities
The Yearbook of English Studies

www.mhra.org.uk
www.legendabooks.com

GERMANIC LITERATURES

Germanic Literatures includes monographs and essay collections on literature originally written not only in German, but also in Dutch and the Scandinavian languages. Within the German-speaking area, it seeks also to publish studies of other national literatures such as those of Austria and Switzerland. The chronological scope of the series extends from the early Middle Ages down to the present day.

APPEARING IN THIS SERIES

Managing Editor
Dr Graham Nelson, 41 Wellington Square, Oxford OX1 2JF, UK
www.legendabooks.com

Isak Dinesen Reading
Søren Kierkegaard

On Christianity, Seduction, Gender, and Repetition

❖

MADS BUNCH

l

LEGENDA

Germanic Literatures 13
Modern Humanities Research Association
2017

Published by Legenda
an imprint of the Modern Humanities Research Association
Salisbury House, Station Road, Cambridge CB1 2LA

ISBN 978-1-781884-93-5

First published 2017

Copy-Editor: Dr Birgit Mikus

CONTENTS

❖

To B.

ACKNOWLEDGEMENTS

❖

A number of people have been very helpful and supportive throughout the eight years it has taken me to complete this work. I would like to give a very special thanks to my mentor and friend Poul Behrendt for his tireless feedback over the years on the work presented in this book. Also for everything I have learned from him during many profound and inspiring conversations the past decade. Thanks also goes to Ivan Ž. Sørensen for kindly sharing his material about Dinesen and Kierkegaard in the early stage of this project. Thanks also to Marianne Wirenfeldt Asmussen for giving me access to the Karen Blixen (Isak Dinesen) Archive at The Royal Library in Copenhagen, to Marianne Juhl for valuable information about the letters concerning Kierkegaard in the new 2013 edition of Dinesen's letters (Blixen 2013), to Bruno Svindborg at Håndskriftssamlingen at The Royal Library and to Anne-Sofie Tiedeman Dal and Catherine Lefebvre at Rungstedlund Museet for giving me access to Karen Blixen's library and for their general interest and support. Thanks also goes to Jakob Stougaard-Nielsen for valuable feedback on the book proposal and a very special thanks to John E. Andersen, Department Head in the Department of Nordic Studies and Linguistics, University of Copenhagen for his excellent support in the final process of finishing this book. I am delighted and grateful that *Scandinavica* and Norvik Press, *Scandinavian Studies* and University of Illinois Press, and *European Journal of Scandinavian Studies* and De Gruyter have given me permission to reuse material from the articles I have published in these journals. I would also like to express my gratitude to Dr Graham Nelson, Professor Ritchie Robertson and Dr Birgit Mikus at Legenda for an excellent feedback and editing process. Thanks also to Lars Gundersen for graphic work done on the cover photo. As a non-native speaker writing in English, I am grateful to Dr Mark Mussari for his proofreading and editing help over the years and his translations of the many Danish quotes in this particular book. I would also like to thank my students at the University of British Columbia (2006–11) and at the University of Copenhagen for valuable and inspiring discussions on Dinesen and Kierkegaard over the years. Finally, I would also like to give a special thanks to my parents Henning V. Jensen and Vibeke Bunch, and my sister Lise Bunch, who have all been very supportive over the years.

M.B., Copenhagen, January 2017

TEXTUAL NOTES

❖

English and Danish Editions

Dinesen wrote all of her works following *Seven Gothic Tales* (1934) in English except *Gengældelsens Veje* (1944) (*The Angelic Avengers*) (1946/1947) and then translated and reworked the English versions into Danish herself. It is extraordinary that a writer writes in her non-native language and then translates and reworks her non-native writing into her own native language. Dinesen initially picked the Danish author Valdemar Rørdam to translate *Seven Gothic Tales* into Danish but his translations of 'The Roads Round Pisa' and 'The Old Chevalier' were not approved by Dinesen (Blixen 1996a: 142–43). Instead she undertook the task herself: 'I Vinter oversætter jeg ganske stille min Bog til dansk, det maa gøres af mig selv' [This winter I will quietly translate my book into Danish, it must be done by me][1] as she writes in a letter dated 23 August 1934 (Blixen 1996a: 165). *Syv fantastiske Fortællinger* (1935) thus seems to be the first example of self-translation of world literature included in the Western canon from a literary non-native language publication (English) to a native language (Danish).[2] Thus, I will use the English originals to quote from and only juxtapose passages from the Danish editions when the connections to Kierkegaard's works have been enhanced or made clearer, which we do find a couple of examples of. (I will provide notes with references to the Danish translations after each English quotation if not followed by a Danish quotation in the running text.) The works of fiction written before *Seven Gothic Tales* were, however, all written in Danish. Thus, I will quote the original Danish version of *Sandhedens Hævn* (1926) (*The Revenge of Truth*) (1986) in Danish followed by the English translation.

Kierkegaard's works, which — on the contrary — were originally written in Danish, will be quoted in Danish followed by the English translation. I have used the latest edition of Søren Kierkegaard's collected works *Søren Kierkegaards Skrifter* (1997–2013) edited by Niels Jørgen Cappelørn and others. The page numbers I am referring to in the running texts are from the printed volumes but the quotes can easily be found in the online edition <www.sks.dk> [accessed 29 August 2016] using the search field. The English translations of Kierkegaard's works are all from the Princeton series *Kierkegaard's Writings*, Series Editors: Howard V. Hong and Edna H. Hong. The page numbers refer to the revised online editions published 21 April 2013, except for *Two Ages* and *The Point of View*, which are the 2009 editions.

Translations

It has been necessary to make new translations of a substantial number of Danish quotes into English since most of Dinesen's letters and some of Kierkegaard's late journal entries have not yet been translated. The same applies to Georg Brandes's (1842–1926) Kierkegaard biography from 1877 *Søren Kierkegaard. En kritisk Fremstilling i Grundrids* [Søren Kierkegaard. A Critical Study] and most of Danish philosopher Harald Høffding's (1843–1931) writings. Unless otherwise stated in the notes, Dr Mark Mussari has kindly provided the major part of the translations of the Danish quotes into English and Dr Gísli Mágnusson has been in charge of the translations of the German quotes into English.

The Author Names: Isak Dinesen and Karen Blixen

In the article 'Dobbelteksistensen. Firmaet Dinesen & Blixen i det 21. århundrede' [The Double Existence. The Firm Dinesen & Blixen in the Twenty-first Century] Danish Dinesen-scholar Poul Behrendt thoroughly treats the use of the two author names 'Isak Dinesen' and 'Karen Blixen' in connection to the Danish and English editions (Behrendt 2014). In the following I will use the information from this article to sum up the key points with regard to the long and complex story of pseudonymity and self-translation in Dinesen's authorship.

The author name 'Isak Dinesen' was used for both the English and the Danish edition of *Seven Gothic Tales* (1934) / *Syv fantastiske Fortællinger* (1935). In Dinesen's second book, the autobiographical novel *Den afrikanske Farm* (1937), Dinesen, however, chose the name 'Karen Blixen' instead of 'Isak Dinesen', since she in this particular work was not writing fiction, but was instead dealing with real people and real events (Blixen 1996a: 127). The autobiographical book titled *Out of Africa* in English came out the same year in the UK (with the correct author name 'Karen Blixen' on the cover) and the year after in the US (1938) but in the US, contrary to the author's wish, under the author name 'Isak Dinesen'. This meant that the idea of switching between the two author names and use 'Isak Dinesen' for fiction writing and 'Karen Blixen' for autobiographical writing was lost in the American editions. The publisher in the US did not find it to be a good marketing idea to change the name of their bestselling author from 'Isak Dinesen' to 'Karen Blixen' and insisted that the name was not changed and Dinesen had to give in.

After the publication of *Syv fantastiske Fortællinger* at C. A. Reitzels Forlag in 1935, Dinesen had decided to move to Gyldendal and let them publish *Den afrikanske Farm*. Shortly after the move, Gyldendal purchased all the publishing rights to Dinesen's works from C. A. Reitzel. Before the publication of *Vinter-Eventyr* (*Winter's Tales*) (1942) Gyldendal suggested that Dinesen's future works in Denmark should be published under the author name 'Karen Blixen', which was a condition Dinesen, much against her own will, had to accept. *Vinter-Eventyr* became the first example of Dinesen's fiction writing in Denmark published under the author name 'Karen Blixen' but Gyldendal also insisted that all future reprints of *Syv fantastiske Fortællinger* should bear the author name 'Karen Blixen'; first example being the fourth edition of *Syv fantastiske Fortællinger* published in 1943 by Gyldendal.

From now on the author name 'Isak Dinesen' was forever lost in Denmark.[3] In the US, the opposite, however, became her fate: 'Isak Dinesen' became the author name for all of her works and nobody knew who 'Karen Blixen' was up until the 1980s when the Academy Award winning film *Out of Africa* (1985) came out following the publication of Judith Thurman's popular biography in 1982. Thurman's title reads *Isak Dinesen. The Life of a Storyteller* (1982) but she is using the name Karen Blixen throughout the biography, in order to underline that it is in fact a woman with a very special life story hiding behind the male pen name. In the 2001 Penguin Classics paperback editions containing a line-up of selected works by Dinesen 'Karen Blixen' has been added, so the cover reads: Isak Dinesen (Karen Blixen). The author 'Isak Dinesen' has, however, been the preferred author name for the scholarly work done on Dinesen in the English-speaking world, both in the UK and in the US, with only a few exceptions.[4] This also applies to the latest scholarly monograph done in English that deals with Dinesen's fiction works *Understanding Isak Dinesen* (2002) by Susan C. Brantly.

Choosing Isak Dinesen

The author name 'Isak Dinesen' is, however, much more than just a pen name. For Dinesen it was also a liberating mask: 'Jeg vil være fri i min ytringsform — jeg, dvs. Isak Dinesen — vil være fri i sin ytringsform' (quoted in Behrendt 2014: 27) [I want my form of expression to be free — I, that is to say, Isak Dinesen — want to be free in the way I express myself][5] and one of the main elements embedded in this position was irony as Behrendt correctly points out: 'Der er således til Isak Dinesens navn og fortællekunst knyttet en alt gennemtrængende ironi' (27) [Thus, a pervasive and all-encompassing irony is connected to the name and the narrative art of Isak Dinesen].[6] This means that the author name Isak Dinesen must be regarded as an emblem of a particular voice, or a worldview, that includes irony, the right to poke fun at everything, truth seeking, and complete artistic freedom both thematically and style wise, which Dinesen also outlines in a couple of crucial letters from Africa in 1926 (see Chapter 2). It is the combination of 'Isak Dinesen' as Dinesen's preferred author name when writing fiction and the irony and freedom this position entails, also in relation to Kierkegaard, that have led me to choose the author name Isak Dinesen over Karen Blixen in this book. To that we can add that it holds significance that 'Isak Dinesen' has been, and still is, the established author name in the English-speaking world, as she herself wanted it. Thus, I have decided to consistently use the name Dinesen in this book, also when I am referring to the biographical Karen Blixen (and her non-fiction writing: the letters and essays). This, I do in order not to confuse things further, even though I am aware that it would have been a more precise choice to switch between the two names.

Notes

1. Author's translation.
2. Other examples of self-translating authors, translating works they have written in their non-native language into their native language, are Samuel Beckett, who started translating his works written in French back into English in the late 1940s, and Vladimir Nabokov, who started translating his works written in English into Russian in the 1950s. Neither Beckett nor Nabokov, or other bilingual authors such as Joseph Conrad and Milan Kundera, however, moved back to their native country and kept writing in their non-native language as Dinesen did.

3. Only exception being the tale 'Spøgelseshestene' ('The Ghost Horses') that came out in Denmark in 1955 under the author name 'Isak Dinesen'.
4. For example: Marianne T. Stecher, *The Creative Dialectic in Karen Blixen's Essays* (Copenhagen: Museum Tusculanum Press, 2014).
5. Author's translation.
6. Author's translation.

INTRODUCTION

❖

Over the past decade it has become more and more clear from my work with Isak Dinesen's tales in relation to Søren Kierkegaard (Bunch 2012, Bunch 2013a, Bunch 2013b and Bunch 2014) that one of Dinesen's major ways of becoming a part of world literature was to deliberately deal with important works from it in her tales, for the most part in a subversive way. In her tales we find an unusually high, almost excessive, number of allusions to world literature, Shakespeare above all, the Bible and Greek mythology, and in her Danish versions also numerous allusions to Danish literature (primarily nineteenth century writers). In Bernhard Glienke's important work from 1986: *Fatale Präzedenz. Karen Blixens Mythologie* we find a section called 'Das Referenzinventar' (Glienke 1986: 98–158) where Glienke meticulously lists the allusions in Dinesen's tales to works from Danish and world literature that he has been able to find in Dinesen's oeuvre including the essays and letters. This gives us a good idea of the huge role that other literature plays in Dinesen's works but for the most part Glienke is not able to coherently analyze how Dinesen in her narratives, through these allusions, inverts characters and plots from the works she alludes to, which means that the potential the allusions have, as keys to understanding Dinesen's works in relation to her literary precursors, is not fully developed. Allusion is here understood as the term is defined by Gerard Genette in *Palimpsestes* (1982) (*Palimpsests*): 'allusion: that is, an annunciation whose full meaning presupposes the perception of a relationship between it and another text, to which it necessarily refers by some inflections that would otherwise remain unintelligible' (Genette 1997: 2). When reading Dinesen it is easy to go astray in all the allusions that often seem to blur the picture more than they clarify. But when subjecting these allusions, plots and characters to an in-depth analysis and combining the analysis with extra textual historical and literary historical knowledge it is, however, often possible to uncover the underlying plan (see also Behrendt 2007; Behrendt 2010).

Previous research focusing on *Winter's Tales* (*Vinter-Eventyr*) has shown that Dinesen in the tale 'The Heroine' ('Heloïse') reverses the female character and the plot in order to criticize Guy de Maupassant's famous short story 'Boule de Suif' ('Ball of Fat') from 1880.[1] Here Dinesen's heroine, contrary to Maupassant's overweight character, is an incredibly beautiful, slim nude dancer, who — instead of being ruined by — triumphs over both the German officer and her fellow travelers, when Dinesen reverses the character and the plot of Maupassant's story.[2] We also know from Dinesen's own pen (which is extremely rare) that 'The Pearls' ('En Historie om en Perle') was (also) a response to *Kristin Lavransdatter* (1920–22): 'En Historie om en Perle', der i sin Tid er skrevet som en Slags Replik til Sigrid Undsets

Mesterværk 'Kristin Lavransdatter' (Blixen 1996b: 393)[3] ['The Pearls', written at the time as a kind of response to Sigrid Undset's masterpiece 'Kristin Lavransdatter'] and Behrendt has shown that the character Alkmene from the tale of the same name can be perceived as Dinesen's tragic version of Shakespeare's character Perdita from his play *The Winter's Tale* (Behrendt 2010: 404). Both 'Alkmene' from *Winter's Tales* and 'Tempests' from *Last Tales* (1957) are significant counter-stories to Shakespeare's plays with very detailed and well thought through character- and plot reversals. Dinesen is skeptical of the happy endings in these two tales, and instead creates two tragedies out of Shakespeare's comedies. In 'Alkmene' love does not prevail over the mésalliance, and in 'Tempests' Dinesen creates a female Ariel and connects her to the element of the water instead of air. Finally, she subjects her female Ariel to suicide (Selboe 1996: 130) instead of freedom, which is how Shakespeare's *The Tempest* ends for his male Ariel. The title of Dinesen's collection *Winter's Tales* is also a way of realizing the potential in Mamillius' sentence from Shakespeare's *The Winter's Tale*: 'a sad tale's best for winter' (Act 2, Scene 1). Thus, Dinesen used the title of Shakespeare's comedy and the statement in the play to create a collection of tragedies.[4]

It is, however, important to pay attention to the fact that Dinesen often in her literary responses does not mention the literary precursor or the literary background text in the tale. This, of course, makes the task of tracing the background texts and untangling the interplay between the background text and Dinesen's counter-story a rather challenging task. When it comes to Kierkegaard, she sometimes has direct references, for example in 'Carnival' (1926–27) and *Shadows on the Grass* (1960), but the most common strategy of her Kierkegaard counter-stories is that they through subtle and elusive allusions and reversals of plot- and/or characters carry a hidden interpretation of the characters and the story-world in the literary background text.

This book on Dinesen and Kierkegaard differs from the previous work I have done in the following ways:[5] Material from the expanded three volume publication of Dinesen's letters from Africa (Blixen 2013) has now been included, which (fortunately) has strengthened both the specific connections to Kierkegaard and the general observations regarding Dinesen's oeuvre I have made in my earlier work. The two most important scholars who inspired Dinesen to form her view on Kierkegaard, Georg Brandes and Harald Høffding, have each gotten a separate chapter, and the material from the three previous articles I have written on Dinesen and Kierkegaard have been broken up, re-developed and organized thematically in five separate parts: 'Dinesen and Kierkegaard', 'Christianity', 'Seduction', 'Gender', and 'Repetition'. The analysis of 'Babette's Feast' has also been thoroughly expanded and material from Harold Bloom's influential work *The Anxiety of Influence* (1973) has been added in order to better understand Dinesen's subversive approach to her great precursor and fellow countryman Søren Kierkegaard.

'Modhistorier' [Counter-Stories]

Danish scholar and personal friend of Isak Dinesen, Aage Henriksen, discovered Dinesen's subversive narrative strategy at a very early stage in their relationship. He then, audaciously, began to send her 'modhistorier' [counter-stories] as literary comments to her own tales. For example 'Vejene omkring Thunersøen' [The Roads Round the Thuner Lake] that he sent to her in a letter 20 December 1953 as a counter-story to 'The Roads Round Pisa' (Dinesen 1934) ('Vejene omkring Pisa') (Dinesen 1935).[6] He also had plans of developing a counter-story to 'Tales of Two Old Gentlemen' (Dinesen 1957) ('To gamle Herrers Historier') (Blixen 1957) before it was published as we know from another letter to Dinesen from 25 September 1956: 'Jeg har også tænkt mig en modhistorie lagt i munden på de to herrers fælles tante, Mædea [...] Jeg begyndte også at skrive på den, men synes så ikke, at det var ulejligheden værd, men hvis de vil høre den engang så skal jeg fortælle den' (Blixen 1996b: 327). [I have also imagined a counter-story told from the point of view of Medea, the two gentlemen's aunt [...] I also began to write it but did not think it was worthwhile. But if you want to hear it sometimes, I will tell it]. To Henriksen's idea of a story as a counter-story Dinesen dryly replied:

> 'En Modhistorie,' sagde hun, 'det er en ting, der ikke eksisterer. Der er heller ikke noget der hedder sådan.' [...] 'Nu skal jeg vise Dem, hvordan en historie ser ud,' sagde hun så og tegnede et pentagram. 'Sådan, her er intet at tilføje og intet at trække fra. På samme måde er historien færdig, når den er forbi.' (Henriksen 1985: 98)

> ['A counter-story,' she said, 'is something that does not exist. There is no such a thing.' [...] 'Now, I'll show you how a story looks like,' she said, drawing a pentagram. 'Like this. There is nothing to add and nothing to subtract. The story is finished in the same way — when it is over.']

Dinesen's answer is both right and wrong since most of her tales are *both* counter-stories *and* at the same time completely original and fully finished pieces of literature in their own right as Dinesen's pentagram analogy is meant to show us. In this quote Dinesen, however, chose to focus exclusively on the latter, probably annoyed with Henriksen's nosey behavior and his counter-stories that suddenly subjected her to her own strategy. The right answer would be a combination of Henriksen and Dinesen's view on Dinesen's stories, thus a matter of both/and rather than either/ or (to allude to Kierkegaard). Dinesen was of course inspired by (and loved) many writers of world literature and absorbed and adapted some of their ideas and made them her own, but it doesn't show very much in her tales. This means that it is very difficult to directly detect the positive influence from the writers of world literature in her works compared to the tales that are polemical and subversive.

Subverting Kierkegaard

Aside from the numerous articles about Dinesen's tale 'Ehrengard' that state the obvious; that the novella is a counter-story to Kierkegaard's 'Forførerens Dagbog' from *Enten — Eller. Første Deel* (1843) ('The Seducer's Diary' from *Either/Or. Part I*) scholarly attempts to tackle Dinesen's approach to Kierkegaard's works have so far been focusing on establishing similarities rather than pointing out differences. What most of the observations have in common is that they — for the most part with little success — try to show how Dinesen adapted Kierkegaard's various ways of thinking and his narrative strategies.[7] This is the overall conclusion I draw in the research survey over the scholarly work done on the connections between Kierkegaard and Blixen (Dinesen) that I have presented in Bunch 2013a.[8] As I also point out in this research survey, very little energy has so far been invested in reflecting upon how the opposite might be the case: that Dinesen used Kierkegaard in her tales only insofar as she subjects him to critique by ironically subverting significant ideas and/ or characters from his works to a degree so it often borders sheer parody. Or, more precisely, what Genette defines as 'serious parody':

> I simply mean to bring it out into the open, if only to make room, for example, for a form of hypertextuality whose literary significance cannot be reduced to that of the pastiche or of canonical parody, and which I shall for now call *serious parody*. The yoking here of these two terms — which in ordinary usage would form an oxymoron — is deliberate, intended to indicate that certain generic formulas cannot be accounted for within a purely functional definition [...] Parody does not actually subjects the hypotext to a degrading stylistic treatment but only takes it as a model or template for the construction of a new text (Genette 1997: 26–27)

In my opinion the blind spot within the scholarship has been that most scholars have expected that Dinesen would just adapt her great fellow countryman's and precursor's ideas and points of view, since she in her letters, essays and tales often shows affinity for him. In a letter to her brother Thomas Dinesen from 1924 she writes: 'Læs forresten ogsaa Søren Kierkegaard [...] Vi har i hvert Fald 'Enten-Eller' hjemme. Jeg tror ikke, at noget Menneske kan læse ham med Eftertanke uden at gribes af ham. Han var et ærligt Menneske og led under det' (Blixen 2013: 1860) [And by the way, read Søren Kierkegaard, too [...] I know that we have 'Either-Or' at home, anyway. I do not think that anyone can read him closely without being gripped by him. He was an honest person and suffered for it] (Dinesen 1981: 225–26). In the early tale 'Carnival' (1926–27), which Dinesen wrote the major part of when she was still living in Africa, we find this passage: 'For all students of Soren [*sic*] Kierkegaard will know his deep and graceful work *The Seducer's Diary*. In it the hero Johannes [Johannes Forføreren] brings to play all his ingeniousness and his great powers of mind, to obtain one single night of love with the heroine, and then leaves her forever' (Dinesen 1977: 82) and finally, almost thirty-five years after, we find this passage in *Shadows on the Grass* about hunting: 'It is a fine and fascinating art, in the spirit of that masterpiece of my countryman Sören [*sic*]

Kierkegaard, *The Seducer's Diary*' (Dinesen 1960: 45). It is, understandably, easy to be led astray by these statements, but Dinesen was, just like Kierkegaard, a master of subtext and irony. When this general position of irony and subversion in Dinesen's approach to Kierkegaard is first discovered, things suddenly fall into place, and we discover that a hidden polemic to Kierkegaard and his works runs as a significant undercurrent all the way through Dinesen's oeuvre from 'Carnival' (1926–27) to 'Ehrengard' (1963).

This leads us to the main aim of this book, which is to uncover how Dinesen in her tales interprets, critiques and subverts major ideas, characters and plots from Kierkegaard's aesthetic-pseudonymous authorship (1843–46).[9] This also means that her tales, instead of just taking over the ideas presented in Kierkegaard's works, as most scholars have so far believed, offer a whole new interpretation of them. That said it is of course also obvious that Dinesen integrated parts of Kierkegaard's thinking in her own view on life and in her artistic oeuvre, without necessarily showing it in the tales. This applies to Kierkegaard's dialectical way of thinking, the idea that the individual must undertake a special effort to become 'oneself' and Kierkegaard's narrative strategies and pseudonymity,[10] but when she alludes to him in her tales, it is always to present another point of view and/or to poke fun.

Before continuing, I must stress that the views and opinions on Kierkegaard presented in this book are *not my view or opinions* on Kierkegaard. *They are exclusively Dinesen's views on Kierkegaard* (or rather *my interpretations of Dinesen's view on Kierkegaard*) — and often they are not very nuanced. One could even say that Dinesen at times is reading Kierkegaard — to use a popular phrase — like the Devil reading the Bible. Or to put it in context: as a 20th century modern atheist woman targeting the aspects in Kierkegaard's aesthetic-pseudonymous authorship (1843–1846) that have to do with Christianity and nineteenth century notions of gender that she found to be questionable or flawed. Even though Dinesen herself insisted that her pseudonyms should be respected as points of view not representing her own private opinions, she does not make the same distinction when it comes to Kierkegaard and *his* pseudonyms and character narrators. In this approach she is following the path of Georg Brandes, but in his case it is easier to understand and explain when taking the dominant reading methods of his time into account (biographical-psychological). In Dinesen's case Harold Bloom might hold the key to understanding Dinesen's disrespect for Kierkegaard's pseudonyms, and her unwillingness to view his works with the complexity they deserve. This passage from his influential work *The Anxiety of Influence* (1973) describes Dinesen's distorted approach in a very precise way:

> Poetic Influence — when it involves two strong, authentic poets, — always proceeds by a misreading of the prior poet, an act of creative correction that is actually and necessarily a misinterpretation. The history of fruitful poetic influence, which is to say the main tradition of Western poetry since the Renaissance, is a history of anxiety and self-saving caricature, of distortion, of perverse, willful revisionism without which modern poetry as such could not exist. (Bloom 1973: 30)

Notes to the Introduction

1. Henriksen 1998, p. 232; Sørensen 2002, p. 24–25; Selboe 2008, p. 25 and Bunch 2013a, p. 24.
2. This is hidden behind the ironical allusion to Abelard and Heloïse that Dinesen established in the Danish version, when she changed the title from 'The Heroine' to 'Heloïse'. From a letter dated 13 January 1928 we also understand that Steen St. Blicher and Jacob Wassermann inspired Dinesen with regard to this particular plot reversal (Blixen 2013: 1296–97).
3. The story as a literary response to *Kristin Lavransdatter* has been treated more in depth by Aage Henriksen in Henriksen 1956, p. 17 and Henriksen 1998, p. 232.
4. The two tales 'The Fat Man' (written in the 1950s, but not published until 1977) (Dinesen 1977) and 'Converse at Night in Copenhagen' (Dinesen 1957) both deal with Shakespeare's *Hamlet* (Mads Bunch: '"Samtale om Natten i København". Hamlet og Shakespeare i Karen Blixens fortællinger', lecture given at the Karen Blixen Summer Course at Rungstedlund 28 June 2016). A full study of Shakespeare's influence in Dinesen's oeuvre is still to be conducted but should be rewarding.
5. Bunch 2012; 2013a; 2013b and 2014.
6. The whole story is reprinted in Henriksen 1985 (128–51).
7. Exceptions being: Selboe, Anz, Makarushka, Sørensen and Behrendt.
8. Readers who are interested in an in depth and thorough evaluation of the entire Kierkegaard/ Blixen (Dinesen) scholarship up until 2013 can consult this section (Bunch 2013a: 7–32).
9. Behrendt's convincing articles 'An Essay in the Art of Writing Posthumous Papers' (Behrendt 2003) and 'Det pseudonyme firma: om juridiske fiktioner — et dobbeltportræt' (Behrendt 2004) [The Pseudonymous Company: juridical fictions — a double portrait] point to the fact that Kierkegaard's entire body of work must be considered pseudonymous. Thus, I will adopt and use the term 'aesthetic-pseudonymous' referring to the first part of Kierkegaard's authorship covering the years 1843–46.
10. Within the Dinesen-Kierkegaard scholarship Poul Behrendt is right when he points out that Dinesen learned from Kierkegaard with regard to her narrative elusiveness (unreliability), use of secret notes, and pseudonyms (Behrendt 2007, 2010a and 2011).

PART I

❖

Dinesen and Kierkegaard

CHAPTER 1

❖

Dinesen's Interest in Kierkegaard before *Seven Gothic Tales* (1934)

In this chapter, I will show that Dinesen was very occupied with Kierkegaard in the 1920s, and already formed her critical opinions of him, long before her international debut in 1934. As we understand from her letters from Africa in the period 1923–1929, and the early tale 'Carnival', which she started to write in 1926, her interest in Kierkegaard and her ironical approach to him, which would later become her trademark, already emerged in these years. The many Kierkegaard allusions in 'Carnival' that supplement the mentions of Kierkegaard in the letters tell us that Dinesen was indeed very familiar with the main ideas from Kierkegaard's aesthetic-pseudonymous works 1843–1846, before she wrote *Seven Gothic Tales*. The letters also show that she eagerly discussed Kierkegaard with her sister Ellen Dahl, who was a big admirer, and that these discussions fuelled Dinesen's interest, even though their opinions on Kierkegaard would turn out to be very different.

Kierkegaard in Dinesen's Letters

From Dinesen's letters we know that she was much occupied with Kierkegaard already in the first part of the 1920s, when she was living in Africa. In a letter to her mother Ingeborg Dinesen from Africa dated 8 July 1923 Dinesen mentions Kierkegaard for the first time. She writes that she has read Harald Høffding's article 'Pascal og Kierkegaard' (Høffding 1923) [Pascal and Kierkegaard] with great pleasure:

> Der stod for en Gangs Skyld en udmærket Artikel i Tilskueren, af Høffding, om Pascal og Kierkegaard, som Du, — og Thomas — maa læse. Du vil vist le af mig, men jeg tror, at Du ved at læse om Kierkegaard vilde komme til en vis Forstaaelse af Viggo.[1] Jeg tror, at Viggo føler noget af Kierkegaards Blanding af Rædsel over og Tiltrækning ved andre Menneskers Overfladiskhed, — ogsaa vor Families — maaske ikke, som hos Kierkegaard, udelukkende i disses Holdning overfor de evige Værdier. Forresten er det i det hele taget meget interessant, synes jeg, ogsaa i den Maade Høffding taler om Kristendommen, hvor jeg er enig med ham, og det var en af de Ting, som Thomas og jeg plejede at diskutere. (Blixen 2013: 623)

> [For once, there was an excellent article in *The Spectator,* by Høffding, about

Pascal and Kierkegaard, which you — and Thomas — must read. I'm sure
you will laugh at me, but I think that by reading Kierkegaard you will arrive
at a certain understanding of Viggo. I think that Viggo feels something of
Kierkegaard's blend of horror over and attraction for other people's superficiality
— even our own family's — perhaps not, as in Kierkegaard, exclusively in their
attitudes toward the eternal values. Besides, by and large, it is very interesting,
I think, also the way Høffding talks about Christianity, in which I agree with
him — and that was one of the things Thomas and I used to discuss.]

In the above passage she not only implies that she has already read Kierkegaard
but also concludes that she agrees with Høffding's critical view on Christianity in
connection to his analysis of Kierkegaard and Pascal. In his article Høffding also
mentions *Enten — Eller* and *Stadier paa Livets Vei* (1845) (*Stages on Life's Way*) as the
most important works in the first part of Kierkegaard's oeuvre:

> Hvad de forskellige Maader at tage Livet paa angaar, anvender han en lignende
> Fremgangsmaade som Pascal, idet han forsøger at karakterisere visse Typer.
> Vi kan her holde os til dem, han har fremstillet i sine mest populære Skrifter
> ('Enten-Eller' og 'Stadier paa Livets Vej' [sic]). (Høffding 1923: 423)

> [With regard to different ways of approaching life, he uses the same method
> as Pascal when trying to characterize certain types. Here, we will stick to the
> ones, he has depicted in his most popular writings ('Either/Or' and 'Stages on
> Life's Way').][2]

A year later Dinesen again encourages Thomas Dinesen to read Kierkegaard. In a
letter from Africa dated 3 August 1924 she also mentions that they have *Enten —
Eller* in the library at home at Rungstedlund:

> Læs forresten ogsaa Søren Kierkegaard, selv om Du maaske vil synes han er lidt
> indviklet (maaske ogsaa lidt gammeldags for Dig!) Vi har i hvert Fald 'Enten-
> Eller' hjemme. Jeg tror ikke, at noget Menneske kan læse ham med Eftertanke
> uden at gribes af ham. Han var et ærligt Menneske og led under det; maaske
> vil Du i hans Opfattelse af 'Den Enkelte' finde noget af Dig selv. (Blixen 2013:
> 860)

> [And by the way, read Søren Kierkegaard, too, even though you may find
> him a little complicated (he may be a little old-fashioned to you, too!); I know
> that we have 'Either-Or' at home, anyway. I do not think that anyone can
> read him closely without being gripped by him. He was an honest person and
> suffered for it; you may perhaps see something of yourself in his concept of 'The
> Individual'.] (Dinesen 1981: 225–26)

In the quote Dinesen focuses on the fate of the biographical Kierkegaard but she
also mentions that she is gripped by him and finds his ideas about 'The Individual'
interesting. Two years after, on 4 July 1926 (after having met Georg Brandes in
Copenhagen in October 1925, see Chapter 2), she, however, makes an ironical
allusion to Kierkegaard's *Gjentagelsen* (1843) (*Repetition*) in a letter to Mary Bess
Westenholz:

> Det kan jo godt være, at Opholdet herude ikke vilde blive saa morsomt for
> Moder som sidst, fordi Tommy ikke er med, og vi jo begge vil savne ham
> gruligt, men paa den anden Side er der jo saa mange Ting her, som det nu vil

more at gense, og det hele er jo ikke saa fremmed for hende. Jeg er egentlig
ikke bange for selve 'Gentagelsen', og at det skulde blive en mat Afglans af det
forrige vellykkede Besøg, jeg tror nok, at jeg skal kunne præstere et Indhold
deri for Moder. (Blixen 2013: 1012)

[Mother's stay out here might not turn out as amusing for her as last time,
because Tommy will not be joining, and we both will miss him terribly, but
on the other hand there are so many things here that it will make her happy
to see again, and it is after all not that foreign to her. I am actually not afraid
of 'Repetition' and the idea that her stay would become a dull afterglow of her
previous successful visit, since I am convinced I will be able to offer her content
and substance.][3]

In the quote Dinesen is alluding to the main character and author of *Gjentagelsen*,
Constantin Constantius, who worries a great deal before going to Berlin for the
second time in order to find out if repetition is possible and whether something
gains or losses in being repeated:

Da jeg i længere Tid havde beskæftiget mig, leilighedsviis idetmindste, med
det Problem, om en Gjentagelse er mulig og hvilken Betydning den har, om
en Ting vinder eller taber ved at gjentages, faldt det mig pludselig ind: Du kan
jo reise til Berlin, der har Du engang før været, og nu overbevise Dig om en
Gjentagelse er mulig og hvad den har at betyde. (Kierkegaard 1843c: 9)

[When I was occupied for some time, at least on occasion, with the question
of repetition — whether or not it is possible, what importance it has, whether
something gains or loses in being repeated — I suddenly had the thought: You
can, after all, take a trip to Berlin; you have been there once before, and now
you can prove to yourself whether a repetition is possible and what importance
it has.] (Kierkegaard 1983a: 99)

The ironical letter passage occurs during a time when Dinesen had started
working on 'Carnival' that was first intended to be a marionette comedy but was
instead developed into a tale. In the Karen Blixen Archive at the Royal Library in
Copenhagen we find a list of the characters and two brief outlines in a household
account book from 1926.[4] She also mentions in a letter to her sister Ellen Dahl
dated 16 May 1926 that she: 'er ved at skrive paa to smaa nye Marionetkomedier'
(Blixen 2013: 980) [I am writing two short new marionette comedies]. 'Carnival'
is a tale about a supper party that takes place in Copenhagen in 1925 after a great
masked ball has taken place and one of the characters, Annelise, is dressed as 'the
young Soren Kierkegaard': 'The party consisted of, to take the ladies first: Watteau
Pierrot, Arlecchino, the young Soren [sic] Kierkegaard — that brilliant, deep and
desperate philosopher of the forties, a sort of macabre dandy of his day — and
Camelia' (Dinesen 1977: 57). We find major ideas/themes in the tale to pop up in
Dinesen's letters during the fall of 1927 and the first part of 1928, suggesting that the
tale was still a work in progress. In a letter to Thomas Dinesen 19 November 1927,
Dinesen writes about seduction and the gender roles of 'the smart set' (Blixen 2013:
1260–61) and she also mentions Harlequin and the Copenhagen spirit in a letter to
Ellen Dahl 13 January 1928 and the term 'Flapper' (that Dinesen uses in the tale) in
a letter to Ingeborg Dinesen on 15 January 1928 (Blixen 2013: 1301). At that time

we also find a critical allusion to another of Kierkegaard's works *Begrebet Angest* (Kierkegaard 1844) (*Concept of Anxiety*) in one of Dinesen's letters to her mother Ingeborg Dinesen dated 22 January 1928:

> Mohr og jeg diskuterede, — med al Respekt for Søren Kierkegaard, — 'Begrebet Angst' [sic], nærmest i Anledning af min Røverbande her; jeg synes at jeg selv i Livet er kommet til det Resultat, at al Angst i Virkeligheden er nervøs, fordi der *ikke er noget at være bange for.* D.v.s.: man kan naturligvis have Lov til at være bange for at blive slaaet ihjel, for at faa Lungebetændelse, køre sin Automobil i Grøften etc. — alle disse Risks existerer naturligvis i Tilværelsen, — men man kan ikke have Lov til at være *rædselsslagen* for dem, — fordi der er ikke i Livet noget at være *rædselsslagen* for (hvis man ikke tror paa Djævlen, i saa Fald kan man naturligvis have Ret til at være det altid). Naar jeg f. Ex. ikke er rædselsslagen for Natives og ikke vilde være det, selv om jeg jo meget godt kunde tænkes at vide, at de stod udenfor Døren og var bestemt paa at slaa mig ihjel, og selv om jeg troede at det vilde lykkes dem, saa kommer det af, at de ikke selv vilde være rædselsslagne for at slaa mig ihjel, d. v. s.: hverken de eller jeg tror paa Djævlen, og det hele kunde meget snarere jævnføres med en Jagtepisode, f. Ex. med at drive en Bjørn ud af Hiet, som ikke har noget rædselsslagende for Jægerne, om de ogsaa ved, at de kan risikere at blive slaaet ihjel, og vistnok hellerikke for Bjørnen, hvor vred den saa kan være og bestemt paa at put up a fight. Al Rædsel er mere eller mindre Mørkerædsel: bring Lys, og det maa naturnødvendigt fortage sig, fordi det vil vise sig at der ikke er noget at nære Rædsel for. Men vi har i saa mange Aar troet paa Helvede og Djævlen og kyst hinanden op til at se noget rædselsindgydende i mange Ting, at der sidder os en Helvedes Frygtagtighed i Blodet, og den kan rejse Hovedet ved de mest urimelige Lejligheder. (Blixen 2013: 1305)

> [Mohr and I have been discussing, — with due respect to Kierkegaard, — 'the concept of anxiety', really arising out of my bandits here; I think that I myself have come to the conclusion in life that all fear in reality is nervous, because there is nothing to be afraid of. That is to say: naturally one may be afraid of being killed, of getting pneumonia, driving one's car into the ditch and so on — all these risks naturally exist in life, — but one must not be *terrified* of them, — because there is nothing in life to be terrified of (unless one believes in the Devil in which case one has the right to be afraid always). For instance, when I am not terrified of natives and would not be so even though I could be imagined to be aware that they were outside my door planning to put me to death, and even though I thought they would succeed, that is because they themselves would not be terrified of killing me, that is: neither they nor I believe in the Devil, and the whole situation would much more resemble a hunting episode, such as driving a bear out of its lair, which does not seem anything terrifying to the hunters even though they know there is a risk of their getting killed, nor probably to the bear, however enraged it might be and determined to put up a fight. All terror is more or less terror of the dark: bring light, and it must of necessity pass, because it will be shown that there is nothing to be feared. But for so many years we have believed in hell and the Devil and worked each other into a state in which so many things inspired us with fear that there is a hellish pusillanimity in our very blood, and it can raise its head on the most unreasonable occasions.] (Dinesen 1981: 338–39)

In this passage Dinesen is very critical of Christianity and blames it for creating anxiety that has no ground in reality, in fact as the very *reason* for people feeling anxious. A few months later, Kierkegaard is mentioned once again in a letter to Ellen Dahl dated 13 March 1928:

> Jeg har saa tit undret mig over, at Moster Bess, som har saa megen Interesse for og Forstand paa Literatur, har læst saa grulig lidt. Ikke alene er jo hele den klassiske, den franske og tyske Literatur, helt en lukket Bog for hende, men ogsaa den allerstørste Del af den engelske og den danske, Holberg, Oehlenschlæger [sic], Søren Kierkegaard, Drachmann, — jeg kunde jo nævne mange flere. (Blixen 2013: 1353)

> [It has always seemed strange to me that Aunt Bess, who has so much interest in and understanding of literature, has read so terribly little. Not only is the whole of Classical, French and German literature an utterly closed book for her but also far the greater part of English and Danish literature, Holberg, Oehlenschlæger, Søren Kierkegaard, Drachmann, — and many more that I could name.] (Dinesen 1981: 349)

In the same letter, we also find a couple of interesting allusions to Kierkegaard regarding marriage:

> Som jeg vist før har udviklet: man kan efter min Opfattelse 'leve for' Menneskeheden, eller for fattige Børn i Sengeløse, men man kan ikke 'leve for' Hr. Petersen, da ikke uden at fordærve ham eller gøre ham ulykkelig, i Reglen begge Dele. Jeg tror ikke der er nogen Mennesker, som vil tage imod eller kan udholde, at et andet Menneske paa den Maade 'lever for' dem; det kan kun tænkes derigennem at begge — det ene Menneske direkte, det andet gennem ham, — lever for en Idé. (Blixen 2013: 1349)

> [I have probably spoken before of my view that one can 'live for' humanity, or for the poor children of Sengeløse, but one cannot 'live for' Mr. Petersen, at least without spoiling him or making him unhappy, usually both. I do not think any human being will accept or can tolerate another person 'living for' him in this way; it is only possible, I think, when both, — one person directly, the other through him, — live for an idea.] (Dinesen 1981: 347)

The term 'leve for' occurs seven times in Judge William's essay on marriage 'Ligevægten mellem det Æsthetiske og Ethiske i Personlighedens Udarbeidelse'[5] ('The Balance Between the Aesthetic and the Ethical in the Development of the Personality') in *Enten — Eller. Anden Deel* and 'Hr. Petersen' five times in Constantin Constantius's speech about marriage in 'in vino veritas' from *Stadier paa Livets Vei* (Kierkegaard 1845: 41).

On 6 May 1928 Dinesen writes that: 'Jeg kan saa godt forstaa, hvad Du skriver om "Romanlæsning", selv om jeg for Tiden er mere inde paa at læse andre Ting, helst enten Digte eller Philosofi' (Blixen 2013: 1375) [I understand so well what you write about 'novel reading,' even though at present I am more inclined to read other things, preferably either poetry or philosophy] (Dinesen 1981: 358). With all the mentions of Kierkegaard and the allusions to his works in Dinesen's letters at a time when she is also working on 'Carnival' where 'the young Soren Kierkegaard' appears as one of the characters, it seems safe to conclude that it is the 'Philosofi' of Kierkegaard she is hinting at.[6] On 29 June 1928 she once again alludes to *Gjentagelsen* in one of her ongoing discussions about marriage with Mary Bess Westenholz: 'En Gentagelse af Madam Dickens nedigennem Aarhundrederne kan være et meget respektabelt Foretagende, — men oprigtig talt tror jeg ikke, at det vejer stort til den ene eller anden Side i Menneskehedens Vægtskaal' (Blixen 2013: 1428) [A repetition of Madame Dickens down through the centuries maybe a respectable undertaking, — but in all sincerity I don't think that it will affect the balance on one or the other side of the human scales to any great extent] (Dinesen 1981: 372). Two months later, on 13 September 1928, fueled by her interest in Kierkegaard, Dinesen tells her sister Ellen Dahl that she is eager to read more of him and asks Ellen for recommendations:

> [Tilføjet]: Undskyld, at der er saa mange Fejl i Skriften, dette Brev er skrevet ved Lyset af en meget daarlig Lampe. Hvilken [sic] af Søren Kierkegaards Bøger er det, Du har læst og særlig blevet grebet af? Jeg vilde grulig gerne have dem.[7] (Blixen 2013: 1470)

> [Continued] I'm sorry that there are so many mistakes in the writing. This letter is written by the light of a very bad lamp. Which of Søren Kierkegaard's books have you read and were you particularly moved by? I would terribly much like to have them.]

This is the last mentioning of Kierkegaard in Dinesen's letters from Africa.

Ellen Dahl

From the letter we also understand that Ellen Dahl was much occupied with Kierkegaard too in the last part of the 1920s even though we don't know what books by Kierkegaard Dinesen is referring to in this letter to her sister. Dinesen was, however, back in Denmark for a period of seven months (18 May — 25 December) in 1929 (Blixen 2013: 1527) half a year after she wrote the above letter, which means that it would not take long before Dinesen was able to discuss Kierkegaard with Ellen Dahl in person and borrow her books. They did meet and Ellen had a surprise in waiting for Dinesen's departure, as we understand from this letter sent from the ship S/S Tanganyika dated 31 December 1929:

> Du siger nok, at vi aldrig var sammen i Sommer, men jeg synes dog, at vi var det, næsten saa meget som aldrig før, og jeg tænker med Glæde baade paa Peter Lieps Hus og Hotel Du Pont. — Det var en Skam, at Du først saa sent aabenbarede Dig som Paracelsus, thi der havde været noget, vi burde have gennemgaaet og fordybet os I, nu maa det blive pr. Korrespondance, naar jeg rigtig faar læst Parablerne. (Blixen 2013: 1532–33)

> [You seem to suggest that we never spent time together this summer, but I think, we did, almost more than ever, and I think with joy on our visits to Peter Liep's House and Hotel du Pont. — It was, however, a shame that you revealed yourself to be Paracelsus so late, since it could have been something we could have looked into and immersed ourselves in but now it has to be through letter correspondence after I have gotten to really read the Parables.][8]

In 1932 Ellen Dahl published another essay-collection under the same pseudonym 'Paracelsus' that she used as the author name for her first book *Parabler* (1929)

[Parables], which is the work that Dinesen is referring to in the letter. It was called *Introductioner* [Introductions] and it came out at a time (1932) when Dinesen had moved back to Denmark and was now working on *Seven Gothic Tales*. The book consists of three different essays about Goethe, Kierkegaard and Ewald, shaped as didactic prose narratives. The middle essay about Kierkegaard is titled 'Melancolia'. Here we find the female protagonist to be stopping in at an inn while traveling in Northern Zealand. In the evening she is alone in the room reading Kierkegaard's 'in vino veritas' from *Stadier paa Livets Vei*. The female protagonist is full of praise and calls Kierkegaard a great eroticist:

> Husker De, Læser, Stadierne og da især den Del deraf, som hedder *in vino veritas*? Hvis ikke, saa find Bogen frem fra Deres Hylde og sæt Dem til at læse. Hvor jeg misunder Dem den Nydelse, der forestaar Dem, — som man misunder den, der tiltræder den samme herlige Rejse, man nylig selv har tilendebragt. Hvilken Rigdom for Aanden! [...] overvældet, aandeløs lægger man tilsidst Bogen fra sig — mere overvældet end noget Pigebarn ved Læsningen af en Skillingsroman — og saa? Mon De saa, som jeg, vil sige til Dem selv: Men du milde Gud, Kierkegaard er jo sletikke Filosoffen, Teologen eller Moralisten — han er selve Erotikeren af Guds Naade. (Dahl 1932: 38–39)

> [Do you remember reader, the Stages and especially that part of them known as *in vino veritas*? If not, take the book down from your shelves and sit down to read. How I envy you the pleasure that lies ahead — as you envy one who is beginning the same glorious journey you have only recently completed. What richness for the spirit! [...] overwhelmed, breathless, you finally set down the book — more overwhelmed than any schoolgirl reading a romance novel — and so? I wonder if you, like me, will say to yourself: But dear God, Kierkegaard is certainly not at all the philosopher, the theologian, or the moralist — he is the very eroticist of God's Mercy.]

While reading, the protagonist is suddenly approached by a young ghost-like figure in the shape of a young girl, who calls herself Melancolia. The young maiden then goes on to talk about the role she has played in Kierkegaard's life (his 'tungsind' [melancolia]) as his 'hemmelighed' [secret] that explains his solitary life, religious quest and prolific production. The last part of the essay contains an imagined dialogue between Kierkegaard, who is lying on his deathbed, and 'Mortensen, Gaardskarlen fra Gammeltorv' [Mortensen, the outdoor servant from Gammeltorv] (Dahl 1932: 63). The essay concludes with three students discussing the concept of melancholia after Kierkegaard has finally taken his last breath. In general, the essay is permeated by Ellen Dahl's compassion, admiration and praise of Kierkegaard. Since *Stadier paa Livets Vei* was the book that Ellen picked for her Kierkegaard-essay in *Introductioner* published in 1932 it seems likely that it was one of the books that Ellen Dahl was 'særligt grebet af' [particularly moved by] as Dinesen phrases it in the letter from 13 September 1928. Thus, it seems very plausible that Dinesen got to know this work by Kierkegaard through Ellen during the seven months she spent in Denmark in 1929. In a letter from 10 April 1931, just four months before Dinesen had to give up the farm for good and go back to Denmark, she writes to Thomas Dinesen:

Saa har jeg, i disse vanskelige Maaneder, foretaget mig, hvad vi Søskende gør, naar vi ikke ved, hvad vi ellers skal gøre, — jeg er begyndt at skrive en Bog. Jeg skrev paa engelsk, fordi jeg tænkte at det skulde betale sig bedre, men da jeg var bange for, at Sproget skulde blive en stor Vanskelighed, sendte jeg en Del af den hjem til en Ven af Mohr, en Forlægger som hedder Morley, og bad om hans Mening derom. Han udtalte sig opmuntrende. (Blixen 2013: 1659)

[So, during these difficult months, I have begun to do what we brothers and sisters do when we don't know what else to resort to, — I have started to write a book. I have been writing in English because I thought it would be more profitable, but as I was afraid that the language would prove a great difficulty, I sent a section of it home to a friend of Mohr's, a publisher called Morley, and asked for his opinion. He was encouraging.] (Dinesen 1981: 419)

'Carnival' is the first tale by Dinesen written in English. It has been dated to 1926–1927 but the above quotes from the letters rather suggest that the tale was a work in progress in the last five years Dinesen spent in Africa (1926–1931). Thomas Dinesen also mentions in a letter to Dinesen on 7 October 1932 that he has read 'Carnival' (Blixen 1996a: 97) and the tale underwent its final revision in the spring of 1933[9] at a time when Dinesen had either read, or was very familiar with, the main ideas presented in *Stadier paa Livets Vei* — at least through Ellen's *Introductioner* from 1932, or from her stay in Denmark in 1929. This means that Dinesen had plenty of time to get to know most of Kierkegaard's aesthetic-pseudonymous authorship (1843–1846), including 'in vino veritas' from *Stadier paa Livets Vei* that plays a significant role as a backdrop piece for 'Carnival', before making the final version of the tale in 1933.

Ellen Dahl also brought up another work by Kierkegaard in her letter correspondence with Dinesen in the fall of 1933, when she was giving Dinesen feedback on *Seven Gothic Tales*. Here she compared the special feeling she got from reading 'The Poet' ('Digteren') with Kierkegaard's review of Thomasine Gyllembourg's (Fru Heiberg's) novel *To Tidsaldre* (1845) (*Two Ages*) in the separate book *En literair Anmeldelse*.[10] *To Tidsaldre, Novelle af Forfatteren til »en Hverdagshistorie«, udgiven af J. L. Heiberg* (Kierkegaard 1846a) (*Two Ages. The Age of the Revolution and the Present Age. A Literary Review*) (Kierkegaard 1978):

Jeg maa lykønske dig til 'Digteren', som er langt den bedste af dine Historier [...] Jeg har tit en Følelse af, at Forfattere ikke selv ved, naar de er at their best. Der kommer pludselig i deres Bøger ligesom en stærkere Strøm, en Varme eller Kulde, som gennemrisler en, — det er det, jeg kalder Inspiration, det eneste, jeg virkelig troer paa i Kunst. Gang paa Gang gribes man paa den Maade i 'The Poet' [...] Det er det, der giver Kunst Perspektiv. Kierkegaard giver det rammende Udtryk for det i sin Anmeldelse af Fru Heiberg (jeg har desværre ikke bogen her, den er på Mols), idet han siger at man føler sig *tryg*, man ved, der er mere bagved, end det man ser.[11] (Blixen 1996a: 116–17)

[I must congratulate you on 'The Poet.' It is by far the best of your stories [...] I often get the feeling that authors do not themselves know when they are at their best. There suddenly appears in their books a warmth or a chill, like a stronger current sending a thrill through you — it is what I call inspiration, the only thing I truly believe in in art. Time and again, one is affected that way in 'The Poet' [...] That is what gives art perspective. Kierkegaard offers the precise expression for it in his review of Mrs. Heiberg (unfortunately, I don't have the book here, it's on Mols); he says that you feel *safe,* you know there is more behind what you see.]

Here Ellen Dahl is more right than she thinks with regard to 'Digteren' ('The Poet') when sensing that something is hiding under the surface ('there is more behind what you see') but, ironically, she doesn't know what that 'more' is (which is Kierkegaard's *Gjentagelsen,* see Chapter 14). Ellen Dahl also mentions Kierkegaard in connection to her reading of one of the other *Seven Gothic Tales* to be ('The Monkey') that she, in this passage, is rather critical of:

> Forfatteren lader os imidlertid ikke i Ro. Først skal vi se for os, ikke blot den vide Udsigt, de store Skove, som Priorinden har talt om, og det smukke Efter-aarslandskab, men også en Flok Enhjøringer. Lad gaa! Det kan vi nok. Men samtidig skal vi, — og er det ikke formeget forlangt? — drøfte med os selv, hvordan Vorherre indretter ikke alene Jordelivet, men selve Paradiset! Hvad nu Ideen med dette Paradis angaar, er Tanken interessant, yderst subtil, og kunde være en Kierkegaard værdig. Men ikke netop nu og paa dette Sted, den unge Mand har saamænd nok at tænke paa. (Blixen 1996a: 120–21)

> [The author, however, does not leave us in peace. First, we must visualize not only the wide vista, the great forests, which the Prioress has spoken of, and the beautiful autumn landscape, but also a flock of unicorns. All right! We can certainly do that. But at the same time we must discuss among ourselves — and is it not too much to ask? — how the Lord designs not only earthly life but the very paradise! Whatever this idea of paradise involves, the thought is interesting, extremely subtle, and worthy of a Kierkegaard. But not right now and in this place; I am sure the young man has enough to think about.]

Dinesen actually very rarely integrated any of Ellen Dahl's critiques in the revised drafts, but she might have felt it a compliment when her sister here compared the level of her thinking to the quality of Kierkegaard. As already mentioned, Dinesen revised 'Carnival' around the time (April 1933), when Ellen Dahl was giving her feedback on the drafts of *Seven Gothic Tales* (Bunch 2012: 75). In 'Carnival' we find a less flattering, to put it mildly, allusion to her sister: 'And if it came to that, he might run the Ellen Dahl aground some morning, as the sun was coming up — she was a moldering old barge' (Dinesen 1977: 90), which points to Dinesen's many reservations towards her sister. In her letters we also find less flattering passages where Dinesen is suggesting that Ellen is a hysteric (Blixen 2013: 1395), an anti-Semite (Blixen 2013: 1513) and dishonest ('Lumske Elle', Blixen 2013: 1213, 1220). The conclusion is that Ellen Dahl had influence with regard to Dinesen's *interest in* Kierkegaard in the sense that she called attention to Kierkegaard's works and encouraged Dinesen to read it, but their views on him certainly turned out very different.

Notes to Chapter 1

1. Viggo is the nobleman and landowner Viggo de Neergaard (1881–1965), proprietor of the estate Valdemarskilde near Slagelse. He was the husband of Dinesen's oldest sister Inger Benedicte (Ea), who had just died in 1922.
2. Author's translation.
3. Author's translation.
4. In 'Kps. 97' (Capsule 97) in the Karen Blixen Archive. It is also mentioned in the online archive registrant here <http://www.kb.dk/permalink/2006/manus/692/dan/9> [accessed 29 August 2016].
5. From now on just referred to as 'Ligevægten'.
6. She, however, also read Max Nordau's *Biologie der Ethik* (1916) in the beginning of 1928 (Blixen 2013: 1326).
7. An examination of the original letter in the Karen Blixen Archive at the Royal Library in Copenhagen in the stack of letters labeled: '45. Håndskr. Afd. Utilg. 727. Ellen og Knud Dahl. D. II. 1–3' showed that there is a mistake in the transcript of the hand-written passage in Blixen 2013, p. 1470. The correct word is 'hvilke' so there is pluralis agreement with the last pronoun 'dem' [them].
8. Author's translation.
9. In capsule 137 in the Blixen Archive in the Royal Library in Copenhagen we find a brown envelope with black pen and Karen Blixen's handwriting, saying: 'Carnival 3.4. 1933. Thomas Dinesen Vænget, Hillerød'. See also Bunch 2012.
10. Thomasine Gyllembourg (Fru Heiberg) published twenty-five novels and longer short stories called *Hverdagshistorier* (1827–1845) under the pseudonym 'Af Forfatteren til en Hverdags-Historie'.
11. The word 'tryg' [safe] does *not* occur directly in Kierkegaard's *En literair Anmeldelse* but must be Ellen Dahl's interpretation of Kierkegaard's review. It could be based on this passage: 'Men hvilken er da denne Forfatters Magt, hvormed han udretter Dette, naar der ikke er Spørgsmaal om det Enkelte i den enkelte Novelle, ikke om hans Fortrinlighed som Novellist, men om ham som Repræsentant for en bestemt Livs-Anskuelse, og dette er netop det Mere, han væsentligen har fremfor Novellister i Almindelighed, og et andet Fortrin end det, han indenfor Bestemmelsen Novellist comparativt maa hævdes' (Kierkegaard 1846a: 21) [But then if it is not a matter of something specific in a particular novel or of his superiority as a novelist that enables the author to do this, what is it but his being a representative of a specific life-view, and that is precisely the something more which he essentially has over novelists in general, a point of preference quite different from what may be claimed for him by comparison within the novelist category] (Kierkegaard 1978: 18).

CHAPTER 2

❖

Kierkegaard, Brandes, and Dinesen: Lucifer's Fire

In this chapter, I argue that Georg Brandes played a much bigger role as a decisive influence in Dinesen's oeuvre than has so far been recognized by Dinesen-scholarship. This holds true for her interest in Kierkegaard as well, since Georg Brandes' Kierkegaard biography from 1877 had major impact on Dinesen's perception of Kierkegaard, which I will go on to show in this chapter, as well as in Chapter 5. Dinesen actually managed to meet Brandes twice when she was back in Denmark in 1925, even though there is no mention of these meetings anywhere in her letters. The meetings fuelled Dinesen's ambition to finally become a writer and gave her new momentum in 1926, when she started writing on the Kierkegaard-critical tale 'Carnival' and a couple of marionette comedies. The most important overall impact is that Dinesen adopted Brandes' notion of Lucifer as the (atheist) angel of light and truth, which would later become an integrated symbol in Dinesen's oeuvre representing her critical approach to Christianity in general — and Kierkegaard in particular.

Dinesen and the Role of Brandes

Mentions of Georg Brandes in Dinesen's letters from Africa are limited to the period 1923 to 1927. All of them are positive. In the first letter from 14 January 1923 Blixen is defending Brandes in connection to a recent love affair he had in Lucerne and concludes: 'det er dog egentlig beundringsværdigt, at der er saa megen Kraft i den Olding [...] Herudefra kan man dog ikke lade være at se paa Brandes som en af dem, som i de sidste 25 Aar har kastet Glans over Danmarks Navn' (Blixen 2013: 548) [it is actually admirable that there is so much energy left in the old man [...] From my point of view from out here one cannot help looking at Brandes as one of the few who has lent brilliance to the name of Denmark the past 25 years].[1] The year after in a letter to Mary Bess Westenholz dated 19 April 1924 Dinesen mentions the fatal blow she suffered as a young girl when she was scorned by her family for sending flowers to Georg Brandes who was lying ill at a hospital in Copenhagen. Here we find Dinesen's great admiration for him most clearly expressed:

> Jeg kan her tage et Exempel fra min tidlige Ungdom, hvorved jeg i sin Tid
> blev bebrejdet Uoprigtighed, men hvor jeg nu ønsker at jeg havde haft Energi

til at handle mere paa egen Haand. Det var, da jeg som ganske ung Pige en Gang sendte nogle Blomster til Georg Brandes, som den Gang var syg og laa paa Communehospitalet. Jeg kan sige at dette var gjort ud af et ungt Hjertes inderlige Begejstring for, hvad der da stod for mig som den første Aabenbaring af Aand og Snille; jeg havde længe levet i Brandes' Bøger, og kan sige at det er ham, som har aabenbaret Literaturen for mig. Min første *personlige* Begejstring for Bøger, — for Shakespeare, Shelley, Heine, — fik jeg gennem ham. Rent objektivt set var jo Brandes en af mit Lands største Aander, og en gammel syg Mand [...] Saa snart som I overhovedet kom ind i det, stoppede I al videre Udvikling; jeg kom aldrig til at skrive til Brandes igen, eller høre fra ham, eller se ham, som jeg saa umaadelig gerne vilde. Ved min Underfundighed havde jeg dog i det mindste opnaaet én eneste Gang at skrive til ham og 'yde ham min Hyldest', og det var jeg dog senere mange Gange glad ved at tænke paa. Jeg havde ikke Kraft eller Evne til at slaa et større Slag herfor, og det havde vel knapt ogsaa nyttet, skønt min Beundring for ham var lige stor. Den Gang var det mig en stor Sorg, og nu regner jeg det for at have været et stort Uheld for mig. Den Gang havde min Ungdoms brændende Kærlighed til 'Aand', som jo i mit daglige Liv var temmelig 'starved', haft en Chance; det er den eneste Gang, at en Mulighed har aabnet sig for mig til at komme i personlig Berøring med en af Danmarks store Aander, og jeg tror nu, at Brandes kunde have gjort en Forfatter eller Kunstner ud af mig, som han gjorde med saa mange, — ja, der er vel ingen af Danmarks Kunstnere og Forfattere i de sidste 50 Aar, som ikke mer eller mindre er blevet det gennem ham, — og min Ungdom kunde være blevet præget af Aandsarbejde og Begejstring for Kunst og 'Snille'. Havde jeg den Gang realiseret, hvor meget der stod paa Spil, saa havde jeg vel, hvis jeg ikke havde Kraft til at sætte det officielt igennem, haft Kraft til at narre eder, og jeg ønsker at jeg havde haft det. (Dinesen 2013: 811)

[I can give an example here from my own early youth, when I was once reproached for insincerity, although I now wish that I had had the strength to act more on my own initiative. It was when I was quite young and once sent some flowers to Georg Brandes, who was lying ill in the city hospital. I had done this with all the fervent enthusiasm of a young heart for what was to me the first revelation of intellectual genius; I had been immersed in Brandes's books for a long time and I can say that it was he who revealed literature to me. My first *personal* enthusiasm for books, — for Shakespeare, Shelley, Heine, — came to me through him. From a purely objective point of view Brandes was of course one of the greatest minds of my country, and a sick old man [...] as soon as you had anything to do with it, you put a stop to any further development; I never wrote to Brandes again, or heard from him, or saw him, which I would so much have liked to do. At least my cunning action had resulted in my writing to him this one time and 'rendering him homage', and the thought of that often made me happy later on. I had neither the strength nor the ability to strike a harder blow then, and probably nothing would have come of it anyway, although my admiration for him never slackened. This was a great grief to me then and now I consider it to have been a great misfortune. It would have been a chance for my youthful fervor for 'intellect' which was after all rather 'starved' in my everyday life; it is the only time in my life when there has been a possibility for personal contact with one of the great minds of Denmark, and I believe that Brandes might have made a writer or artist of me, as he did with so many, — indeed, probably none of the artists and writers of

Denmark during the last fifty years have been without his influence to a greater or lesser extent, — and my youth might have been blessed with intellectual work and enthusiasm for art and 'genius'. If I had realized at that time how much was at stake I would probably, if I had not had the strength to carry it through openly, have had strength enough to deceive you, and I wish that I had had it.] (Dinesen 1981: 209–10)

About a year after sending this letter to Mary Bess — on 5 March 1925 — Dinesen left Mombasa for Denmark. Through Marseilles she traveled to Paris, where she stayed for the month of April before arriving in Denmark in early May (Blixen 2013: 887–903). She then stayed with her mother at Rungstedlund for eight months and finally — after waiting more than twenty years — got the chance to meet Georg Brandes. Influenced by Dinesen's strong letter about the incident with Brandes, Mary Bess Westenholz had decided to make it up for her young niece and managed to arrange a meeting. The meeting between Dinesen and Brandes based on solid evidence (the notes from Georg Brandes' diary) was first described by Kristensen 1981 in the article 'Karen Blixen og Georg Brandes' [Karen Blixen and Georg Brandes] in *Blixeniana* 1981 (pp. 177–85) and later by Knudsen 2004 in his Brandes biography *Georg Brandes. Uovervindelig taber* (Vol. II: 486–89) [Georg Brandes. Invincible Loser]. A search conducted in Georg Brandes' diary from 1923 to 1926[2] revealed that Dinesen and Brandes met and talked on 14 October 1925 and that Brandes *also* had dinner with Dinesen the day after on the evening of 15 October, which is a fact that both sources seem to overlook. From his diary we understand that Brandes was fascinated with Dinesen's life in Africa. He also mentions that she had divorced her husband and calls her 'vakker dame' [beautiful lady]. All in all he seems very amused and entertained by her company (Brandes 1923–26: 84–85). The meetings seem to have had a big impact on Dinesen. In one of the most important letters from Africa, dated 3 April 1926, written a few months after she had returned from Denmark where she met Georg Brandes, Dinesen is making a decisive leap with regard to her writing and life view:

> Jeg kommer til at tænke paa, at jeg vist burde nærmere forklare, hvad jeg mener med det symbolske Udtryk: Lucifer, for at det ikke skal forstaas som om jeg længtes efter noget vildt dæmonisk, eller misforstaas paa anden Maade. Jeg opfatter det som om det betyder: Sandhed, eller Søgen efter Sandhed, Stræben mod Lys, Kritik, — ja, vel det man kalder *Aand* [...] Og sammen hermed [...] en sense of humour, som ikke er bange for *noget*, men *efter sin Overbevisning* tør gøre Nar ad alt, og Liv, og nyt Lys, Vekslen. (Blixen 2013: 953)

> [It occurs to me that I ought perhaps to explain in more detail what I mean by the symbolic expression Lucifer, so that it does not appear as if it means that I am longing for something wild and demonic, or be misunderstood in some other way. I conceive of it as meaning: truth, or the search for truth, striving toward the light, a critical attitude, — indeed, what one means by *spirit*. [...] And in addition to this [...] — a *sense of humor* which is afraid of *nothing*, but has the *courage of its convictions* to make fun of everything, and life, new light, variety.] (Dinesen 1981: 249)

Behind this notion of Lucifer we find Georg Brandes to be the inspiration. In a

'Fakkeltale' [Torch Speech] Brandes gave in Odd Fellow Palæet, Copenhagen in 1891, we find this verse about Lucifer:

> [...] Lucifer, Ildens Ophav og Flammens Bærer og Luernes Aand [...]
> er selve den Livets Gnist, der gløder i Blodet; det er selve den Kundskabens
> Stjerne, der lyser paa vor Himmel; det er den gode Aand. Han er en Lysets
> Engel. Tro aldrig den Løgn, at Lysets Engel nogensinde faldt eller kunde falde!
> [...] (Brandes 1891: 271)[3]

> [Lucifer, source of fire and bearer of the flames and spirit of the flames [...]
> is the very spark of life that glows in the blood; it is the very star of knowledge
> that glows in our sky, it is the good spirit. He is the angel of light. Never believe
> that lie that the angel of light ever fell or could fall!]

In the same letter to Thomas Dinesen where Dinesen mentions Lucifer as her new-found ally, she continues with a very important statement about *Sandhedens Hævn* that connects Lucifer's fall and Dinesen's notion of what is necessary to become an independent individual and artist: 'Jeg kan ikke, jeg kan *umuligt* skrive noget, som der er det mindste ved, uden at bryde med Paradiset, og nedstyrtes til mit eget Rige. 'Sandhedens Hævn' er vel et Miniatur-Forsøg herpaa; den skrev jeg i Rom' (Blixen 2013: 949). [I cannot, I cannot *possibly* write anything of the slightest interest without breaking away from the Paradise and hurtling down to my own kingdom. 'The Revenge of Truth' is a miniature of that, you know; I wrote it in Rome] (Dinesen 1981: 246). Dinesen had already mentioned *Sandhedens Hævn* in a letter to Thomas Dinesen on 24 February 1926 shortly after returning to Africa:

> Jeg ser, at 'Tilskueren' endnu ikke har indeholdt 'Sandhedens Hævn'. Mon de
> skulde have betænkt sig og slet ikke vil tage den? Kan du ikke faa det at vide af
> dem, og ligeledes fravriste Holstein 'Jaques', — hvorom han dog gerne kunde
> have givet Livstegn? *Hvis* imidlertid 'S. H.' kommer ud i Enden, vil Du saa ikke
> sende den tilligemed indlagte Brev til gamle Georg? — jeg ville dog gerne at
> han skulde se den, og muligt have et Ord fra ham derom. Selv om den skulde
> været kommet i Martshæftet, vil jeg bede Dig sende ham Brevet; Du kunde da
> maaske føje nogle Ord til det, om at jeg havde sendt Dig det, men det var blevet
> uventet forsinket. (Blixen 2013: 928).

> [I see that 'Revenge of Truth' has still not appeared in 'Tilskueren' magazine.
> I wonder if they have changed their minds and not accepted it after all? Please
> could you find out from them, and also tear 'Jaques' away from Holstein, — he
> might have shown some kind of reaction to it, don't you think? However, *if*
> 'T.R.O.T' does finally come out, would you please send it together with the
> enclosed letter to old Georg? — I would like him to see it and perhaps have a
> word from him about it. Even if it should have appeared in the March number
> I would like to ask you to send him the letter; you could then perhaps add a few
> words to it saying that I had sent it to you but that it had been unexpectedly
> delayed.] (Dinesen 1981: 239)

The passage indicates that Brandes and Dinesen had discussed *Sandhedens Hævn* in Copenhagen in October 1925. It is also possible that Brandes put in a good word for her to the editors of *Tilskueren* paving the way for the publication, even though we have no solid proof of that. We also understand from the line dated 24 February 1926: 'Jeg ser, at "Tilskueren" endnu ikke har indeholdt Sandhedens Hævn' that Dinesen had expected her play to be published in the January or February 1926 issue of *Tilskueren*. In letters dated 16 May and 23 May Dinesen complains that she still hasn't heard a word from the editors about the publication of *Sandhedens Hævn*. Thus, the final reworking and submission of the manuscript must have taken place in 1925 in Denmark before she left for Africa on 25 December 1925, and not in 1926 as has been commonly accepted.[4] For Christmas 1925, just a day before Dinesen started her travel back to Ngong and a few months after the meetings with Brandes, Knud Dahl (Ellen Dahl's husband) gave Dinesen Brandes' work *Hovedstrømninger i det 19de Aarhundredes Litteratur. Det unge Tyskland* (second edition from 1898)[5] (*Main Currents in Nineteenth Century Literature. VI Young Germany*) (1906) as a Christmas present (Blixen 2013: 914) Brandes chose a quote from Balzac as the motto for his book:

> Dersom Kunstneren ikke styrter sig ned i sit Værk som Curtius sprang ned i Afgrunden, og dersom han ikke arbejder i dette Krater som en Grubearbejder, over hvem Jorden er styrtet sammen; dersom han giver sig til at betragte Vanskelighederne istedenfor at overvinde dem en for en, saa bliver han Vidne til sit Talents Selvmord. (Brandes 1890)[6]

> [If the artist does not throw himself into his work as Curtius sprang into the gulf [...] and if when he is in the crater he does not dig on as a miner does when the earth has fallen in on him; if he contemplates the difficulties before him instead of conquering them one by one [...] the artist looks on at the suicide of his own talent.][7]

These ideas we find echoed in Dinesen's letter to her brother Thomas dated 1 April 1926 just two months after returning to Africa from Denmark: 'Det samme er Tilfældet med mit ynkelige "Forfatterskab". Jeg kan ikke, jeg kan *umuligt* skrive noget, som der er det mindste ved, uden at bryde med Paradiset, og nedstyrtes i mit eget Rige' (Blixen 2013: 949) [The same is true of my pathetic 'authorship'. I cannot, I cannot *possibly* write anything of the slightest interest without breaking away from the Paradise and hurtling down into my own kingdom] (Dinesen 1981: 246). In the letter a few months later, dated 23 May 1926 Dinesen expresses her gratitude to Mary Bess for setting up the meeting with Brandes: 'Jeg var ude i Somalibyen for at se at finde en eller anden Ting at sende til gamle G. B., som jeg tænker paa med stor Venlighed; jeg er dig meget taknemmelig for, at Du hjalp mig med at træffe ham' (Blixen 2013: 983) [I was out in the Somali village to look for a thing to send to old G.B. who I am thinking of with great affection; I am very grateful that you helped me to meet him].[8]

Retrospectively, 1925 turned out to be the turning point in Dinesen's career as a writer. She met Georg Brandes and the final version of *Sandhedens Hævn* that she had been working on for decades (!) was finally submitted to *Tilskueren*. Brandes also seems to have inspired the formation of her Lucifer life view and fueled her artistic ambitions that eventually led her to write with much more determination and discipline from May 1926. On that note, it should be mentioned that Georg

Brandes was also the decisive force behind the publication of Dinesen's father's *Jagtbreve* (1889) [Hunting Letters] (Buk-Swienty 2014: 50) published under the pseudonym Boganis (the letters had been published in Danish Newspaper *Politiken* as a serial and Brandes found them terrific). Brandes and Captain Dinesen had personal contact from 1889 onwards where Captain Dinesen received the first of a number of excited and praising letters from Georg Brandes (Buk-Swienty 2014: 392–93).

Georg Brandes: *Søren Kierkegaard. En kritisk Fremstilling i Grundrids* (1877)

Combining Dinesen's strong interest in Kierkegaard in the period from 1923 to 1928, her meetings with Georg Brandes in 1925, her admiration for him and the obvious alignment in their perception of 'Lucifer' and the critical Kierkegaard-tale 'Carnival' she started working on in 1926, it seems very likely that Dinesen was familiar with Brandes' book about Kierkegaard: *Søren Kierkegaard. En kritisk Fremstilling i Grundrids* from 1877, which at the time was one of the main works on Kierkegaard. Heinrich Anz mentions Brandes' Kierkegaard book as *the work* about Kierkegaard that has had the most influence on the reception of Kierkegaard among Scandinavian writers:

> Brandes' Kierkegaard-Monographie ist eine der wichtigsten und wirkungs-vollsten Biographien innerhalb des literarischen Genres 'Biographie' und seiner skandinavischen Gattungsgeschichte: Eine Werkbiographie, die Kierkegaard als die große Dichterpersönlichkeit herausstellt und die zugleich die von Kierkegaard postulierte innere Notwendigkeit in der reflexiven Bewegung der Stadien aufhebt, ihn also für Richtigstellungen und Weiterführungen freigibt. Die in Brandes' Werkbiographie erreichte große Nähe zu Kierkegaard und zugleich kritische Distanzierung von Kierkegaard prägt die Korrekturen der literarischen Rezeptionsgeschichte. (Anz 1999: 207–08)

> [Brandes' Kierkegaard monograph is one of the most important and influential works within the literary genre of 'biography' in Scandinavia: It focuses on the great personality of Kierkegaard as a poet and, at the same time, eliminates the inner necessity of moving reflectively through the stages; and thereby, he opens up for corrections and continuations. The combination of near proximity and critical distancing found in Brandes' biography has shaped the literary reception history.]

In the article Anz, however, *only* mentions Dinesen and Ibsen as having been parti-cularly influenced by Brandes' book (Anz 1999), but we do know that other writers from the time around the Modern Breakthrough also got to know Kierkegaard through Brandes (for example Strindberg) and it does seem plausible that the huge impact Anz claims that Brandes' book had among Scandinavian writers is true if we modify the claim to account only for the period from the turn of the century and up until World War II. Just before, during and after World War II, I will argue, Brandes' materialistic-critical approach to Kierkegaard was substituted by existentialist-religious approaches e.g. by Kaj Munk and the Heretica-group. Since then many different approaches to Kierkegaard have emerged in which Brandes' critical view on Kierkegaard seems to have drowned.[9]

When juxtaposing the positive and less positive quotes about Kierkegaard and the critical allusions to his works in Dinesen's letters from Africa it seems reasonable to conclude that Dinesen, just like her Kierkegaard-mentor Georg Brandes, had an ambiguous relationship to Kierkegaard and his writings. It also seems that Dinesen's approach to Kierkegaard changed after meeting Georg Brandes in Denmark in 1925 since the mentioning of Kierkegaard and the allusions to his works in the letters from 4 July 1926 onwards became more critical and ironical. Just like Brandes, she respected Kierkegaard's profound wit and courage and how he discovered the subject and the self (as we see from the positive lines from the quotes in the early letters from Africa), but was, on the other hand, highly critical of his views on Christianity and gender. In Brandes' book about Kierkegaard we find this passage to clearly illustrate the core of Brandes' (and later Dinesen's) critique of Kierkegaard:

> Da Kierkegaard forlod den gamle naive Landvei til Troen, fandt han da paa hint Skib, han selv havde bygget, Reflexionens ubanede Vei dertil? Nei, i det Øieblik han raabte Land, var det i Virkeligheden ikke Traditionens Indien, hvortil han var naaet, men Personlighedens, den store Lidenskabs, den store Selvstændigheds Amerika. Hans umiskjendelige Storhed er, at han opdagede dette Amerika, hans uheldbredelige Galskab var, at han haardnakket vedblev at kalde det Indien [...] Men det var en underlig Blindhed, en Sygdom, næsten en Sindssyge af ham at troe, at hint den store Selvstændigheds Amerika var Traditionens gamle Vidunderland, at den Enkelte var eet med den Christne, at hin Inderlighed var en rent specific som en speciel positiv Religion havde forpagtet, eller, for at vende tilbage til vort Udgangspunkt, at hans egen ethiske Collision havde nogen Lighed med Patriarchen Abrahams i det gamle Testamente. (Brandes 1877: 106–07, 109)

> [When Kierkegaard left that old naïve road toward faith, did he then find, on the ship that he himself had built, the untrodden path of reflection? No, in the moment he cried out, Land, he had in reality reached not the India of tradition but of personality, of the great passion, the great America of Independence. His unmistakable greatness is that he discovered this America; his incurable madness was that he continued, stubbornly, to call it India [...] But it was a strange blindness, a sickness, almost an insanity, for him to believe that this America of great independence was the old wonderland of tradition, that the individual was the same as the Christian, that this intensity was a purely specific one that a special positive religion had monopoly on, or, to return to our point of departure, that his own ethical collision had any similarity to that of the patriarch Abraham's in the Old Testament.]

But also his admiration for him:

> Det skal ikke glemmes, at Faa her i Danmark have bidraget saa meget til dens [den intellectuelle Culturs] Fremme og Væxt som han, om hvem vi tale. Han er, som jeg engang har sagt det, vor Filosofis Tycho Brahe; han feilede i sin Opfattelse af Verdenssystemets Midtpunkt; han var paa mange Punkter hildet i sin Samtids Overtro, men han har beriget vort Aandsliv med en Rigdom af selvstændige Iagttagelser og Ideer. (Brandes 1877: 117)[10]

> [It must not be forgotten that few here in Denmark have contributed as much to

its [the intellectual culture's] advancement and growth as he of whom we speak. He is, as I once said, our Tycho Brahe of philosophy; he erred in his perception of the center of the world's system; he was, on several counts, ensnared in the superstition of his time, but he has enriched our intellectual life with a wealth of independent observations and ideas.]

Again, this was a view on Kierkegaard that Dinesen supported, even though she — as Brandes — also reserved her right to be critical.

Notes to Chapter 2

1. Author's translation.
2. Made available online by the Royal Danish Library here <http://www.kb.dk/da/kb/nb/ha/web_udstil/gb_dagbog.html> [accessed 29 August 2015].
3. Georg Brandes, *Samlede Skrifter*, bind 12 (Copenhagen: Gyldendalske Boghandel, 1902), p. 271, available at <http://runeberg.org/gbsamskr/12/0277.html> [accessed 29 August 2016].
4. 'Den første kladde til Sandhedens hævn er fra 1904. Den blev omarbejdet i 1915 og igen i 1926, hvor den blev trykt i tidsskriftet Tilskueren, maj 1926. På samme tid skrev Karen Blixen på to andre marionetkomedier — den aldrig trykte Elmis Hjerte, samt Carneval', quoted from <http://blixen.dk/liv-forfatterskab/karen-blixens-vaerker/marionet-komedier/> [accessed 29 August 2016]. [The first draft of 'The Revenge of Truth' is from 1904. It was revised in 1915 and again in 1926, when it was printed in the journal *Tilskueren* (May, 1926). At the same time Karen Blixen wrote two other marionette comedies — the never published *Elmis Hjerte* [Elmi's Heart], along with *Carneval* [Carnival]].
5. This work was still in Dinesen's library at Rungstedlund when she died (Bondesson 1982: 300).
6. The English translation of this work brings the original French quote without an English translation.
7. Honoré de Balzac, *Cousin Betty*, transl. by James Waring. Release Date: March 1, 2010 [EBook #1749]. Last Updated: April 3, 2013, 425–26 <http://www.gutenberg.org/files/1749/1749-h/1749-h.htm> [accessed 29 August 2016].
8. Author's translation.
9. Brandes book — and his views on Kierkegaard — might, however, get a revival since a reprint of his biography, with a foreword by Frederik Stjernfelt, came out on Gyldendal in 2013. It is surprising that it took hundred and thirty-six years before at second edition of this major work on Kierkegaard was published. It is still to be translated into English.
10. Despite his critique of Kierkegaard, Brandes did a tour of Scandinavia in the fall of 1876 where he gave public lectures about Kierkegaard. His Kierkegaard biography that came out a year later was also soon translated into Swedish and German (Anz 1999: 206) but has curiously enough never been translated into English.

CHAPTER 3

❖

Kierkegaard, Høffding, and Dinesen: Poetics of Irony

This chapter points to the influence of the Danish philosopher Harald Høffding with special attention to Dinesen's notion of irony in relation to Kierkegaard. Høffding finds Kierkegaard's definition of irony in *Om Begrebet Ironie* (1841) (*The Concept of Irony*) too one-sided and negative. Instead he operates with three categories 'the small irony', 'the great irony', and 'artistic irony'. Høffding defines 'the small irony' as an utterance that occurs with apparent recognition and seriousness, although its real quest is to attack and destroy. This is, according to Høffding, similar to Kierkegaard's notion of irony that he made absolute and saw as disintegrating and devoid of any positive content. Contrary to Kierkegaard, Høffding introduces a positive form of irony that he calls 'the great irony', which he argues has constructive and creative qualities and is similar to humour. Høffding then uses Shakespeare as an example when he defines 'artistic irony' as an irony that connects to art's great task: to offer concrete and individual portraits of characters and destinies, not abstractions and utopias. In the chapter, I argue that Dinesen's overall approach, to her predecessors in general, and Kierkegaard in particular, belongs to that of 'the great irony' and that her materialistic counter-stories very precisely fit Høffding's notion of 'artistic irony'.

Høffding and Dinesen

In the early 1900s Dinesen met Høffding in person when she was studying painting in Copenhagen at 'Kunstakademiet' [The Royal Art Academy] (1903–1905). In this passage from a small essay that was first published in Danish newspaper *Berlingske Aftenavis* on 24 June 1950 Dinesen recollects him with great sympathy:[1]

> Her var jeg engang Watteau'sk Pierrot paa et meget vellykket Karneval,[2] og her oplevede jeg, som en Slags Værtinde i Foreningen, at have Professor Høffding til Bords, da denne store, gamle Mand venligt kom og holdt Foredrag for os. Jeg kan ikke huske, at jeg den Aften følte mig det allermindste trykket af min prominente Stilling, jeg tror, at Høffdings blide, vise Elskværdighed lige straks har faaet mig til at føle mig hjemme ved hans Side. (Blixen 1951: 22)

> [One time here I was Watteau's Perrot at a very successful Carnival, and, as a kind of hostess in the society, I experienced having Professor Høffding to

dinner, when the large, old man kindly came and lectured to us. I cannot remember that evening feeling in the least bit pressured by my prominent position. I believe that Høffding's mild, wise kindness immediately made me feel at ease by his side.]

About ten years before, in 1892, Høffding had written a book about Kierkegaard called *Søren Kierkegaard som Filosof* [3] [Søren Kierkegaard as a Philosopher] that was only the second monograph about Kierkegaard succeeding Georg Brandes' work from 1877. Høffding's book came out in a second edition in 1919. Dinesen was indeed very familiar with the work of Høffding around that time, as we know from the letter about Pascal and Kierkegaard from 1923, even though it is hard to determine with certainty whether she read Høffding's monograph or not. In the polemical essay 'Fra lægmand til lægmand' [From layman to layman] (that has still not been translated into English), first printed in Danish newspaper *Politiken* 11 May 1954, Dinesen gives an answer to a group of young doctors, who have arrogantly suggested that she is not familiar with the ethics of Kant and Høffding:

> De unge medicinere må dog nok forestille sig, at jeg har hørt om Kant og Høffding. — Ja, [...] jeg har hos Høffding læst: 'Etiske domme er ikke blot teoretiske kuriositeter.' [...] Jeg kan også bruge nogle ord af selve Høffding: '... den forfærdelige isolation som fremkommer, hvor delen sætter sig i helhedens sted'. (Blixen 1954: 233–34, 247)

> [The young doctors should be able to picture to themselves that I have heard about Kant and Høffding. — Yes, [...] In Høffding I have read: 'Ethical judgments are not just theoretical curiosities.' [...] I can even use a couple of Høffding's own words: 'the terrible isolation that emerges when the part becomes the substitute for the whole'.][4]

Høffding's Notion of Irony

In his book *'Gid De havde set mig dengang'* [I Wish You Had Seen Me Then] that contains a long an interesting analysis of 'Ehrengard' including a chapter on the connections to Kierkegaard, Ivan Ž. Sørensen suggests that Dinesen had read Høffding's work *Den store Humor* [The Big Humour] from 1916 (Sørensen 2002: 155). It seems very likely, especially when reading the chapter titled 'Ironi og Humor' where Kierkegaard's concept of irony[5] is thoroughly treated and criticized by Høffding in ways that fit very well with the artistic strategy of irony we find in Dinesen's works:

> Til Satirens Midler kan den ironiske Form høre. Den optræder da med tilsyneladende Anerkendelse og Alvor, skønt dens egentlige Stræben er at angribe og tilintetgøre. En indirekte Angrebsform afløser da den direkte. Ironien er her kun Middel, betegner ikke en særlig Livstype. Det er, hvad man kunde kalde den lille Ironi, medens den store Ironi ikke blot er Form og Middel, men et Livsstade. Forskellen vil bl.a. bestaa i, at medens det ved Ironi som Form eller Talefigur maa tilstræbes, at de Andre forstaa, at det er Ironi, at Alvoren ikke er alvorligt ment, forholder det sig anderledes ved den store Ironi [...] Medens Satiren støder Genstanden bort, eller kun fastholder den for atter og

atter at støde den bort, kan Ironien være en Vej, ad hvilken det bliver muligt at trænge ind i Genstanden og oprette et Fællesskab med den. Selv hvor Ironien tjener Selvhævdelsen, er den ikke en Frastøden, men en Unddragen, en Vej til at holde Sindets Helligdom fri for Omverdenens Indtrængen [...] Kierkegaard konstruerede i sit geniale Ungdomsskrift (Om Begrebet Ironi [sic], med særligt Hensyn til Sokrates. 1841) en absolut Ironi, hvorved han mente en Ironi af rent negativ Art. Det var den lille Ironi, han gjorde absolut, istedetfor at gøre den stor. Han betragtede Ironien blot som opløsende, som blottet for ethvert positivt Indhold. Han fraskriver den baade indre Fylde og det sympatiske Element. (Høffding 1916: 61, 63 and 64)

[Ironic form can belong to Satire's means. It occurs then with apparent recognition and seriousness, although its real quest is to attack and destroy. Thus, an indirect form of attack replaces the direct one. Irony in this case functions only as a means; it does not denote a specific way of living. It is what one might call the small irony, whereas the great irony is not only a form or a means but also a stage in life. The difference will consist of, among others, that while irony as a form or figure of speech aim for that others understand that it is irony, that nothing serious is intended; it is a different matter with the great irony [...] Whereas satire pushes the object away, or retains it only to, again and again, push it away, irony can be a way by which it becomes possible to penetrate the subject and establish fellowship with it. Even when irony serves self-assertion, it is not something repulsive, but rather an evasion, a way to hold the sanctity of the mind free of incursions from the outside world [...] In his brilliant youthful document (*The Concept of Irony, with Continual Reference to Socrates.* 1841), Kierkegaard constructed an absolute irony, whereby he meant an irony of purely negative nature. It was absolutely the small irony he was creating, rather than the large one. He viewed irony solely as disintegrating, as devoid of any positive content. He renounces both the inner abundance and the sympathetic element.]

The notion of 'kunstnerisk ironi' [artistic irony] that Høffding then goes on to present in the quote below, with Dinesen's favorite writer Shakespeare as the prime example, also fits very well as a description of Dinesen's preferred artistic method with regard to how she makes the abstract ideas we find presented in Kierkegaard's works concrete in her ironical counter-stories:

Ogsaa Shakespeare har man villet gøre til Ironiker [in the negative Kierkegaardian sense of the word] [...] Herimod indvender en af de ypperste nyere Shakespeareforskere [footnote in the text: '*Dowden: Shakespeare. His Mind and Art.* (1880) p. 345'] med Rette, at Shakespeare's Upartiskhed overfor Personer og Skæbner ikke betyder Ligegyldighed og Fjernhed, men netop udspringer af hans Interesse for Emnerne, af den faste Villie til at lade enhver af deres Sider komme til sin Ret; hans Begejstring svækkes ikke ved de Skranker, menneskelige Handlinger og Skæbner ere underlagte. Der gives en kunstnerisk Ironi, som hænger nøje sammen med Kunstens store Opgave, den at give konkrete og individuelle Billeder af Karakterer og Skæbner, ikke Abstraktioner og Utopier. (Høffding 1916: 67)

[People have also wanted to turn Shakespeare into an ironist [...] To the contrary, one of the finest of the recent Shakespeare scholars objects correctly that Shakespeare's impartiality toward persons and destinies does not indicate indifference or remoteness, but stems precisely from his interest in his subjects, of that steadfast will to let each one of their sides come into its own. His enthusiasm is not weakened by these limitations; human actions and destinies are ascribed. An artistic irony is provided that connects precisely to art's great task, to offer concrete and individual portraits of characters and destinies, not abstractions and utopias.]

Høffding then goes on to point out the following differences between 'Ironi' [irony] and 'Humor' [humour]:

> Forskellen mellem Ironi og Humor er ofte udtrykt saaledes, at i Ironi er der Spøg bag Alvor, i Humor Alvor bag Spøg [...] I ironien gaas der tilsyneladende ind paa Værdier og Bestræbelser, men Ironikeren foretager kun denne Bevægelse for at bevare sit Indre frit, eller — i den pædagogisk [sic] Ironi — for at udløse psykisk Energi hos den, der vedkender sig visse Værdier og Formaal. At der er Spøg bag Alvoren, behøver blot at betyde, at Ironikeren har sin Alvor i andre Retninger end hans Omgivelser. (Høffding 1916: 68–69)

> [The difference between irony and humour is often expressed as such — that in irony there is jest behind seriousness, in humour, seriousness behind jest [...] In irony, values and efforts are seemingly agreed to, but the ironist only makes this move to preserve his mind freely, or — in pedagogical irony — to provoke mental energy in the one who acknowledges certain values and purposes. That there is jest behind the seriousness need only mean that the ironist maintains his seriousness in other directions than his surroundings.]

Høffding proceeds to state that 'den store Ironi' equals 'Humour' using formal logic as a method to prove it:

> Derfor kan Ironien være en ydre Form for Humor, saa at vi faa følgende Skema (hvor Tegnet < betyder 'Middel' eller 'Udtryk for'):
>
> (Alvor < Spøg) = Ironi < Humor = (Spøg < Alvor)
> eller simplere Alvor < Spøg < Alvor
>
> Den Spøg, i hvilken Humoristen skjuler sin Alvor, bestaar da netop i Anvendelse af Ironi. Eller Simplere: bag den Spøg, der i Ironien er skjult i Alvor, ligger igen Alvor Skjult. Paa denne Maade gaar den store Ironi, som Form for Selvhævdelse eller for Opdragende Omsorg, over til Humor. (Høffding 1916: 69)

> [Therefore, irony can be an exterior form of humour, so that we get the following schemata (in which the symbol < indicates 'means' or 'expression for'):
>
> (Seriousness < Jest) = Irony < Humour = (Jest < Seriousness)
> or, more simply, Seriousness < Jest < Seriousness
>
> That jest, in which the humorist hides his seriousness, consists then precisely in the use of irony. Or more simply: behind that jest, which in irony is hidden in seriousness, seriousness lies again, hidden. In this way, the great irony transforms into a form of self-assertion or, for educational solicitude, into humour.]

Høffding finally concludes his essay with regard to Kierkegaard and his notion of irony, humour and the religious:

> I det nævnte Skrift [*Om Begrebet Ironie*] (og i Optegnelser, der ere samtidige med det) opfattede Kierkegaard Forholdet mellem Ironi og Humor som

Modsætninger. Ironien skal være egoistisk, og den skal være stedt i stadig Kamp mod Verden. Humoren derimod skal være befriet fra Verden; den staar som Udtryk for en religiøs Livsalvor og for Bevidstheden om at høre ind under en stor Helhed. Ironien skal være aristokratisk og polemisk, men Humoren er forsonet med Verden og hviler i en Tro, som fastholdes trods alle Absurditeter. (Skrifter XIII p. 35–119.) Senere derimod, efter det definitive Brud md [sic] den spekulative Teologi, betragter Kierkegaard ikke mere Humor som et religiøst Stade. Den staar for ham nu som det sidste humane Stade før det religiøse Stade, — som Udtryk for det højeste rent Menneskeliges Grænse. (Høffding 1916: 74)

[In the mentioned work [*The Concept of Irony*] (and in notes contemporaneous with it) Kierkegaard perceived the relationship between irony and humour as opposites. Irony must be egotistic, and it must be present in a constant battle against the world. Humour, on the other hand, must be liberated from the world; it is an expression for a religious seriousness and for the consciousness of belonging under a great oneness. Irony must be aristocratic and polemical, but humour is reconciled with the world and rests in a faith that is maintained, despite all absurdities. (Skrifter XIII p. 35–119) Later, on the other hand, after the definitive break with speculative theology, Kierkegaard no longer views humour as a religious stage. It now becomes for him the last human stage before the religious stage — an expression for the highest purely human limitation.]

Dinesen's overall approach to irony clearly fits Høffding's category of the great irony (which he also calls humour). An example from 'Ehrengard' is that the serious and embarrassing moment she subjects Cazotte to, when he blushes, also carries a joke (the great artist and rumoured Don Juan, who is in fact a virgin), which then again has seriousness behind it with regard to the more grave insights into art, omnipotence, manipulation and sexual sublimation that the tale has to offer. I will, however, favour the term irony (Høffding's 'great irony'), when describing Dinesen's overall approach to Kierkegaard, since it better describes the serious core in Dinesen's approach to Kierkegaard (her counter-stories as 'serious parodies' as defined by Genette) and the important fact that we can only understand the parodic elements and the humour after we have understood the serious alternative interpretations that the subversions offer. But, admittedly, the discourse in Dinesen's tales often shifts between irony and humour to such a degree that at times they cannot be clearly separated.[6]

It is easier to directly connect Dinesen's artistic and practical approach, when crafting her Kierkegaard counter-stories, to Høffding's notion of artistic irony, since her stories precisely offer 'concrete and individual portraits of characters and destinies' compared to Kierkegaard's theoretical and philosophical 'abstractions and utopias'. In *Sandhedens Hævn*, Abraham is a common murderer (not the 'founder of faith'), in 'The Diver' Thusmu is a very beautiful dancer of flesh and blood (not an angel), in 'The Dreamers' Pellegrina is an opera diva (not Don Juan as the embodiment of music), and in 'Babette's Feast' the Berlevaagians are not given an hour of the millennium by the grace of God, but by the grace of the artist Babette and the intoxication of fine champagne and wine, just to mention a few examples.

Notes to Chapter 3

1. Subsequently in the small book *Karen Blixens Tegninger. Med To Essays af Karen Blixen* (Blixen 1951) published by Frans Lasson.
2. Which is the same costume that the main protagonist, Mimi, is wearing in 'Carnival'.
3. Høffding's book on Kierkegaard has, just like Brandes critical study from 1877, never been translated into English.
4. Author's translation.
5. It is not possible to prove that Dinesen read Kierkegaard's *Om Begrebet Ironie* (1841), but it is very likely that she was familiar with his concept of irony through Brandes' Kierkegaard book and this work by Harald Høffding.
6. Genette notes that the shifts between irony and humour in connection to 'serious parody' seem to be a trademark for great literary works: 'Thomas Mann oscillates too constantly between irony and humor: hence a new gradation, a new blurring, for so it goes with great literary works' (Genette 1997: 29).

CHAPTER 4

❖

Dinesen's Combined
Knowledge of Kierkegaard

In an article from 2010, Anz mentions that:

> Blixens Kierkegaardlektüre ist schwer zu rekonstruieren. Es lässt sich nicht eindeutig ausmachen, welche Werke Kierkegaards Blixen selbst gelesen hat und wie viel bei ihr sekundär über allgemein verbreitete Vorstellungen bürgerlicher Bildung vermittelt ist [...] Explizite Bezüge innerhalb einzelner Erzählungen, wie die nachgelassenen Erzählungen *Karneval* und *Ehrengard*, verweisen auf eine Lektüre von *Diapsalmata* vielleicht von *Skyggerids* und mit Sicherheit von *Forførerens Dagbog* und damit wohl insgesamt auf die Papiere des Ästhetikers im ersten Band von *Enten. Eller.* Die Hiobreferenzen im Kontext der Dichterexistenz verweisen möglicherweise auf *Gjentagelsen*, alles andere bleibt so unspezifisch wie geflügelte Worte. Und auch die in ihren Texten selbst explizit etablierten Bibliotheken und die rekonstruierten Bibliotheken in ihren afrikanischen Farmhaus und in Rungstedlund bringen lediglich den Aufschluss, dass Kierkegaard in Blixens Bibliothek nicht vorkommt. (Anz 2010: 421–22).

> [It is difficult to reconstruct Blixen's reading of Kierkegaard. It is not possible to establish decidedly which of Kierkegaard's works were actually read by Blixen and how much was mediated through commonly known bourgeois cultural notions [...] Explicit references within specific tales — e.g. the posthumous tales *Karneval* and *Ehrengard* — indicate that she has read *Diapsalmata,* maybe *Skyggerids*, and for certain *Forførerens Dagbog* and probably all of the papers of the aesthete from the first volume of *Enten. Eller.* The mentioning of Hiob within the context of the poet's existence possibly refers to *Gjentagelsen*, everything else is as vague as popular sayings/dictums. Additionally, an investigation of the libraries that are explicitly mentioned in her texts and the reconstructed libraries of her African farmhouse and in Rungstedlund only lead to the conclusion that Kierkegaard is not represented in Blixen's library.]

Anz is partly correct in his first claim that 'Blixens Kierkegaardlektüre ist schwer zu rekonstruieren', since it, indeed, at times can be difficult to figure out how much Dinesen knew about Kierkegaard from secondary literature and common knowledge and how much we can attribute to her own readings of his works. But after mentioning the works that Dinesen had read, or might have read, which I all agree with, Anz concludes: 'everything else is as vague as popular sayings/dictums', which I will go on to show is a premature conclusion. The concluding line is particularly curious: 'that Kierkegaard is not represented in Blixen's library' since a closer look in Bondesson's registrant (Bondesson 1982) very precisely tells us that the following books by — or about — Kierkegaard were in Dinesen's library when she died. From the books in Dinesen's library, listed here below in chronological order according to publication date, we get the following information about Dinesen's 'Kierkegaardlektüre'. Comments, if any, under each title:

> Kierkegaard, Søren
> Enten — eller: et Livs-Fragment / udg. af Victor Eremita — 3. Udg. København: C. A. Reitzels forlag, 1865. Ejersignatur med blyant i bind I: Wilhelm Dinesen [signature of owner written in pencil in volume I: Wilhelm Dinesen]. (Bondesson 1982: 179)

According to Clara Selborn this copy of Enten — Eller, which had belonged to Dinesen's father, was given to Dinesen by her sister Ellen Dahl (Bondesson 1982: 179). In the first volume there are no pencil markings whereas in volume two (not mentioned by Anz) we find eight substantial passages underlined, all mentioned in their full length by Bondesson (Bondesson 1982: 179–80).

> Kierkegaard, Søren
> Synspunktet for min Forfatter-Virksomhed : en ligefrem Meddelelse, Rapport til Historien / Ved A.B. Drachmann. — 2. Udg. Kjøbenhavn: Gyldendal, 1906 (Bondesson 1982: 343)

> Kierkegaard, Søren
> Lillien paa Marken og Fuglen under Himlen : tre gudelige Taler. Kjøbenhavn: Haase, 1922 (Bondesson 1982: 238) Dedication: 'Ellen Westenholz af H. Molbech.' [Ellen Westenholz from H. Molbech]

> Bruun Andersen, K.
> Søren Kierkegaard og kritikeren P. L. Møller. København : Munksgaard, 1950.

From a letter to Dinesen we know that Aage Henriksen gave her this small book about the feud between Kierkegaard and P. L. Møller in August 1955 (no specific date), while she was hospitalized at 'Militærhospitalet' in Copenhagen (Blixen 1996b: 298–99).

> Hansen, P. Emanuel
> Dagbogsoptegnelser: omkring Søren Kierkegaard / indledning og noter ved Julius Clausen. Sønderborg : [s.1.], 1950. (Bondesson 1982: 343)

> Søren Kierkegaards dagbøger / i udvalg ved Peter P. Rohde; udg. af Dansk-lærerforeningen. København : Gyldendal, 1953 (Bondesson 1982: 344).

Peter P. Rohde visited Rungstedlund from time to time in the early fifties until (at least) 1960 (Selborn 1974: 166). Dinesen herself mentions in a letter that Peter Rohde and Tage Skou-Hansen were visiting on 11 September 1953 to talk her into contributing to the new literary magazine 'Vindrosen' published by Gyldendal (Blixen 1996b: 156). We find the initials 'KW.J.' inscribed with pencil on the inside of the cover, which are the initials of Dinesen's friend Knud W. Jensen. Knud W. Jensen might have given the copy to Dinesen, or, alternatively, she borrowed it and never returned it.

Henriksen, Aage
Kierkegaards Romaner. København : Gyldendal, 1954.

Given to Dinesen by Aage Henriksen in 1954 upon publication (Bondesson 1982: 343). Dinesen had a copy of the manuscript at Rungstedlund for most of the summer of 1953 that she read very closely before it went to press.[1] The thesis was published on 5 October (Blixen 1996b: 236) and defended by Aage Henriksen three weeks later, on 26 October 1954.

The combination of the early letter passages concerning Kierkegaard, the library listings and the many additional allusions we find in Dinesen's Kierkegaard counter-stories (that I will go on to show), we can deduce that Dinesen was well versed in the major works from Kierkegaard's aesthetic-pseudonymous authorship (1843–1846) before she finished *Seven Gothic Tales* in 1934. She must have read, or at least, through secondary literature, been familiar with the main ideas presented in the following works: *Enten — Eller. Første Deel* (Kierkegaard 1843a) and *Anden Deel* (Kierkegaard 1843b), *Gjentagelsen* (Kierkegaard 1843c), *Frygt og Bæven* (Kierkegaard 1843d), *Begrebet Angest* (Kierkegaard 1844), 'in vino veritas' from *Stadier paa Livets Vei* (Kierkegaard 1845) and *En literair Anmeldelse* (Kierkegaard 1846a). In the library we also find two later works by Kierkegaard: *Synspunktet for min Forfatter-Virksomhed: en ligefrem Meddelelse, Rapport til Historien* (1848, published posthumously in 1859) (*The point of view, on my work as an author, the point of view for my work as an author, armed neutrality*) and *Lillien paa Marken og Fuglen under Himlen. Tre Gudelige Taler af Søren Kierkegaard* (1849) (*The Lily in the Field and the Bird of the Air*). Dinesen deals with the ideas about 'the aesthetic' and 'the religious' presented in the first work in 'Babette's Feast' (see Chapter 15) but the second title does not seem to have played any particular role in Dinesen's counter-stories.

As we can see from the library listings, Dinesen also conducted studies of the most influential non-theological secondary literature about Kierkegaard that was published in her lifetime. In the 1920s it was the works of Georg Brandes and Harald Høffding and when her interest in Kierkegaard peaked for the second time in the 1950s while working on 'Ehrengard' (1952–1962). It was works by Frithiof Brandt,[2] K. Bruun Andersen, Aage Henriksen and the Kierkegaard's diary entries in Peter Rohde's selection that she studied. Dinesen's renewed interest in Kierkegaard in the early 1950s was sparked by Aage Henriksen whom she met for the first time in April 1953 after having corresponded with him in letters from the summer of 1952 (Blixen 1996b: 99). From the letter passages we understand that they eagerly discussed Kierkegaard in the years 1953 to 1955 (Blixen 1996b: 130, 299) while Henriksen was working on his doctoral thesis about Kierkegaard, and Dinesen on her Kierkegaard-tale 'Ehrengard'. These conversations with Aage Henriksen and the new works she read inspired by their discussions informed her view on Kierkegaard in a way that would come to play a role in 'Ehrengard' with regard to Kierkegaard and sexuality as I will go on to show in Chapter 10 and 11.

The range and implications of Dinesen's extensive interest in Kierkegaard's works, and maybe, and particularly, the secondary literature about Kierkegaard in Dinesen's oeuvre have, until now, not been fully understood and documented.

Notes to Chapter 4

1. From 13 June to 29 July 1953 (Henriksen 1985: 106, 111).
2. In a letter to Aage Henriksen she mentions that she has borrowed Frithiof Brandt's Kierkegaard biography *Den unge Søren Kierkegaard* (1929) on the library in July 1953 (Blixen 1996b: 147).

PART II

❖

Christianity

CHAPTER 5

❖

Kierkegaard, Christianity, and Dinesen: Influence from Brandes and Høffding

In this short chapter I will compare a couple of crucial letters where Dinesen explains her critical view of Christianity to passages from the works of Brandes and Høffding. All in all Dinesen is in line with Brandes' and Høffding's anthropological-materialistic view of Christianity, which suggests that the Bible is just a collection of stories and myths from certain Middle Eastern Tribes and not historical facts. Dinesen is in line with Høffding when he stresses that the great religions have their origin, just like culture, in human nature ad human conditions. Thus, Christianity is nothing more than a figment of the human imagination, created by humans in order to explain human longings (the quest for immortality), to justify gender roles and to account for the organization of (patriarchal) society.

'I must ask these Christians: Why do you believe this?'

That Kierkegaard was a Christian and did everything he could to fit in his new philosophy of the individual under the umbrella of Christianity is one of Dinesen's major points of critique. In fact, she already agrees with Høffding's critical view on Christianity and Kierkegaard in 1923 as we saw in the letter passage in Chapter 1. The core of Høffding's critic of Kierkegaard and Christianity in the article can be summed up in these quotes:

> Med to Aarhundreders Mellemrum mødtes to Tænkere [Pascal og Kierkegaard], som begge med hele deres Sjæls Inderlighed klamrede sig til Kristendommen, i den Maade, paa hvilken de gjorde op med deres Religion, saaledes som denne havde udviklet sig gennem Tiderne. (Høffding 1923: 412)

> [Within the space of two centuries, we encounter two thinkers [Pascal and Kierkegaard], both of whom with all their soul's fervor, clung to Christianity in the manner in which they broke from their religion, such as it had evolved through the ages.]

Høffding then goes on to ask:

> Kan den oprindelige Kristendoms Livsopfattelse og Livsførelse fastholdes sammen med Tilegnelse af og Arbejde for den aandelige og materielle Kultur, som Kristendommen ikke har frembragt, men som — før og efter Kristendommens Opstaaen — har udviklet sig efter sine egne love? (Høffding 1923: 424–25)

[Can original Christianity's conception of life and conduct be maintained along with the acquisition of and work toward spiritual and material culture, which Christianity has not engendered but which has developed — before and after the emergence of Christianity — according to its own laws?]

In the essay Høffding perceives any religion as a cultural and anthropological pheno-menon. Religion is a product of the psychology of certain people living in certain parts of the world under certain conditions, which means that religion ultimately derives from human beings and is a sort of anthropological fantasy, representing the ideals of a people:

> De store Verdensreligioner har nu engang, ligesom Kulturen, deres Udspring i menneskelig Natur og menneskelige Livsforhold, og hvad der af Ædelt, Stort og Skønt har udviklet sig indenfor Religionerne, tilhører derfor tilsidst Menneskeslægten som Helhed, ikke en enkelt Sekt, selv om denne har nok saa stor en Udbredelse. (Høffding 1923: 432–33)

> [The great world religions have their origin, after all, just like culture, in human nature and human conditions, and that which is noble, great, and wonderful in religions belongs, therefore, ultimately to humankind as a whole, not as a single sect, even though this has had a wide distribution.]

In his book *Søren Kierkegaard. En kritisk Fremstilling i Grundrids* Brandes is very cri-tical of the way Kierkegaard engaged Christianity, as I have already mentioned. Instead of dismissing Christianity as an illusion based on all the paradoxes he discovered, Kierkegaard directed his critique towards the leaders of the church. This was, according to Brandes, a blind spot and a severe mistake:

> Da Kierkegaard nu var naaet saa vidt i Udvikling, at den Opposition mod Undervisningen, der var at forudse, kom til Udbrud, kom han følgelig ved denne Revolte ind i en rent tilfældig og hurtigt forældet Polemik, der desværre strækker sig gjennem hele hans Forfatterliv [...] Ikke mod en Strauss, ikke mod en Feuerbach rettede han sine Slag, men mod en Marheineke, en Martensen og deres Disciple! Han agtede ikke paa, at medens han stod paa Volden og forsvarede Fæstningen mod uskadelige Speculanter, trængte Fritænkerne ind bag hans Ryg og erobrede Pladsen. (Brandes 1877: 24–25)

> [When Kierkegaard reached the point in his development that the expected opposition toward the teachings erupted, he entered, because of this revolt, into a purely random and quickly outdated polemic, one which unfortunately stretched throughout his entire life as an author [...] Not against a Strauss, not against a Feuerbach did he direct his blows, but toward a Marheineke, a Martensen and their disciples! He never noticed that, while he was standing on the ramparts and defending the fort against innocent speculators, the free thinkers were penetrating behind his back and capturing the site.]

Not without a significant element of disappointment Brandes concludes: 'Og ikke blot at Kierkegaard blev Theolog, men han levede hele sit Liv igjennem i en fuldstændig theologisk og theologiseret Dunstkreds' (Brandes 1877: 23) [And not only that Kierkegaard became a theologian, but he lived his entire life in a totally theological and theologized atmosphere]. As I have shown, Dinesen openly admitted that she admired both Brandes and Høffding's writings and ideas and subscribed to their critical views on Christianity. This was an opinion she kept all her life. We find it most clearly formulated in a letter to Johannes Rosendahl from 15 January 1952, during a period where her interest in Kierkegaard peaked for the second time (1950–1955) and she wrote two major tales that relate to Kierkegaard's ideas: 'Babette's Feast' (1950) ('Babettes Gæstebud') (1958) and the first draft of 'Ehrengard' (spring 1952). In the letter Dinesen explains very clearly to Rosendahl, how she sees Christianity as an illusion and why she has to be critical of it. Her explanation is completely in line with the anthropological and sociological approaches to religion and Christianity propagated by Brandes and Høffding, which, as I shall argue in the next chapter, Dinesen had already adopted before she finished her first significant work *Sandhedens Hævn*:[1]

> Det var ifølge min Opfattelse galt, at Ordet *Tro* Aftenen igennem kom til at stå for *kristen Tro*, som om disse Begreber givetvis faldt sammen. Mennesker har i Tusinder af Aar *troet* uden at være Kristne; Millioner af Mennesker har i Dag en *Tro*, som ikke er Kristendom. Hvorfor vælger nu Mennesker, — altsaa nærmere bestemt Mennesker i Danmark og i Aaret 1951, — at bestemme deres Tro som Kristendom? [...] Kristendom er Troen paa, at i et historisk bestemt Aar en af de tre Personer i en treenig Guddom blev Menneske [...] Nu spurgte jeg altsaa, fra min Stilling udenfor Kristendommen, de Kristne: Hvorfor tror I dette? Jeg har jo før spurgt og har da ofte faaet Svaret: 'Fordi det staar i Bibelen'. Her har jeg da igen maattet spørge: 'Hvorfor vælger I i ganske særlig Grad at sætte eders Lid til et lille østerlandsk, og selv fjerntstaaende, Folks Samling af mytologiske Forestillinger og Fortællinger? Der er i Verden, og i Tiden, nedskrevet mangfoldige saadanne, uden at I i mindste Maade tillægger dem Betydning som Oplysning om den hele Universet gældende Sandhed' [...] til dette maa jeg føje, at jeg ikke kan grunde et Livssyn paa en historisk Begivenhed, og at jeg ikke tror, at noget Menneske er i Stand dertil, eller egentlig vil give sig ud for at være i Stand dertil. En Mangfoldighed af anerkendte historiske Begivenheder, — Folkevandringen, det romerske Riges Undergang, den franske Revolution, ja, og i denne Sammenhæng ogsaa den kristne Kirkes Historie, — har bidraget til at danne mit Syn paa Menneskelivets Sammenhæng, uden derfor at havde givet mig en absolut Forklaring paa selve Livets og Universets Væsen. (Blixen 1996b: 75–77)

> [In my opinion, it was wrong that throughout the evening the word *Faith* came to mean *Christian faith,* as if these two concepts naturally coincided. For thousands of years, people have *believed* without being Christians; millions of people today have a *faith* that is not Christianity. Why do people now choose — more specifically, people in Denmark in the year 1951 — to identify their faith as Christianity? [...] Christianity is the belief that in a historically determined year one of the three persons of the tripartite God became man [...] Now, I must ask these Christians, therefore, from my position outside of Christianity: Why do you believe this? I have certainly asked before and have often gotten the answer: 'Because it is in the Bible'. And I had to then ask once again: 'Why have you chosen, to such a special degree, to put your trust in a small Eastern, even remote, people's collection of mythological ideas and stories? Throughout the world, and throughout time, numerous such stories have been recorded, yet you have not in any way attached any meaning to them about enlightenment applicable to the entire universe' [...] to this I must add that I cannot base a

view of life on one single historic occurrence, and that I do not believe that any person is capable of doing so, or really would pretend to do so. A multitude of renowned historical events — the Exodus, the fall of the Roman Empire, the French Revolution, yes, and in this connection also the history of the Christian church — have helped to form my view of the context of human life, without therefore having given me an absolute explanation on the very being of life and the universe.]

Thus, the next chapter is dedicated to an analysis of *Sandhedens Hævn* with particular attention to Kierkegaard and Christianity.

Notes to Chapter 5

1. Which we also find very adamantly formulated in some of the letters from Africa in 1923 and 1924 (Blixen 2013: 595, 719 and 730).

CHAPTER 6

❖

The Gospel of Nature and Joy:
Sandhedens Hævn and *Frygt og Bæven*

In this chapter, I argue that Dinesen's marionette play *Sandhedens Hævn* (1926) (*The Revenge of Truth*) is highly critical of Christianity and instead propagates the gospel of nature and joy. The play also deals with — and mocks — certain ideas put forward by Johannes de Silentio in *Frygt og Bæven* (1843) — especially de Silentio's idolization of Abraham as the founder of faith and the ethical model of humanity. Here Dinesen seems inspired by Brandes' critique of this particular work in his Kierkegaard biography from 1877. In *Sandhedens Hævn*, Abraham is a materialistic-comical subversion of this biblical character from *Frygt og Bæven*, a simple cowardly villain, and not a hero. Dinesen also subverts Johannes de Silentio's notion of eternal consciousness as the highest, and human passions as something dark and destructive, when Fortunio concludes the play with a tribute to love, danger, music and wine. It is also no coincidence that the omnipotent character in Dinesen's marionette comedy is a Pagan witch, Amiane, and not the usual omnipotent authority: the male Christian God that we also find in *Frygt og Bæven*.

In *Sandhedens Hævn*, Dinesen also suggests that the art of becoming oneself cannot happen through a religious movement, but that the individual, on the contrary, must break free from the pangs of anxiety and the sense of guilt that Christian ethics and the religious have subjected mankind to, and instead follow the uncorrupted seeds of human nature that express our natural sensuousness, playfulness, and creativity. Here Dinesen also draws on P. M. Møller's (1843) notion of 'affektation' [affectation] (to do what others expect you to do, instead of what you want to do) and how to break away from it. Another profound insight the play gives us is that the choices we did not make in life (and not just the ones we made as Kierkegaard maintains) have a much bigger influence on our lives than we normally tend to think. The play is also, in various ways, as I shall go on to show, an early version of Dinesen's notion of Nemesis.

An Atheist's Point of View

In a letter to Mary Bess Westenholz dated 1 April 1914 just a few months after she arrived in Kenya and now residing at the MBagathi Estate in Ngong Hills, we find this very important, but up until the publication of the expanded letter collection

Karen Blixen i Afrika (2013), hitherto unknown passage:

> Angaaende 'Sandhedens Hævn', saa vil jeg ikke forandre noget i den; derimod tror jeg, der er ringe Chance for, at den nogensinde kommer ud. Jeg synes ikke, der er noget blasfemisk i den, kun skrevet lige ud fra en Atheists Standpunkt.[1] Jeg tror, det er umuligt at skrive, hvis man skal tage Hensyn til hvem som læser det. (Blixen 2013: 29)

> [Regarding 'The Revenge of Truth': I would not change anything in it; on the other hand, I believe there is little chance of it ever being published. I do not think there is anything blasphemous in it; it is just written directly from an atheist's point of view. I think it is impossible to write if you have to be considerate about everyone who reads it.]

Sandhedens Hævn is the first substantial example of Dinesen's critique of Christianity, which later came to run as a significant current in her entire oeuvre.[2] In the play we find the murderous innkeeper to bear the value-laden name of Abraham — the founder of faith according to Christian mythology. Dinesen of course knew the story of Abraham and Isaac from The Bible and as this letter passage from Africa dated 14 September 1930 shows, she had not much good to say about the characters in the Old Testament:

> [Han [Grigg] er saa stor Shakespearedyrker, saa vi taler altid meget ivrigt om ham, — ogsaa meget stiv i det gamle Testamente, som efter min Erfaring tidt følges ad, ikke for mit Vedkommende, thi jeg kan ikke faa nogetsomhelst ud deraf og synes, det var en Samling Skurke.] (Blixen 2013: 1625)

> [He is such a great devotee of Shakespeare, so we always talk very enthusiastically about him, — also well up on the Old Testament, two interests that often go together, although not in my case, for I can get nothing whatsoever out of it and think they were a lot of scoundrels.] (Dinesen 1981: 410)

In his book about Kierkegaard Brandes is extremely critical of Johannes de Silentio's idealized depiction of Abraham (Brandes 1877: 109–12).[3] The essence of Brandes' critique is:

> Det er godt nok at beundre Abraham. Men der er intet redeligt Menneske, som af Vane eller Magelighed vil kalde det stort hos Abraham, som han vilde stemple ganske anderledes, ifald det skete i vore Dage, ifald det f. Ex. udførtes af en stakkels udannet Haandværkssvend. (Brandes 1877: 110)

> [It is fine to admire Abraham. But no honest person, either out of habit or impudence, would call that great in Abraham which he would brand quite differently if it happened in our day — if, for example, it was carried out by some poor, uneducated journeyman.]

Brandes continues with an anthropological reading of the story and concludes by accusing Kierkegaard of exploiting this biblical story (among others) as a means to depict his own inner condition and existential pangs:

> Historien om Abraham er en af de flere gamle skjønne Legender, i hvilke Menneskeslægten paa sin Vandring gjennem Historien har nedlagt sin Erindring om de ældste Tiders Menneskeofringers Overgang til Dyreofre, men er det redeligt, er det sundt, er det ethisk, at prise Abraham som det store

ethiske Mønster for Slægten og som Troens Fader, naar man dog blot vil bruge ham til at udskamme en lidenskabsløs Samtid og til at stille sine egne indre Erfaringer i et elektrisk Lys? (Brandes 1877: 112)

[The story of Abraham is one of several old beautiful legends in which humankind, in its wandering through history, has preserved its memory of the oldest age's transition from human to animal sacrifices; but is it honest, is it healthy, is it ethical, to praise Abraham as the great ethical model for humanity and as the father of faith, when one only wants to use him, however, to embarrass a dispassionate contemporary time period and to highlight his own inner experience?]

In *Sandhedens Hævn* Dinesen depicts the great founder of faith Abraham as not only a villain, but also a coward, who from time to time asks his henchman Mopsus to kill the guests at the inn for him, so he can take their money.[4] He is in no way a noble and admirable person as Johannes de Silentio depicts him in Kierkegaard's *Frygt og Bæven*. Dinesen's Abraham is the materialistic-comical subversion of this biblical character that supports Brandes' view that Abraham should be judged as a common murderer. Dinesen is doing here what Johannes de Silentio suggests would be the result if we looked at Abraham without counting in the notion of faith and the religious perspective:

Kan Troen ikke gjøre det til en hellig Handling at ville myrde sin Søn, saa lad den samme Dom gaae over Abraham som over enhver Anden. Mangler man maaskee Mod til at gjennemføre sin Tanke, at sige, at Abraham var en Morder, da er det vel bedre at erhverve dette Mod, end at spilde Tiden paa ufortjente Lovtaler. (Kierkegaard 1843d: 126)

[If faith cannot make it a holy act to be willing to murder his son, then let the same judgment be passed on Abraham as on everyone else. If a person lacks the courage to think his thought all the way through and say that Abraham was a murderer, then it is certainly better to attain this courage than to waste time on unmerited eulogies.] (Kierkegaard 1983b: 40)

This is exactly what Dinesen does in *Sandhedens Hævn*. She shows everyone that she has the 'Mod' [courage] to take this position and even tops it by ridiculing Abraham when casting him in the role of a comical villain in a marionette comedy. The following passage in *Frygt og Bæven* also seems to have inspired both the plot and the title, since 'Sandhedens Dom' [the judgment of Abraham] is exactly that Abraham is a 'Morder' [murderer] who in Dinesen's play has 'sovet sig til Navnkundighed' [slept his way to fame], in this case to his wealth and power, since Mopsus is running around in the night killing the guests for him while he himself is asleep:

Hvis jeg havde erkjendt det for Sandhedens Dom, at Abraham var en Morder, da veed jeg ikke, om jeg havde kunnet bringe min Pietet for ham til Taushed. Havde jeg imidlertid tænkt det, saa havde jeg formodentlig tiet dermed; thi i slige Tanker skal man ikke indvie Andre. Men Abraham er intet Blendværk, han har ikke sovet sig til sin Navnkundighed, han skylder den ikke en Lune af Skjebnen. (Kierkegaard 1843d: 126)

[If I had acknowledged as true the judgment that Abraham was a murderer, I am not sure that I would have been able to silence my reverence for him. But if

I did think that, I probably would have said nothing, for one should not initiate others into such thoughts. But Abraham is no illusion, he did not sleep his way to fame, he does not owe it to a whim of fate.] (Kierkegaard 1983b: 41)

Abraham even falls victim of 'en Lune af Skjebnen' [whim of fate] when the witch Amiane casts the spell that every lie told that night, will come true, which in the end becomes the main reason for Abraham's demise. In the Biblical story God rewards Abraham with numerous descendants and abundant prosperity for being willing to follow his command to kill his own son. In *Sandhedens Hævn* Dinesen subjects Abraham to the opposite fate, when all his money disappears as a cloud of bats into the sky and his only daughter runs away with the gossip journalist and alcoholic Jan Bravida.

The Gospel of Nature and Joy

In one of the first paragraphs 'Lovtale til Abraham' [Eulogy on Abraham] in *Frygt og Bæven* we find a passage where Johannes de Silentio is praising consciousness and spirit over nature:

Dersom der ingen evig Bevidsthed var i et Menneske, dersom der til Grund for Alt kun laae en vildt gjærende Magt, der vridende sig i dunkle Lidenskaber frembragte Alt, hvad der var stort og hvad der var ubetydeligt, dersom en bundløs Tomhed, aldrig mættet, skjulte sig under Alt, hvad var da Livet Andet end Fortvivlelse? Dersom det forholdt sig saaledes, dersom der intet helligt Baand var, der sammenknyttede Menneskeheden, dersom den ene Slægt stod op efter den anden som Løvet i Skoven, dersom den ene Slægt afløste den anden som Fuglesangen i Skoven, dersom Slægten gik gjennem Verden, som Skibet gaaer gjennem Havet, som Veiret gjennem Ørkenen, en tankeløs og ufrugtbar Gjerning, dersom en evig Glemsel altid hungrig lurede paa sit Bytte, og der var ingen Magt stærk nok til at frarive den det — hvor var da Livet tomt og trøstesløst! (Kierkegaard 1843d: 112)

[If a human being did not have an eternal consciousness, if underlying everything there were only a wild, fermenting power that writhing in dark passions produced everything, be it significant or insignificant, if a vast, never appeased emptiness hid beneath everything, what would life be then but despair? If such were the situation, if there were no sacred bond that knit humankind together, if one generation emerged after another like forest foliage, if one generation succeeded another like the singing of birds in the forest, if a generation passed through the world as a ship through the sea, as wind through the desert, an unthinking and unproductive performance, if an eternal oblivion, perpetually hungry, lurked for its prey and there were no power strong enough to wrench that away from it — how empty and devoid of consolation life would be!] (Kierkegaard 1983b: 33)

In the closing lines of the song that concludes *Sandhedens Hævn* Fortunio propagates the exact opposite view on nature compared to that of Johannes de Silentio. Fortunio does not subscribe to the idea that without 'evig Bevidsthed' [eternal consciousness] and God life is just 'bundløs Tomhed' [appeased emptiness] and 'Fortvivlelse' [despair]. He, on the contrary, propagates a joyous version of materialistic metaphysics, where nature, and the sea in particular, is the superior and eternal element. This point of view is also articulated as a tribute to the bodily pleasures of life, to joy and desire:

> Hejs Sejl. O Haab sid Du tilrors
> Farvel grønne Kyster
> vi har indenbords
> alt hvad Menneskers Sjæle lyster
> Elskov, Fare
> Musik og Alkohol
>
> [...]
> Jeg er det fri Hav
> andre Guder skal I ikke have.
> I Evighed er jeg bestandig ens.
> Mer end Jordens Lyst min Lyst
> og mer end Jordens Smerte er min Smerte
> en og udelt er jeg.
> Kom o frie Hjerter til mit Hjerte.
>
> [...]
> Ekko efterlod
> vi bag Mil og Maane
> lad Din Sjæl, Dit Blod
> min sit Ekko laane.
> Farvel o Kyst.
> Evig er Havets Lyst
> Evig o evig
> Lyst.
>
> (Blixen 1926: 38–39)

[Hoist the sail. Oh Hope, you are at the helm.
Farewell green shores.
On board we have all which can gladden human heart.
Love, danger,
Music and wine.

[...]
I am the unbounded sea.
No other gods shalt thou have.
For all eternity I remain unchanging.
My pleasure is more than earthly pleasure.
And my sorrow is more than earthly sorrow.
One and undivided am I.
Come, oh free hearts, to mine.

[...]
Echo left we behind,
Miles of distance and the moon also.
Let your soul, your blood
Echo mine.
Oh shore, farewell,
Eternal are the sea's delights,

> Eternal, oh eternal
> Delights.]
> (Dinesen 1986a: 124–25)

The song praises the sea as the only religion: 'Jeg er det fri Hav / andre Guder skal I ikke have' [I am the unbounded sea. No other gods shalt thou have] and 'Lyst' [delights]:[5] 'Evig er Havets Lyst. Evig o evig Lyst' [Eternal are the sea's delights, Eternal, oh eternal Delights] as the highest principle, which is a point of view that subverts the Christian notion of nature, the human body, lust and desire as something, spiritless and dark that has to be rejected, cultivated and controlled. The notion of eternity here is the opposite of the Christian notion of a timeless and eternal paradise in heaven. Instead, Fortunio connects eternity to the sea as the only eternal, infinite, time- and borderless earthly element, which is a materialistic subversion of the lofty Christian idea of a Paradise in Heaven (that we also find in 'The Diver', see Chapter 13). With her usual affinity for gender reversals of Kierkegaard's characters, it is also no coincidence that the omnipotent character in Dinesen's marionette comedy is a Pagan witch, Amiane, and not the usual omnipotent authority: the male Christian God that we also find in Kierkegaard's *Frygt og Bæven*. *Sandhedens Hævn* is the first, yet prominent and very clear, example of Dinesen's subversive strategy with regard to gender and Christianity in relation to Kierkegaard.

To be a Good Marionette

In his essay *Karen Blixen og marionetterne* from 1952 Aage Henriksen made the following connection between Dinesen's marionette motif in *Sandhedens Hævn*, Kierkegaard, and Christianity. The essay was first given as two radio talks in May 1952 (which led Dinesen to make contact with Aage Henriksen) and then published by Wivels Forlag the same summer:

> I begyndelsen af dette essay omtaltes Heinrich von Kleists dialog om marionetterne. Den endte med den vittigt-dybsindige påstand, at absolut ynde har kun marionetten og Gud, d.v.s. de væsner som er ubetinget natur eller ren ånd. På dansk kunne vi sige, at gentagelsen oplever kun marionetten og den kristne, og med det sidste ord føre tanken hen på Søren Kierkegaard, som skrev en bog, der hedder *Gjentagelsen*. I dette begreb kan Søren Kierkegaard og Karen Blixen mødes og i frygten for den dæmoniske æstetiker, men de mødes kun ved, fra denne skikkelse, at gå i modsatte retninger og følge to meget forskellige arter af fromhed. (Henriksen 1952: 32)

> [The beginning of this essay mentioned Heinrich von Kleist's dialog about the marionettes. It ended with the witty-profound claim that only the marionette and God, that is, those beings who are unconditional nature or pure spirit, possess grace. In Danish, we could say that only the marionette and the Christian experience repetition, and that last word leads our thoughts to Søren Kierkegaard, who wrote a book called *Repetition*. Søren Kierkegaard and Karen Blixen converge in this idea — and in fear of the demonic aesthete — but they converge only to depart, from this figure, in opposite directions and to follow two very different types of piety.]

In the last chapter of his doctoral thesis from 1954 *Kierkegaards romaner* [Kierkegaard's Novels] Henriksen, however, develops the ideas presented in the above quote, while quoting a central passage from Dinesen's *Sandhedens Hævn* but without mentioning the source:

> Og det, at have et forhold til en idé i sit liv, er ikke ensbetydende med at leve efter en bestemt overbevisning. Ideen kan så at sige være før og efter lidenskaben, kan være ubevidst eller bevidst. Den idé, som bliver anskuelig i det umiddelbare menneskes skæbne, er 'nedlagt' i det og kan kaldes dets bestemmelse; den idé, som et menneske begejstres for og lidenskabeligt hengiver sig til, er dets personlige ejendom, som det har taget i besiddelse i frihed. Disse to så forskelligartede forhold til ideen skulle ikke i princippet behøve at udelukke hinanden; tværtimod skulle man kunne tænke sig en højere enhed, at et menneske kunne identificere den idé, som var nedlagt i dets væsen, og så bevidst stræbe efter 'at holde forfatterens idé klar, ja, at drive den ud i den yderste konsekvens'. (Henriksen 1954: 175)

> [And that, to have a relation to an idea in one's life, is not synonymous with living according to a certain conviction. The idea can, so to say, exist before and after the passion, can be unconscious or conscious. That idea that becomes evident in the immediate person's fate is 'implanted' in it and can be called his destiny; the idea that a person is excited about and passionately gives himself over to is his personal property, taken freely into possession. These two diverse relations to the idea do not, in principle, need to be mutually exclusive; on the contrary, one should be able to imagine a higher unity, that a person could identify that idea that was implanted in his being, and so consciously strive to 'keep the author's idea clear, yes, to propel it to its utmost consequence'.]

I find Aage Henriksen's interpretation in the above passage correct. In *Sandhedens Hævn* 'Lyst' [desire] is connected to the abilities that have been 'implanted' in us (our 'nature'), which both gives us joy and define who we are. If we don't follow our abilities and desires, the 'idea', 'Naturens Tanker' [the ideas of Nature], is lost and anxiety kicks in:

> Nogle Mennesker gør andet end de har Lyst til og glemmer, hvad de selv er. De forvirrer Naturens Tanker, de plumrer Naturens Kilder op, ja tag jer endelig iagt for dem. Hele Natten i Mørke voxer Træerne i Skoven, ja, hvis det blæser, bevæger deres Kroner sig i Blæsten. Sådanne Mennesker, som jeg taler om, vaagner om Natten, bliver urolige og beskæmmes, naar de tænker derpaa. (Blixen 1926: 9)

> [Some people do things they don't want to do, and they forget what they themselves really are. They upset the ideas of Nature, they make her clear wells muddy, beware of them! In the dark, throughout the night, the trees in the woods are growing. If there is a wind blowing, the tops of the trees sway in it. Such people, as I am talking about, wake at night, become anxious, and feel ashamed when they think about it.] (Dinesen 1986a: 109)

Mopsus' problem in the comedy is precisely that he doesn't do what he wants to do. He doesn't follow his 'nature' but instead does what Abraham and other people tell him to do, thus forgetting who he is. He blames Christian 'Moral' [morality] and his 'Samvittighed' [conscience] for this discrepancy in his individuality that prevents him from following his own 'Lyst' [desire], his own nature and becoming himself:

> min Moder var meget streng. Hun plagede mig med sin Moral [...] Da jeg voxede op, blev min Samvittighed min største Prøvelse [...] Hør nu. O, jeg kan ikke forstaa, hvorfor jeg altid skal have saa forfærdelige Samvittighedskvaler, naar andre Mennesker aldrig har det. (Blixen 1926: 26, 31–32)

> [my mother was very strict. She pestered me with her morality [...] When I grew up, my conscience was my greatest trial [...] Listen. Oh, I don't understand why I always get such terrible pangs of conscience when other people never do.] (Dinesen 1986a: 118–19)

Mopsus also has his doubts with regard to God, since: 'Det er det svære ved at gøre Guds Vilje, at jeg aldrig rigtig kan blive klar over hans Karakter' (Blixen 1926: 28) [The difficulty doing God's will is that I can never be certain about his character] (Dinesen 1986a: 118–19), which sounds reasonable, when thinking about the Abraham-Isaac story and other gruesome, paradoxical stories from the Old Testament. It is true that when one evaluates the character of God outside the discourse of religion (as a concrete character), the main characteristics of his personality are less flattering and could be described with keywords such as narcissism, capriciousness and inconsistency. He is also a liar, since his command to Abraham to kill his son is in fact just a test to see if Abraham has faith and is willing to follow his commands blindly. Had Abraham not trusted God, one could easily imagine that the outcome would have been the exact opposite — that God would have taken Isaac from Abraham to punish him. Since God is normally evaluated within the discourse of religion, he typically evades these types of anthropomorphic evaluations, but not in Dinesen's world, as we also see in a letter to her sister Ellen Dahl from 13 January 1924: 'jeg synes, at den Gud hun [Mary Bess] omtaler og tror paa, er ubeskrivelig frastødende, saa langt som muligt fra ethvert Begreb om Gentlemanliness'[6] (Blixen 2013: 730) [I think the God she is speaking of and believes in is so indescribably repulsive, and as far as possible from any idea of Gentlemanliness.][7]

The idea of staying true to one's nature that Dinesen develops in *Sandhedens Hævn* may derive from Kierkegaard's mentor P. M. Møller and his ideas about 'Affektation' [affectation] and 'Naturen' [nature]:

> Affektation kommer oftest af, at man ej har Kraft til at lægge sig ud med Verden for at vise sin Personlighed sand. Derfor er det godt, at somme komme til at staa i trodsig Opposition til Livet. I Naturstanden levede hver adskilt og udviklede sig trodsig en Personlighed, da han ej forstyrredes af mange. Nu danner man sig ved Abstraktion en almengyldig Person, et Selskabsideal uden Kanter, et Ideal uden Individualitet. (Naturen gør da sin Ret gældende i Bøger som Baggesens Genganger.) Enhver har af Naturen sit dybe Præg, men lader det udslettes for at tækkes andre. Disse andre have i at forkaste de fremstikkende et meget rigtigt Princip; kuns skulde de gøre Forskel imellem de selvraadige og dem, der ere fremstikkende af Pedanteri og Hjælpeløshed. Folk ere ikke det, Naturen bestemte dem til, da det stramt organiserede Borgersamfund udsletter Individualiteten.[8]

[Affectation occurs most often when one lacks the strength to quarrel with the world to reveal one's true personality. Therefore, it is good that some become defiant in their opposition to life. In a state of nature, everyone lived separately, developing a personality defiantly, when not being disturbed by others. Now, people create a generally applicable person by abstraction, a societal ideal without edges, an ideal without individuality. (Nature at least maintains its right in books like Baggesen's Ghost.) By nature, everyone has his profound character, but allows it to be destroyed to please others. By rejecting those who stand out, these others have a very correct principle; but they forget to create a difference between the self-willed and those who stand out from pedantry and helplessness. People are not what nature intended them to be when the strictly organized Bourgeois community of citizens destroys individuality.]

Møller's collected works with numerous passages underlined were in Dinesen's library when she died (Bondesson 1982: 185) but Dinesen could also have gotten the ideas from Høffding's book *Søren Kierkegaard som Filosof* [Søren Kierkegaard as Philosopher] where he describes the essence of Møller's thinking in this way:

> Affektation er efter Poul Møller en forbindelse af falskhed og selvbedrag. Den opstår ved, at man vil være, hvad man efter sin natur ikke kan være, og derfor indbilder sig selv og andre, at man er anderledes end man i virkeligheden er [...] Fast bliver affektationen, når man konsekvent gennemfører det fremmede princip, uagtet det ikke kan få rod i ens personlighed.[9] Både moralsk følelse, selvfølelse og immoralitet kan på denne måde være skaller, man skjuler sig i over for sig selv og andre, idet man finder behag ved dem uden dog virkelig at udfylde dem [...] Poul Møller går endog så vidt i sin hævden af vigtigheden af overensstemmelse mellem det indre og det ydre, at han erklærer, at 'ingen Livsytring har Sandhed, uden deri ligger skabende Selvvirksomhed'. (Høffding 1892: 32–33)

> [According to Poul Møller, affectation is a combination of falsehood and delusion. It occurs when one wants to be what, by one's own nature, one cannot be, and therefore makes oneself and others believe that one is different that one is in reality [...] Affectation becomes fixed when one consistently implements the foreign principle, despite the fact that it cannot take root in one's personality. In that way, moral sense, self-esteem, and immorality can all become shells in which one hides, from oneself and from others, as one finds comfort in them without, however, actually filling them in [...] Poul Møller even goes so far in his assertion of the importance of agreement between the inner and the outer that he declares that 'no utterance in life has truth unless there lies therein creative self-activity'.]

To return to Henriksen's idea 'that one should be able to imagine a higher unity, that a person could identify that idea that was implanted in his being, and so consciously strive to 'keep the author's idea clear, yes, to propel it to its utmost consequence' in relation to Kierkegaard and the Christian, we understand that Kierkegaard identified this 'idea' in *Om Begrebet Ironie* as Christianity and the obligation of the true Christian individual to develop these seeds in accordance with God's idea:

> men netop skal udvikle de Spirer, Gud selv har nedlagt i Mennesket, da den Christne veed sig som den, der har Realitet for Gud. Her kommer den Christne

ogsaa Gud tilhjelp, bliver ligesom hans Medarbeider i at fuldføre den gode
Gjerning, Gud selv har begyndt. (Kierkegaard 1841: 316)

[but is specifically supposed to develop the seeds God himself has placed in
man, since the Christian knows himself as that which has reality for God.
Here, in fact, the Christian comes to the aid of God, becomes, so to speak, his
co-worker in completing the good work God himself has begun.] (Kierkegaard
1992: 186)

In *Sandhedens Hævn* Dinesen propagates the opposite: that it is the seeds of nature
in the shape of creative abilities, joy, desire and inspiration that human beings must
stay true to and develop in order 'to reveal his true personality', follow 'the ideas
of nature' and become a true individual (in accordance with Møller). In the play
she also blames Christian-Bourgeois societal norms for rejecting and corrupting
these seeds of nature that are connected to the pagan, since: 'Begrebet Skyld og
Synd kommer ikke frem i dybeste forstand i Hedenskabet' (Kierkegaard 1844: 400)
[The concepts of guilt and sin in their deepest sense do not emerge in paganism]
(Kierkegaard 1980: 73).

Dinesen here puts forward another notion than Kierkegaard that the art of
becoming oneself is to break free from the pangs of anxiety and the sense of guilt
that Christian ethics and the religious have subjected mankind to and instead
follow these uncorrupted seeds of human nature that are expressions of our natural
'Sandselighed' [sensuousness], playfulness and creativity. This is very similar to how
the character A describes the Pagan Greeks in *Enten — Eller. Første Deel* and their
relation to 'Sandseligheden' [the sensuous] and the individual:

I Græciteten var Sandseligheden behersket i den skjønne Individualitet, eller
rettere sagt, den var ikke behersket; thi den var jo ikke en Fjende, der skulde
undertvinges, ikke en farlig Oprører, der skulle holde i Ave, den var frigjort til
Liv og Glæde i den skjønne Individualitet.[10] (Kierkegaard 1843a: 69)[11]

[In Greek culture, the sensuous was controlled in the beautiful individuality, or,
to put it more accurately, it was not controlled, for it was not an enemy to be
subdued, not a dangerous insurgent to be held in check; it was liberated to life
and joy in the beautiful individuality.] (Kierkegaard 1987a: 50)

This is a notion that Dinesen clearly supported.

Nature and the Poet as God

In 1854, towards the end of his life, Kierkegaard made a very interesting comparison
between God and the poet in one of his diary entries:

Mine Tanker er: Gud er som en Digter. Deraf forklares det saa ogsaa at han
finde sig i baade det Onde og alt Vrøvlet og Ubetydelighedens Jammerlighed
og Middelmaadighed o: s: v:. Saaledes forholder jo en Digter sig ogsaa til sin
Digter-Frembringelse (der ogsaa kaldes hans Skabning) han lader det komme
frem. Men som man jo i høi Grad feiler, naar man troer, at hvad den enkelte
Person i Digtet siger eller gjør, er Digterens personlige Mening: saaledes feiler
man jo ogsaa ved at antage, at hvad der skeer, derved at det skeer, er af Gud
samtykket. O, nei, han har sin Mening for sig. Men digterisk tillader han alt

Muligt at komme frem, selv er han overalt tilstede, seer til, digter videre, i een Forstand, digterisk (upersonlig), ligeligt opmærksom paa Alt, i en anden Forstand, personligt, sættende den frygteligste Forskjel som den mellem Godt og Ondt, mellem det at ville som han vil og ikke at ville som han vil. o: s: v: o: s: v: Det Hegelske Sludder om, at det Virkelige er det Sande, er derfor aldeles ligesom den Forvexling, at paanøde en Digter, at hans dramatiske Personers Ord og Handlinger ere hans personlige Ord og Handlinger. Kun det maa fastholdes, at hvad der, om jeg saa tør sige, bestemmer Gud til at ville saaledes digte, ikke er, som Hedenskabet meente, for Tidsfordriv, nei, nei, just deri ligger Alvoren, at det at elske og at ville elskes er Guds Lidenskab, ja fast — uendelige Kjerlighed! — som var han selv bunden i denne Lidenskab. (Kierkegaard 1854: 266–67)

[My thoughts are: God is like a poet. That explains why he puts up with both the evil and all the nonsense and wretchedness and mediocrity of insignificance, etc. In the same way a poet relates to his poetic productions (which are also called his creation), which he allows to be produced. But as one would certainly make a major mistake in believing that what the individual person says or does in a poem is the poet's personal meaning, he also makes a mistake in assuming that what happens, simply because it happens, is approved by God. Oh, no, he has his own opinion. But as a poet he allows everything possible to be produced, he is everywhere, watching, as a poet, in a sense, producing poetically (impersonally), equally aware of everything, in another sense, personally, making the most fearful distinction as that between good and evil, between willing and not willing what he will, etc., etc. The Hegelian nonsense that the real is the true is, therefore, entirely like the confusion imposed onto a poet that his dramatic characters' words and actions are his personal words and actions. Only it must be maintained firmly: that what God, if I may put it so, wills to produce poetically is not, as paganism thought, a pastime — no, no, this is the serious point — that to love and be loved are God's passion, yes, steadfast — infinite love! — as if he himself were bound in this passion.]

In Dinesen's world there is no Christian God behind it all, which also means that God can't be the author of our destinies. But who is the author then? With her affinity for materialistic inversions and her obligation to offer 'konkrete og individuelle Billeder af Karakterer og Skæbner, ikke Abstraktioner og Utopier' (Høffding 1916: 67) [concrete and individual portraits of characters and destinies, not abstractions and utopias] in her tales, Dinesen substitutes God and The Divine Creation with The Poet and Nature as the logical materialistic answers to the omnipotent Christian God.[12] Only nature and poets create with the omnipotence of a God, which means that God is not like a poet, but, conversely, that the poet is like a God. We human beings are in the hands of nature just like the characters in a tale are in the hands of the omnipotent poet:

Sandheden er, at vi alle spiller med i en Marionetkomedie [...] Hvad det, mine Børn gælder om i en Marionetkomedie er at holde Forfatterens Idé klar. Det er en Hemmelighed, som jeg dog vil fortælle Dig, at dette er den sande Lykke, som Folk leder om paa andre Steder [...] o [sic] I mine Medspillende, hold Forfatterens Idé klar, ja driv den ud i dens yderste Konsekvens. (Blixen 1926: 10)

[The truth is that we are all acting in a marionette comedy [...] My children, what is more important than anything else in a marionette comedy is to keep the author's idea clear. I will tell you, even though it is a secret, that this is the real happiness which people seek everywhere else [...] But you, my fellow actors, keep the author's idea clear. Aye, drive it to its utmost consequence.] (Dinesen 1986a: 109)

We can only become ourselves, if we follow our 'nature', implanted in us by 'nature'.[13]

This is the idea that was put down in us that we must follow in order to be good marionettes in the hands of nature, and only then will we be able to embrace our destiny unconditionally and experience 'den sande lykke' [the real happiness]. Just like the character in a story must 'holde Forfatterens Idé klar' [keep the author's idea clear] and follow the idea of the poet and the aesthetic laws of the character to the fullest in order to be a good marionette. The play concludes with Sabine didactically encouraging the audience to reflect on their own life in relation to this particular life view that the play propagates:

SABINE: Jovist, Fortunio, vær ikke bedrøvet, vi har gjort vort bedste, og mere forlanger vi ikke at gøre. Da vi først begyndte, da vidste ingen, hvordan vore Roller var, ja, vi vidste det ikke selv, thi hvem kan vide, hvordan en Karakter tager sig ud på Scenen? Men nu har vi sagt de Repliker, som var i os, ikke en eneste har vi holdt tilbage, og naar Tæppet falder, kan ingen tvivle om, hvad vi egentlig var. O maatte enhver af Tilskuerne engang kunne sige det samme. (Blixen 1926: 36)

[SABINE: Well, Fortunio, don't be sad, we have done our best, and we don't ask to do more than that. When we first began, no one knew what his role was like, indeed, we ourselves didn't know, for who can know what a character will look like on the stage? But now we have said those lines we had in us, we haven't kept a single one back, and when the curtain falls, no one can have any doubt what we really were. Oh I hope that sometime each member of the audience will be able to say the same thing!] (Dinesen 1986a: 123)

In *Begrebet Angest* (1844) Vigilius Haufniensis has the following to say about destiny: 'Om Skjebnen kan man derfor sige, hvad Paulus siger om en Afgud: der er ingen Afgud i Verden; men dog er Afguden Gjenstand for Hedningens Religieusitet' (Kierkegaard, 1844: 400). [Therefore what Paul said about the idol may be said of fate: there is no idol in the world; nevertheless, the idol is the object of the pagan's religiousness] (Kierkegaard 1980: 72). Contrary to Haufniensis, Dinesen supports this point of view and reinstates 'fate', understood as the interplay between nature and the individual, as the only higher principle in life, which she then, as we know, made 'the object of the pagan's [her own] religiousness' in line with Fortunio who concludes his song with praising nature and the sea and commands that 'No other gods shalt thou have'.

Early Nemesis. Truth as the Nemesis of the Lie

When recalling Johannes de Silentio's idea that his world would fall apart if he recognized that 'Sandhedens Dom' [the judgment of Abraham] was that he was just a common murderer, it also seems no coincidence that the title of Dinesen's play is *Sandhedens Hævn*. Here 'Dom' is substituted with 'Hævn', which means that Dinesen's play is not just 'Sandhedens Dom' with regard to the individual Abraham (that he is a common murderer) but also becomes a broader way of looking at truth and lies in connection to the human condition (the play on words is completely lost in the English translation). In *Sandhedens Hævn,* 'Sandhed' [truth] becomes the nemesis of the lie, since that which is told as a lie to cover up the truth actually becomes true in the play. Since 'the lie' is the enemy of 'the truth', the revenge of the truth is precisely that the lie becomes true (as a sort of ironic moral law). Abraham is a wealthy man, but is lying about it. In the end his lie becomes true when he loses all his money and becomes poor. Sabine lies about loving Jan but ends up falling irresistibly in love with him, and Mopsus, by denying all his sins towards the end of the play, ends up finally confessing them. The profound insight of the play is that we can eventually get caught up in society's or other people's expectations to a degree, so they become the foundation of our life, which means that these lies in the end become true — have become the truth of our life, since we live a life in complete 'affectation'. So what Dinesen stages in *Sandhedens Hævn* as a comedic reversal (Amiane's spell that all the lies told that night will become true) is in fact, on the level of human existence, a profound observation of a dynamic in life that applies to all of us. The quote about Lucifer from 3 April 1926 (that I will return to here in a shortened form) is useful when uncovering Dinesen's artistic ideal:

> det symbolske Udtryk: Lucifer [....] Jeg opfatter det som om det betyder: Sandhed, eller Søgen efter Sandhed, Stræben mod Lys, Kritik, — ja, vel det man kalder *Aand* [...] Og sammen hermed [...] en sense of humour, som ikke er bange for *noget*, men *efter sin Overbevisning* tør gøre Nar ad alt, og Liv, og nyt Lys, Vekslen. (Blixen 2013: 953)
>
> [the symbolic expression Lucifer [...] I conceive of it as meaning: truth, or the search for truth, striving toward the light, a critical attitude, — indeed, what one means by *spirit* [...] And in addition to this [...] — a *sense of humor* which is afraid of *nothing*, but has the *courage of its convictions* to make fun of everything, and life, new light, variety.] (Dinesen 1981: 249)

This is also a very good description of Dinesen's rhetorical strategy in *Sandhedens Hævn*, and her other counter-stories concerning Kierkegaard, which is precisely a mix of 'Søgen efter Sandhed' [search for truth] and 'Lys, Kritik' [light, a critical attitude] mixed with a 'sense of humour som ikke er bange for noget' [a sense of humour which is afraid of nothing] and 'tør gøre Nar ad alt' [courage of its convictions to make fun of everything] (Blixen 2013: 953). These are the elements that make the play a remarkable mix of harsh Christianity critique (with clear ties back to Brandes and The Modern Breakthrough), and a new materialistic-metaphysics (destiny based on 'nature') that proposes another version of the Kierkegaardian notion of how to become oneself, wrapped in the guise of a marionette comedy in the tradition of the young J. L. Heiberg.[14]

Dinesen's attempt to break away from Christian-Bourgeois norms (and woman's role as a mother and homemaker) and become 'herself' by following her own nature and become an artist is analog to Lucifer's revolt against God. As was the case for Lucifer, such a decision comes at a price, but in order to become an independent artist (Dinesen) or intellectual (Brandes) this is indeed a necessary movement. This was the movement that Kierkegaard also made, but the irony was — according to Brandes and Dinesen — that he fell subject to the illusion that his ally in this project of becoming 'himself' was God.

With all this in mind, it is of course understandable that Dinesen was furious when she discovered that Levin had published *Sandhedens Hævn* under her married name Karen Blixen-Finecke instead of under her Pagan pen name 'Osceola', as we see from this letter to her mother dated 13 June 1926:

> Tak for 'Sandhedens Hævn', — det er aldeles forkert og uforskammet, at Levin har sat mit Navn derpaa; det er stik imod Aftalen, og jeg fremhævede for ham, at hvis jeg sendte ham nogle Skildringer herfra Afrika kunde han sætte mit navn derpå, men ikke paa den slags Skønliterair Produktion. (Blixen 2013: 999)

> [Thank you for 'The Revenge of Truth', — it is altogether wrong and rude that Levin has put my name on it, contrary to our agreement, and I stressed to him that if I sent him any accounts from here in Africa that he could put my name on them — but not on that kind of literary production.]

Using this Pagan pseudonym was of utmost importance for Dinesen in order to underline the critique of Christianity that permeates the play, but we also understand from the passage that Dinesen already back in 1926 was very conscious about using different author names for fiction writing and autobiographical writing. From a letter to Moster Bess 23 May 1926 we also know that Dinesen already around the time of publication was well aware that *Sandhedens Hævn* was a very difficult piece and that the readers would have difficulties understanding it: 'Elle skrev at hun mente, der var en Chance for at faa "Sandhedens Hævn" opført; det ville more mig i allerhøjeste Grad, om det kunde blive af, og maaske den vilde være lettere opfattelig paa en Scene!' (Blixen 2013: 983) [Elle wrote that she thought there might be a chance of getting 'The Revenge of Truth' performed; it would give me the greatest pleasure if it could be done, and perhaps it would be easier to understand on the stage!] (Dinesen 1981: 258). The full range of Dinesen's profound thinking and the critique of Kierkegaard's *Frygt og Bæven* in *Sandhedens Hævn* have so far, as I have shown in this chapter, not been fully understood by scholars. Therefore, it is about time that the play is recognized within the Dinesen scholarship as an important piece in Dinesen's production that also outlines significant motives and ideas that came to permeate her entire oeuvre.

Notes to Chapter 6

1. Dinesen's father and Georg Brandes were also ardent atheists (Buk-Swienty 2014: 49).

2. Very significant in 'The Pearls' (1942) that I will analyze in the next chapter. But also poignantly clear in the long and famous tales 'The Deluge at Norderney' (1934) and 'Babette's Feast' (1950) that can be regarded as out right parodies of the flood narrative of Noah from The Old Testament (Genesis, chapter 6–9), respectively the last supper from The New Testament (the four canonical gospels). These two tales also contain a line-up of important allusions to Kierkegaard (see Chapter 13 and 15).

3. Throughout the book Brandes consistently disregards Kierkegaard's pseudonyms and often ascribe the thoughts and ideas presented by the various pseudonyms to the empirical Kierkegaard. Or, alternatively, he uses the pseudonyms as entry points for analyzing the life and psychology of the empirical Kierkegaard.

4. Mopsus was a celebrated seer and diviner in Greek mythology. He also plays a part in Ovid's *Metamorphoses. Book 8*: 'Mopsus the sage, who future things foretold' <http://classics.mit.edu/Ovid/metam.8.eighth.html> [accessed 29 August 2016]. In *Sandhedens Hævn* the name is used for comical purposes. Instead, the only seer of the play is the Pagan witch Amiane.

5. In my view 'delights' is a flawed translation, 'desire' is more correct.

6. This passage has been left out (!) in Born's translation of this letter (Dinesen 1981: 184–86) together with the pages: 728 (starting: 'I det hele') to 731 (ending: 'skal nok ogsaa svare, saa godt jeg kan') in the Danish version of the letter (Blixen 2013: 726–34).

7. Author's translation.

8. P. M. Møller, *Skrifter i Udvalg, 1–2* (Copenhagen: Holbergsselskabet, 1930), vol. 2, p. 291, quoted from <http://adl.dk/adl_pub/pg/cv/ShowPgText.xsql?nnoc=adl_pub&p_udg_id=49&p_sidenr=291> [accessed 29 August 2016].

9. This type of life-principle, where 'affectation becomes fixed', is exactly what the reoccurring character in Dinesen's tales, August von Schimmelmann, is living by as we see in this passage from 'The Poet': 'He had collected flowers, studied music, and had many friends. He had tried a life of pleasure and had been made happy many times. But the road leading from it all into the heart of things he had not found. As time went on a dreadful thing had happened to him: one thing had become to him as good as another. Now, later in life, he had accepted the happiness of life in a different way, not as he really believed it to be, but, as in a reflection within a mirror, such as others saw it [...] Slowly he took to living, so to say, upon the envy of the outside world, and to accept his happiness according to the quotation of the day' (Dinesen 1934: 380).

10. Dinesen seems to use the last part of this phrase in *Sandhedens Hævn* when the Pagan witch Amiane says: 'De gode Gerninger er ligesom de smaa Børn. Tænker I jer længe om, bliver de aldrig til noget, men naar I ingen Hensigt har, men er fulde af Liv og Glæde, gør I dem uden at tænke derpaa' (Blixen 1926: 10) [Good deeds are like little children. If you think too much about them they never come to anything, but when you are only full of the joys of life, and have no real intentions, you manage to create them without thinking about it] (Dinesen 1986a: 109).

11. It is also worth noting that Kierkegaard dedicated *Begrebet Angest* to P. M. Møller. In the dedication he calls him 'Græcitetens lykkelige Elsker' (Kierkegaard 1844: 311) [The happy lover of Greek Culture] (Kierkegaard 1980: 17).

12. In 'The Cardinal's First Tale' from *Last Tales* (1957) Cardinal Salviati talks about God in a way that is very similar to how Kierkegaard describes him in the passage above: "You are aware', he said, 'that I am almighty. And you have before you the world which I have created. Now give me your opinion on it. Do you take it that I have meant to create a peaceful world?' 'No, indeed', answered the youth. 'Or a world easy to live in?' asked the Lord. 'O good Lord, no!' said the candidate. 'Or do you', the Lord asked for the last time, 'hold and believe that I have resolved to create a sublime world, with all things necessary to the purpose in it, and none left out?' 'I do', said the young man. 'Then', said the Master, 'then, my servant and mouthpiece, take the oath!'" (Dinesen 1957: 21–22). Salviati concludes that the only representative on earth, which is conducting the same principle of sublime creation, is the priest and the poet. He also concludes

that none of them can be sure if they are in fact serving God or The Devil: ' "Are you sure," she asked, "that it is God whom you serve?" The Cardinal looked up, met her eyes and smiled very gently. "That," he said, "that, Madame, is a risk which the artists and the priests of the world have to run" ' (Dinesen 1957: 26).

13. In P. M. Møller's version this movement of following one's own nature, however, also contains an element of 'skabende Selvvirksomhed' [creative self-activity] according to Høffding (Høffding 1892: 33) equivalent to Kierkegaard's idea of the good Christian as a 'Medarbeider' [co-worker].

14. Dinesen was inspired by the marionette comedies of the young J. L. Heiberg: *Pottemager Walther* (which she quotes in the closing lines of 'Carnival') and *Don Juan* that came out together in the collection *Marionettheater* (1814). Dinesen had them in her library along with the edition of Heiberg's collected plays: Heiberg, *Skuespil*, VII vols (Copenhagen: Shubote 1833–41) (Bondesson 1982: 68).

CHAPTER 7

❖

The Concept of Christi-Anxiety: 'The Pearls' and *Begrebet Angest*

In this chapter, I investigate the relation between 'The Pearls' and *Begrebet Angest* with particular attention to the way Dinesen in 'The Pearls' connects anxiety to the Christian-Bourgeois way of living. The insight of the tale is that Christianity, in combination with the Bourgeois notion of the self-made individual, becomes the very source of anxiety, not the remedy. Anxiety arises in the main character, Jensine, whenever she is faced with desire and sexuality, which are elements that are to be subdued and rejected in Christian-Bourgeois society, since 'Sandselighed som saadan er Syndighed (Kierkegaard 1844: 363) [sensuousness as such is sinfulness] (Kierkegaard 1980: 50–51) according to Vigilius Haufniensis in *Begrebet Angest*. When Jensine also realizes that the world is not organized according to the common Christian principle: that you get in life what you deserve (since her husband gets away with duelling and gambling), her world almost falls apart. Alexander, being a nobleman, is incapable of feeling anxiety, but Jensine does not see this as a good quality, instead she thinks of him as some sort of demon — a lost soul she has to save from eternal hellfire. In her desperate attempt to teach him anxiety and recreate him in her own image according to her Christian-Bourgeois values, Jensine, however, ends up in the demonic. She does so because Alexander is free, Jensine could have been too, and they could have lived a good life together had it not been for Jensine's anxiety created by Christianity. In *Begrebet Angest*, the demonic is defined as 'anxiety about the good'. The good in the tale are the values represented by the free nobleman Alexander, who is carefree, audacious, and passionate, but the Christian Jensine unfortunately, disregards these qualities, and she ends up in despair and isolation. In this tale, Dinesen wants to prove a point with regard to Christianity, anxiety, and Kierkegaard. She is creating a counter-story that subverts major ideas in *Begrebet Angest*, in order to show that it is in fact Christian ethics, with its notions of sin, guilt, and ideas about what is good and bad in this world, which is demonic.

The Genealogy

In his paper from 2010 Anz correctly observes that anxiety seems to be a theme in 'The Pearls' ('En Historie om en Perle') from Dinesen's *Winter's Tales* (*Vinter-

Eventy) even though he, as he himself mentions, is not able to back it by any specific quotations:

> Auch in meinem zweiten Beispiel ist der Bezug zu Kierkegaard nicht auf der Ebene der Zitation, sondern auf thematisch-motivischer Ebene zu suchen: *En Historie om en Perle* spielt im Kopenhagen der 1860er Jahre unmittelbar vor dem Deutsch-Dänischen Krieg. Den Bezug zu Kierkegaard bildet, so scheint mir, die Genealogie der Heldin Jensine und eins der zentralen Motive: die Angst. (Anz 2010: 424)

> [In my second example, the reference to Kierkegaard is also not on the level of citation, but rather on the thematic-motivic level: *En Historie om en Perle* takes place in Copenhagen in the 1860s just prior to the German-Danish War. In my opinion, both the genealogy of the female protagonist Jensine and the central motif of anxiety refer to Kierkegaard.]

In the above quote, Anz also correctly observes that the description of Jensine's grandfather and father ('the genealogy') in 'The Pearls' has striking similarities with the accounts we have of Søren Kierkegaard's father:

> About eighty years ago a young officer in the guards, the youngest son of an old country family, married, in Copenhagen, the daughter of a rich wool merchant whose father had been a peddler and had come to town from Jutland [...] She had been brought up in an atmosphere of prudence and foresight. Her father was an honest tradesman, afraid both to lose his own money, and let down his customers. Sometimes this double risk had thrown him into melancholia. (Dinesen 1942: 107, 109–10)[1]

Kierkegaard's father, Michael Pedersen Kierkegaard, was a poor child from Jutland who was also a 'Peddler' but later became a very wealthy man in Copenhagen. As the years went on he became increasingly worried about his immortal soul since he, as a poor child in Jutland, on one particular occasion had cursed God. There is also reason to believe that he had problems mediating his religious life as a strict Pietist Herrnhuter with his civil life as a crafty and extremely wealthy businessman. At least we know that he, when Kierkegaard grew up, lived in a permanent state of melancholy and anxiety, which he passed down to his son, who, if he did not write for just one or two days, fell into melancholia. Unfortunately Anz's analysis of the tale and the relation to Kierkegaard's *Begrebet Angest* stops where it actually should have begun, but in the following I will try to make up for that.

'The Pearls'

In 'The Pearls', Jensine's father has become a very wealthy man, but as we also know from Matthew 19:24: 'Again I say to you, it is easier for a camel to go through the eye of a needle, than for a rich man to enter the kingdom of God'. As a man belonging to the new, emerging class of the bourgeoisie, where the members, by their own doings and craftiness, are able to create wealth for themselves, the question that arises for Jensine's (and Kierkegaard's) father in connection to Christian morals and ethics is: at what expense? Will I as a very wealthy man that has created my fortune at the expense of others (and maybe cheated them) be able to enter the 'kingdom of God' or am I going straight to hell? There is an inherent (and unsolvable) conflict between the new nineteenth century ideology of individualism and capitalism and the Christian notions about how people are supposed to live in order to get to Heaven.[2] Jensine has inherited her father's Christian-Bourgeois way of thinking that is in conflict with itself and it invades and pollutes her marriage with Alexander, who as a nobleman comes from a completely different environment (the Aristocracy) that does not subscribe to Jensine's Christian-Bourgeois ethics. It is curious that Anz does not point out that Dinesen actually uses the word 'Angst' [anxiety] three times in the Danish version of the tale in situations that precisely confront her with the elements that have been rejected by Christianity (passion and sexuality). Again Kierkegaard and major ideas put forward in several of his works seem to be the targets of criticism. Here a passage by A from *Enten — Eller. Første Deel*:

> under Bestemmelse af Aand er Sandseligheden først sat ved Christendommen. Dette er ganske naturligt; thi Christendommen er Aand, og Aanden det positive Princip, den har bragt ind i Verden. Men idet Sandseligheden sees under Aandens Bestemmelse, saa sees dens Betydning at være den, at den skal udelukkes. (Kierkegaard 1843a: 68)

> [sensuality was placed under the qualification of spirit first by Christianity. This is quite natural, for Christianity is spirit, and spirit is the positive principle it has brought into the world. But when sensuality is viewed under the qualification of spirit, its significance is seen to be that it is to be excluded.] (Kierkegaard 1987a: 49)

And a passage by Vigilius Haufniensis in *Begrebet Angest*: 'Sandselighed som saadan er Syndighed. Efterat Synden er kommen ind i Verden, og hver Gang Synden kommer ind i Verden, bliver Sandselighed Syndighed' (Kierkegaard 1844: 363) [Sensuousness as such is sinfulness. After sin came into the world, and every time sin comes into the world, sensuousness becomes sinfulness] (Kierkegaard 1980: 51). This passage must have sounded like sheer nonsense to Dinesen's ears since 'Syndens skepsis er Hedenskabet aldeles fremmed' (Kierkegaard 1844: 326) [Sin's skepticism is altogether foreign to paganism] (Kierkegaard 1980: 24). What Jensine experiences on her honeymoon in the Norwegian mountains challenges her Christian-Bourgeois worldview that has rejected the part of her human nature that is connected to the sensuous. When she finally experiences the erotic and the sensuous through the consummation of her marriage with Alexander, a state of panic and anxiety emerges in her:

> she held the god of love in great respect, and had already for some years sent a little daily prayer to him: 'Why doest thou tarry?' But now she reflected that he had perhaps granted her her prayer with a vengeance, and that her books had given her but little information as to the real nature of love [...] At first all this was so new to her that she felt her old ideas of the world blown about in all directions, like her skirts and her shawl. But soon the impressions converged into a sensation of the deepest alarm, a panic such as she had never experienced. (Dinesen 1942: 109)

[Hun holdt netop Eros højt i Ære, hendes Ungpige-Bogskab var fyldt med Romaner og Kærlighedsdigte, og hun havde allerede i et par Aar, urolig ved Tomheden i sit eget Hjerte, lønligt anraabt Kærlighedsguden, og hvisket: 'Hvorfor tøver du dog saa længe?' *Men nu følte hun med stigende Angst at Guden*[3] maaske havde givet hende mere, end hun havde bedt om, og at hendes Bøger ikke paa langt nær havde sagt hende ren Besked om Kærligheden [...] Til at begynde med var alt dette hende saa nyt, at hun følte det, som om hendes gamle Verdensbillede blev hvirvlet ad alle fire Verdenshjørner til, med hendes Skørter og Shawl. Men efter nogen Tids Forløb samlede de voldsomme nye Indtryk sig til *en saadan dyb Angst*, som hun aldrig hidtil havde kendt.] (Blixen 1942: 46–47)[4]

In *Begrebet Angest* Vigilius Haufniensis also notes that 'Angest kan man sammenligne med Svimmelhed. Den, hvis Øie kommer til at skue ned i et svælgende Dyb, han bliver svimmel' (Kierkegaard 1844: 365) [Anxiety may be compared with dizziness. He whose eye happens to look down into the yawning abyss becomes dizzy] (Kierkegaard 1980: 52), thus it seems no coincidence when Dinesen describes Jensine's experience in the Norwegian Mountains as 'She was higher than she had ever been, and the air went to her head like wine' (Dinesen 1942: 109) [Hun var højere oppe i *Æteren* end hun nogensinde før havde været, og Luften gik hende til Hovedet som Vin] (Blixen 1942: 47) and later, when she gets the extra pearl and consequently believes that it is the Devil who is playing with her: 'Had the powers of the universe, she thought, combined, here, to make fun of a poor girl' (Dinesen 1942: 120) [Har da alle Magter i Verden,' *tænkte hun svimmel*, 'slaaet sig sammen for at drive en stakkels Pige til vanvid] (Blixen 1942: 57).[5] Aside from the anxiety created by the discovery of Eros (in these highly natural and erotic surroundings), which is the part of human nature that is excluded and neglected within Christian-Bourgeois society, one of the major things that also frightens Jensine and creates anxiety has to do with her husband Alexander, who seems to escape the normal rules and regulations of Christian ethics. In fact he seems to be completely unaware of them:

One day he recounted how he had gambled in Baden-Baden, risked his last cent, and then won. He did not know that she thought, by his side: 'He is really a thief, or if not that, a receiver of stolen goods, and no better than a thief'. At other times he made fun of the debts he had had, and the trouble he had had to take to avoid meeting his tailor. This talk sounded really uncanny to Jensine's ears. For to her debts were an abomination, and that he should have lived on in the midst of them without anxiety, trusting to fortune to pay up for him, seemed against nature. (Dinesen 1942: 111)

[En Dag beskrev han for hende, hvordan han i Casinoet i Baden-Baden havde spillet alle sine Penge bort, sat sin sidste Krone ind, og paa den havde vundet dem alle tilbage, og en pæn Sum foruden. Han vidste jo ikke af at hun, lige ved Siden af ham i sit Hjerte tænkte: 'Han er jo i Virkeligheden en Tyv. Eller om ikke en Tyv, saa en Hæler, — og Hæleren er lige saa god som Stjæleren'. En anden Gang gjorde han Løjer med sin Ungdoms Pengesorger, og udmalede for hende, hvordan han havde maattet løbe om ad Sidegaderne for at undgaa at møde sin Skræder. *En saadan Tale lød rent ud dæmonisk* i Jensines Øren. For hun havde hele sit Liv betragtet Gæld som en Vederstyggelighed, og det forekom hende nu næsten naturstridigt, at hendes Brudgom skulde have levet i mange Aar midt i den Usikkerhed og Uhygge, som den maatte føre med sig, uden Frygt, og i Tillid til, at Skæbnen nok engang skulde hjælpe ham ud af den.] (Blixen 1942: 49)[6]

With her strict moral Christian-Bourgeois upbringing Jensine behaves towards Alexander as 'den fromme Følelse (i Retning af det Ethiske)' [a pious feeling (with an ethical tone)] described in this passage in *Begrebet Angest*:

men den fromme Følelse (i Retning af det Ethiske) giver sig Luft i sin Indignation paa Arvesynden, paatager sig Anklagerens Rolle, og er nu ene bekymret for med næsten qvindelig Lidenskabelighed, med den elskende Piges Sværmerie, at gjøre Syndigheden afskyeligere og afskyeligere og sig selv i den, saa intet Ord er haardt nok for at betegne den Enkeltes Participeren i den. (Kierkegaard 1844: 333)

[but a pious feeling (with an ethical tone) that gives vent to its indignation over hereditary sin. This feeling assumes the role of an accuser, who with an almost feminine passion and with the fanaticism of a girl in love is now concerned only with making sinfulness and his own participation in it more and more detestable, and in such a manner that no word can be severe enough to describe the single individual's participation in it.] (Kierkegaard 1980: 31)

Jensine perceives Alexander as a demonic person, who not only defies the law of Christian moral (that you get in life what you deserve), but she also firmly believes that he will end up in hell if she doesn't save him (since people, in her world view, are punished by God for breaking the Ten Commandments). The main reason why Alexander has no fear and does not seem to understand the categories of good and bad, as they are defined by Christian ethics, has to do with him being a nobleman. He is a man from the aristocracy, who, contrary to Jensine, has been born with the privileges of wealth and power through his family name, his pedigree, which at the same time also make him immortal, since he is already assured of a place in history through his name: the line of genealogy of his family. The interpretation of this condition that the tale offers is that Alexander as an aristocrat has never experienced The Fall of Man, which, as we know, implies that 1) you have to die 2) that you, before you die: 'By the sweat of your face You will eat bread, Till you return to the ground, Because from it you were taken; For you are dust, And to dust you shall return' (Genesis, 3:19) and that 3) you have now been equipped with a consciousness in order to enable you to distinguish between good and evil within the realm of Christian ethics, so that you eventually will be able to return to paradise if you have behaved as a good Christian. Having not been subjected to this fall Alexander, however, neither knows the concept of sin, nor the concept of anxiety, which means that he lives intuitively and follows his 'Lyst' [desires] without any fear or moral pangs. This idea ties into the observation that Vigilius Haufniensis makes about Adam before the fall in *Begrebet Angest*:

Angest er Frihedens Virkelighed som Mulighed for Muligheden. Man vil derfor ikke finde Angest hos Dyret, netop fordi det i sin Naturlighed ikke er bestemmet som Aand [...] At der gives Mennesker, der slet ingen Angest mærke, maa forstaaes ligesom, at Adam ingen vilde have fornummet, hvis han have været blot Dyr. (Kierkegaard 1844: 348, 357)

[anxiety is freedom's actuality as the possibility of possibility. For this reason, anxiety is not found in the beast, precisely because by nature the beast is not qualified as spirit [...] That there may be men who never experience any anxiety must be understood in the sense that Adam would have perceived no anxiety had he been merely animal.] (Kierkegaard 1980: 39, 47)

Yet, Alexander is not an animal, even though he does not know fear or anxiety. He is the earthly, materialistic embodiment of the human condition before the fall, which Dinesen, contrary to Haufniensis, perceives as a natural (and desirable) condition for a human being: as 'det Umiddelbares rene Væren' (Kierkegaard 1844: 343) [the pure being of the immediate] (Kierkegaard 1980: 37).[7] Thus, in 'The Pearls', the male protagonist Alexander is the embodiment of *Adam before the fall* and the female protagonist Jensine is the embodiment of *Eve after the fall* (which is of course the worst mésalliance one can possibly think of). Dinesen creates her narrative around this dichotomy by closely following what Haufniensis outlines in *Begrebet Angest* with regard to the conditions before and after the fall, but with the usual line-up of inversions on the level of gender and Christianity. The story develops when Jensine, in her delusional state of mind where she does not yet understand that it is herself that is the problem, decides to try to save Alexander from the despair and perdition she is convinced is awaiting him (but also in an attempt to save herself since otherwise her world view will fall apart). The method she decides to apply originates from one of the old folk tales collected by the Grimm brothers: 'She recalled the fairy-tale of the boy who is sent out into the world to learn to be afraid, and it seemed to her that for her own sake and his, in self-defense as well as in order to protect and save him, she must teach her husband to fear' [Dinesen 1942: 111) [Hun huskede Eventyret om Drengen, som blev sendt ud i Verden for at lære Frygt at kende, og det kom til at staa for hende, som om hun, paa Liv og Død, for sin egen Skyld ligesaavel som for at beskytte og redde ham, maatte lære sin Brudgom at frygte] (Dinesen 1942: 48). The fairy-tale 'Eventyret om en, der drog ud, for at lære frygt at kende' [The fairytale of the boy who set out to learn fear] collected by the Grimm brothers is also mentioned in Kierkegaard's *Begrebet Angest*:

Man har i et af Grims [sic] Eventyr en Fortælling om en Ungersvend, der gik ud paa Eventyr for at lære at ængstes. Vi ville lade hiin Eventyrer gaa sin Gang, uden at bekymre os om, hvorvidt han paa sin Vei traf det Forfærdelige. Derimod vil jeg sige, at dette er et Eventyr, som ethvert Menneske har at bestaae, at lære at ængstes, for at han ikke enten skal fortabes ved aldrig at have været angest, eller ved at synke i Angesten; hvo der derfor lærte at ængstes retteligen, han har lært det Høieste. Dersom et Menneske var et Dyr eller en Engel, da vilde han ikke kunne ængstes. (Kierkegaard 1844: 454)

[In one of Grimm's fairy tales there is a story of a young man who goes in search of adventure in order to learn what it is to be in anxiety. We will let the adventurer pursue his journey without concerning ourselves about whether he encountered the terrible on his way. However, I will say that this is an adventure that every human being must go through — to learn to be anxious in order that he may not perish either by never having been in anxiety or by succumbing in anxiety. Whoever has learned to be anxious in the right way has learned the ultimate. If a human being were a beast or an angel, he could not be in anxiety.] (Kierkegaard 1980: 110)

Alexander has no anxiety but he is neither a beast, nor an angel or an animal (which he would be according to the quote).[8] This also means that the tale in fact suggests that it is the other way around; that it is Jensine, not Alexander, who is demonic:

> Det Dæmoniske er Angest for det Gode. I Uskyldigheden var Friheden ikke sat som Frihed, dens Mulighed var i Individualiteten Angest. I det Dæmoniske er Forholdet vendt om. Friheden er sat som Ufrihed; thi Friheden er tabt. Frihedens Mulighed er her igjen Angest. Forskjellen er absolut; thi Frihedens Mulighed viser sig her i Forhold til Ufriheden, hvilken er lige det modsatte af Uskyldigheden, der en Bestemmelse hen til Friheden. Det Dæmoniske er Ufriheden, der vil afslutte sig. Dette er og bliver imidlertid en Umulighed, den beholder altid sit Forhold, og selv om dette ganske tilsyneladende er forsvundet, er det der dog, og Angesten viser sig strax i Berøringens Øieblik (Cfr. det Foregaaende i Anledning af Fortællingerne i det N.T.). Det Dæmoniske er *det Indesluttede og det ufrivilligt Aabenbare.* (Kierkegaard 1844: 424)

> [The demonic is anxiety about the good. In innocence, freedom was not posited as freedom: its possibility was anxiety in the individual. In the demonic, the relation is reversed. Freedom is posited as unfreedom, because freedom is lost. Here again freedom's possibility is anxiety. The difference is absolute, because freedom's possibility appears here in relation to unfreedom, which is the very opposite of innocence, which is a qualification disposed toward freedom. The demonic is unfreedom that wants to close itself off. This, however, is and remains impossibility. It always retains a relation, and even when this has apparently disappeared altogether, it is nevertheless there, and anxiety at once manifests itself in the moment of contact [with the good] (see what is said above of the accounts m the New Testament). The demonic is *inclosing reserve* [det Indesluttede] *and the unfreely disclosed.*] (Kierkegaard 1980: 89)

As the narrative unfolds, Jensine has indeed been 'Angest for det Gode' [anxiety about the good] and personified 'Friheden sat som Ufrihed; thi Friheden er tabt' [Freedom is posited as unfreedom, because freedom is lost] and 'Det Dæmoniske er Ufriheden' [The Demonic is unfreedom]. Thus, 'The Pearls' suggests that it is the Christian-Bourgeois Jensine, who is the embodiment of the demonic, which is another audacious subversion on the level of both gender and Christianity. Dinesen wants to prove a point with regard to Christianity and Kierkegaard and show how Christian ethics in a demonic way (with its notions of sin, guilt and ideas about what is good and bad in this world) twists people's notions of love, joy, sexuality and 'Sandselighed' [sensuousness] as something sinful, to a degree so they are forced to live a life in 'Ufrihed' [unfreedom] (opposite of Alexander who is free and without anxiety). This also means *that Christian ethics is the cause of anxiety, not the remedy* as Jensine and most of the people of the day believed until Georg Brandes suggested otherwise in 1871. As Høffding also mentions in his article about Kierkegaard and Pascal in *Tilskueren*: 'Jo mere udpræget en Karakter det religiøse Liv faar, des mindre lever Mennesket i sit naturlige Element, men bliver som en Fisk paa Landjorden'

(Høffding 1923: 423) [The more pronounced religious life gets, the less a human being is able to live in its natural environment and instead become like a fish on dry land],[9] which is exactly what Jensine feels is happening to her, when her Christian world view is questioned by Alexander's non-religious carefree way of living:

> and now she began to think about what she had read about deep-water fish, which have been so much used to bear the weight of many thousand fathoms of water, that if they are raised to the surface, they will burst. Was she herself, she wondered, such a deep-water fish that felt at home only under the pressure of existence? And her father, her grandfather and his people before him, had they been the same? What was a deep-water fish to do, she thought on, if she were married to one of those salmon which here she had seen springing in the water-falls? Or to a flying-fish? (Dinesen 1942: 116)

Thus, the tale also interprets and analyzes a specific historical period with regard to anxiety, the mid-nineteenth century (the tale takes place in 1863), and astutely points to the fact that the combination of Bourgeois individualism and Christian ethics is a particularly explosive anxiety-producing cocktail. In the Feudal society of the seventeenth and eighteenth centuries, people, on the other hand, knew their place and here Christianity could, conversely, be a comfort and consolation, since it guaranteed you an afterlife in Paradise if you played the social role you were given in the hierarchy to the fullest. But when Bourgeois individualism starts to meddle with the categories (earning money, making a career for yourself, breaking the social categories) it challenges the very notion of Christian moral and ethics. Dinesen saw this and created a narrative that, with clear connections to Kierkegaard's *Begrebet Angest*, deals with the notion of anxiety within the Christian-Bourgeois society of the mid-nineteenth century. On that note it is not a coincidence that Kierkegaard's work *Begrebet Angest* (1844) was born under such conditions. It is only one out of a number of narratives belonging to the current of Romanticism that deals with the issue of anxiety in relation to Christianity and the erotic within a Bourgeois environment, most prominent other Danish examples being Steen Steensen Blicher's 'Sildig Opvaagnen' (1828) ('Tardy Awakening') and H. C. Andersen's 'Skyggen' (1847) ('The Shadow').

Many years later Dinesen would prove her point once again in a tête-à-tête conversation with Ole Wivel on her sixty-fifths birthday on 17 April 1950, when she had invited him to come to Rungstedlund alone (Wivel 1972: 212). It turned out that she was furious with him and some of the other Heretics of the day with regard to their approach to the ethical:

> Karen Blixen vædede lige akkurat læberne med vinen i glasset før hun tog ordet igen. Og nu fortalte hun om sin mors slægt og om sin far, om den konflikt imellem et religiøst livssyn og et ateistisk-heroisk som hun ganske vist aldrig selv havde mærket, men senere lært at kende — og lært at leve med. Og var det ikke en af de ting ude i Afrika, som havde henrevet hende, at denne konflikt var overvundet, fuldkommen forsonet? Himmelsk og jordisk kærlighed var derude ikke modsætninger som hos de kristne europæere, som tilsyneladende hos Martin A. Hansen og nu i Heretica, en smitte fra selve den dualismens tradition, vi modigt havde forsøgt at bekæmpe. 'Jeg advarer Dem', sagde hun

'mod Deres moralske valg og tilbøjelighed for det etiske. Har ikke netop dette valg i vores protestantiske kulturer først os stik mod vor egen gode vilje lige i afgrunden? Har ikke kristendommen udelukket henrykkelsen ved dette livs gaver og mysterier og spærret os ude fra åndens verden på de betingelser, som er de eneste vi har?' (Wivel 1972: 214)

[Karen Blixen barely moistened her lips with the wine in her glass before she began to speak again. And now she spoke about her mother's family and about her father, about the conflict between a religious view of life and the atheistic-heroic one that she had never felt herself, but later came to know — and learned to live with. And was that not one of the things in Africa that had fascinated her — that this conflict had been overcome, completely reconciled? Out there, divine and earthly love were not opposites as they are among Christian Europeans, as they are apparently for Martin A. Hansen and now in Heretica, an infection from dualism's very tradition, which we have bravely tried to fight. 'I caution you', she said, 'against your moral choice and your propensity for the ethical. Has not this very choice in out protestant cultures led us directly against our own good will, right into the abyss? Has Christianity not excluded the delight in life's gifts and mysteries blocked us from the world of the spirit on the only conditions [the body] we have?']

Christianity is just a Sign: 'Clothes Mangled Here'

In one of the most quoted and famous allusions to Kierkegaard in Dinesen's work that we find in 'The Poet' ('Digteren'), Dinesen delivers another blow to religion and Christianity. The quote is a reversal of the idea that A coins in 'Diapsalmata' from *Enten — Eller. Første Deel.* In 'The Poet' Dinesen lets August von Schimmelmann re-articulate this quote in a conversation with Councilor Mathiesen:

'When,' he went on after a little pause, 'you and I, on our morning walk, pass a pawnbroker's shop, and, pointing at a painted board in the window, on which is written "Clothes mangled here", you say to me: "Look, clothes are mangled here — I shall go and bring my washing", I smile at you, and inform you that you will find neither mangle nor mangler here, that the painted board is for sale. Most religions are like that board, and we smile at them.' (Dinesen 1934: 384)

['Det er sandt, at hvis De og jeg paa vor Morgentur kommer forbi en Pantelaaners Bod, og De peger paa et malet Skilt i Vinduet, paa hvilket der staar skrevet: "Her rulles" og siger til mig: "Se, her rulles, jeg vil gaa hen og hente mit Vasketøj", saa smiler jeg af Dem og belærer Dem om, at der hverken findes Rulle eller Rullekone, men at det malede Skilt er til Salgs. De fleste Livsanskuelser er som dette Skilt, og vi smiler ad dem.] (Dinesen 1935: 362)

This is, as has been pointed out in the scholarship numerous times since Torgny Segerstedt's review of *Seven Gothic Tales* in July 1934 (see Bunch 2013a), a rephrasing of the notion that character A puts forward in the first section 'Diapsalmata' where the target is the philosophers: 'Det, Philospherne tale om Virkeligheden, er ofte lige saa skuffende, som naar man hos en Marchandiser læser paa et Skildt: her rulles. Vilde man komme med sit Tøi for at faae det rullet, saa var man narret;

thi Skildtet er blot tilsalgs' (Kierkegaard 1843a: 41) [What philosophers say about actuality [*Virkelighed*] is often just as disappointing as it is when one reads on a sign in a secondhand shop: Pressing Done Here. If a person were to bring his clothes to be pressed, he would be duped, for the sign is merely for sale] (Kierkegaard 1987a: 33). In the English version Dinesen substitutes Kierkegaard's 'Philosopherne' with 'most religions' but later modifies it in the Danish version 'Digteren' to 'de fleste Livsanskuelser' [most philosophies of life] so it becomes a more general critique of dogmatic thinking.

The point is of course that we as human beings must make our own experiences and form our own opinions and live by them and not blindly subscribe to an ideology, religion or philosophy created by others. The quote is also a hidden blow to Kierkegaard, who propagated individuality and criticized contemporary philosophy (first and foremost Hegel) but ended up subscribing to a religion, Christianity, which, according to Dinesen, eventually places him in the category of the delusional people who are fooled by the sign. Dinesen also seems to have been particularly critical with regard to Kierkegaard's late religious writings (even though we do not seem to find any traces of them in her tales). In a letter from Bonn dated 27 June 1951 Thorkild Bjørnvig writes that he participates in a study circle where he, in the absence of Dinesen, has been playing the devil's advocate in their discussion of Kierkegaard and his 'sidste meget hellige Skrifter' [final, very holy writings]:

> Endelig deltager jeg ugentlig i en Studiekreds over Kierkegaard, omsider forstaaet som og i Egenskab af at være den eneste Dansker ved Universitetet. Vi gennemgaar nogle af hans sidste meget hellige Skrifter — og for at forfriske Helligheden ved lidt diabolsk Dialektik fører jeg ofte, uden at de mærker det, paa underfundig vis Djævlens Sag, og fornøjer dem derved, uden at de vist rigtigt fatter hvorfor ... Sig saa ikke, at jeg ikke, efter bedste Evne, ogsaa fører Rungstedlunds Farver en Smule her! (Blixen 1996b: 44)

> [I am finally participating weekly in a reading group about Kierkegaard, eventually understood as, and in capacity of being, the only Dane at the university. We are examining some of his final, very holy writings — and to refresh the holiness through a little diabolical dialectic, I often appear, without their noticing it, for the devil, and amuse them thereby, without their rightly sensing why ... So do not say that I am not, to the best of my ability, also bearing the colors of Rungstedlund a little here!]

Here Bjørnvig strongly indicates that he supported Dinesen in her materialistic critique of Christianity (represented symbolically by 'the devil': the materialistic representative of light and truth), which, as I have shown in the above section, became a very significant point of critique in Dinesen's approach to Kierkegaard.

Notes to Chapter 7

1. Blixen 1942: 45, 47.
2. We also have the Biblical story about 'The Rich Man and Lazarus': 'And it came to pass, that the beggar died, and was carried by the angels into Abraham's bosom: the rich man also died, and was buried; And in hell he lift up his eyes, being in torments, and seeth Abraham afar off,

and Lazarus in his bosom. And he cried and said, Father Abraham, have mercy on me, and send Lazarus, that he may dip the tip of his finger in water, and cool my tongue; for I am tormented in this flame. But Abraham said, Son, remember that thou in thy lifetime receivedst thy good things, and likewise Lazarus evil things: but now he is comforted, and thou art tormented', available at <http://adl.dk/adl_pub/pg/cv/ShowPgText.xsql?nnoc=adl_pub&p_udg_id=49&p_sidenr=291> [accessed 29 August 2016).

3. The Pagan God 'Eros'.

4. Author's italics. Note how Dinesen in the Danish version adds 'stigende Angest' [increasing anxiety] and substitutes 'panic' and 'alarm' with 'dyb Angst' [deepest anxiety]. Her Danish rewritings are for the most part significantly longer than the English originals.

5. Note how Blixen in the reworked Danish version decides to use the word 'svimmel' [dizzy] instead of the more neutral 'thought' [tænkte] in the original English version. Also: how she ads the word 'Æteren' [ether] in the previous quote. The two reworked sentences in the Danish version thus establish a stronger connection to Kierkegaard.

6. Author's italics. Note how Dinesen has substituted 'uncanny' with 'dæmonisk' [demonic] in the Danish version. Again making the allusion to Kierkegaard and *Begrebet Angest* stronger.

7. On a biographical note this way of living was what both Hans Blixen, Bror Blixen, and Denys Finch Hatton as noblemen embodied and which was utterly attractive to Dinesen, even though at times unfathomable and baffling to her. She was, on the contrary, brought up in a strict bourgeois Unitarian environment where feelings of guilt and anxiety were used as means to instigate moral values. In *Out of Africa* (1937) she describes Denys as a man, who just like Alexander, lives before the fall: [his] 'absolute lack of self-consciousness, or self-interest, an unconditional truthfulness which outside of him I have only met in idiots' (Dinesen 1938: 301).

8. In a crucial passage in *Shadows on the Grass* Dinesen describes herself and her aristocratic friends in Kenya as belonging to the wild animals: 'We registered ourselves with the wild animals, sadly admitting the inadequacy of our return to the community — and to our mortgages — but realizing that we could not possibly, not even in order to obtain the highest approval of our surroundings, give up that direct contact with God which we shared with the hippo and the flamingo. Nine thousand feet up we felt safe, and we laughed at the ambition of the new arrivals, of the Missions, the business people and the Government itself, to make the continent of Africa respectable' (Dinesen 1961: 18).

9. Author's translation.

PART III

❖

Seduction

CHAPTER 8

❖

Early Female Seducers: 'Carnival' and 'the young Soren Kierkegaard'

In this chapter, I will focus on the early tale 'Carnival' in relation to Kierkegaard and seduction. The analysis of 'Carnival' is supported by significant passages from Dinesen's letters in the 1920s at a time when she was much occupied with the gender roles of the roaring twenties. Dinesen's main point in 'Carnival' is that the common notion of seduction and the (male) seducer is connected to traditional gender roles of the 19th century where man played the role as the active and cunning part in a seduction, and woman the passive and innocent part. This does not fit with the reality of the roaring twenties where gender roles and approaches to sexuality and birth control were rapidly changing, at least among the upper class (the smart set) and in artistic, bohemian circles. Thus, in 'Carnival' we find not only one, but two young female seducers, Annelise and Polly. In the tale Annelise is dressed as 'the young Soren Kierkegaard' after having attended a masked ball. She is an artist and aesthete and a female version of Kierkegaard's Johannes Forføreren, but even more radical. She also believes that both parties must be in on a seduction, in order for it to be a proper seduction and not a deceit. Contrary to Annelise, who enjoys and embraces her role as a seducer and aesthete, Polly discovers in the closing scene in 'Carnival' that she has seduced Zamor, and suffers from it, which is the feeling that most of Dinesen's female seducers experience (see also the section 'Tragedy, Irony, and Gender' in Chapter 10). In a passage in the tale Kierkegaard is also described as 'a macabre dandy', which I argue has to do with him being a virgin. This claim I will elaborate further on in Chapter 11.

The Roaring Twenties

Already in 1924, when Dinesen was working on the essay 'Moderne ægteskab og andre betragtninger' (On Modern Marriage and Other Observations),[1] we find many of the ideas about gender and seduction in her letters (Blixen 2013: 739, 757–79) that would later reappear as artistically developed material in the tale 'Carnival'. More ideas were developed in the summer of 1926 inspired by Denys Finch Hatton's letters on lesbianism (Blixen 2013: 1025) and his gift of the book *China under the Dowager Empress* (Blixen 2013: 1045) that contains depictions of power hungry eunuchs and homosexual brothels. In the last part of 1927 and the first part of 1928 she again brings topics related to 'Carnival' up in her letters, for example: ideas about the Danish smart set and seduction in a modern world (Blixen 2013: 1261), the 'Flapper' (Blixen 2013: 1301) and Harlequin (Blixen 2013: 1293). In this chapter I will, however, focus exclusively on seduction in connection to Kierkegaard and reserve most of the more general gender aspects of the tale for Chapter 12. In a letter dated 27 January 1924 where Dinesen explains how the concept of seduction is outdated in the modern world of the roaring twenties where free love relationships and birth control have become the norm:

> I gamle Dage existerede der Begreber som 'at forføre', 'Forførelse' etc., men jeg tror sletikke at de mere findes i nogen moderne ung Mands eller Piges Tankegang, og et moderne Menneske kan overhovedet vanskeligt udtale disse Ord, uden at der 'i Stemmen skælver et Gran af Ironi'. Hvis man vil se nærmere paa disse Begreber, saa maa det vel forstaas saaledes at en 'Forfører' i et Forhold, for sit eget Formaals Skyld, overtalte den anden Part til, eller ledede den ind paa noget, som paa en eller anden Maade matte skade, ødelægge eller nedværdige denne, som 'Forføreren' vidste at den 'Forførte' vilde komme til at angre, og som tillige overhovedet nedsatte 'den Forførte' i *Forførerens egne Øjne*; thi en Mand kaldtes ikke en Forfører, fordi han overtalte en Pige til at gifte sig med ham. I de mere grove Forhold kunde det vel ogsaa forstaas saaledes, at Forføreren indlod sig paa at love noget, — fx Ægteskab, — som han vidste han ikke vilde holde; men dette ligger vist udenfor det egentlige Begreb. Nutildags fører 'et Kærlighedsforhold' ikke til nogensomhelst af de nævnte Konsekvenser, og derfor er hele Begrebet (hvad dette Forhold angaar, thi det kan vel endnu findes f. Ex. i Politik) ganske naturligt udgaaet af Menneskehedens Ordbog. [...] Det var i gamle Dage en vis Antagelse, at en Kvinde satte mere Følelse ind i et Kærlighedsforhold, end en Mand i Almindelighed gjorde; men Gud ved, om den har meget paa sig, hvor Kvinderne i deres Liv udenfor Kærlighedsforholdet har ligesaa mange Ressourcer som Mændene. (Blixen 2013: 757)

> [In previous times there were such concepts as 'to seduce', 'seduction', etc., but I do not think that these exist at all any more in the way of thinking of modern young people, who have difficulty in uttering these words at all without 'a shade of irony in the voice.' If one looks more closely at these concepts, they must surely be understood to mean that a 'seducer' in a relationship persuaded the other partner to, or led her into doing, something for his own purposes, that in some way or other would injure, destroy, or degrade her, which 'the seducer' knew that 'the seduced' would regret having done and which also demeaned 'the seduced' in *the seducer's own eyes;* for a man was not deemed a seducer for persuading or pestering a girl to marry him. In the cruder instances there could be cases where the seducer went as far as to promise something, — marriage, for instance, — which he had no intention of fulfilling but this probably lies outside the main concept. Nowadays a love affair does not lea d to any of these consequences and thus the whole concept (as far as this sphere is concerned, for it is still to be found in politics, for instance) has quite naturally disappeared from current usage [...] In former times it was probably assumed that a woman put more feeling into a love affair than a man generally did; but heaven knows whether there is still anything in that when women have just as many resources in their lives apart from love affairs.] (Dinesen 1981: 188–89)

Dinesen uses this notion as a framework to create a scenario in 'Carnival' where seduction plays a role but in the new ways that fit the historical conditions of the contemporary 1920s. With the introduction of birth control in the 1920s the risk — and the possible dire consequences — for women engaging in a non-marital sexual relationship were reduced. Becoming pregnant without being married had up until then ruined many a woman's life and made her a social outcast. A fate that Johannes's Cordelia — in the aftermath of the affair with Johannes — might very well have faced, making Johannes undertaking a less noble affair and very un-gentlemanlike in the eyes of Dinesen, thus an example of: 'a "seducer" [who] in a relationship persuaded the other partner to, or led her into doing, something for his own purposes, that in some way or other would injure, destroy, or degrade her' that she mentions in the letter quoted above.

Annelise and 'the young Soren Kierkegaard'

Annelise is the first of Dinesen's female variations on Kierkegaard's Johannes Forføreren, which was a character she would later return to in her last tale 'Ehrengard' (see Chapter 10). Annelise is an artist. She is writing modern poetry and earns a living on the side posing as a nude model for the painters of the day. From this passage in the tale we understand why she has chosen her costume and what the connections to 'Forførerens Dagbog' are and what the nature of her proposal to Tido is:

> She had put on her costume tonight to accentuate the situation. For all students of Soren Kierkegaard will know his deep and graceful work *The Seducer's Diary*. In it the hero Johannes brings into play all his ingeniousness and his great powers of mind, to obtain one single night of love with the heroine, and then leaves her forever. The modern young woman had been at one with the old poet in the fundamental principle — which he laments himself in that exquisite passage: 'Why cannot such a night last for ever', etc. — that with one night the cup of love is emptied, the rest is dregs. But she had her own views upon the book, and had maintained, and lectured to him [Tido] upon, the idea that the triumph of Johannes is not complete as long as he keeps Cordelia in the dark as to his prospects of leaving her forever at daybreak, and that the name of seducer is falsely assumed where you are in any way deceiving your partner. More honest than Kierkegaard's seducer, she has presented her problem straight to him [Tido], this night of love was *à prendre ou à laisser*. This ultimatum she had delivered only a few days ago, now her costume as a dandy of the forties brought it home to him (Dinesen 1977: 82–83)

The element of seduction lies in the offer. Does the offer hold enough seductive quality to take? Tido can get the whole world in a short night, but consequently lose everything the following morning. Or, if he does not take it, he will never spend a night with his beloved. It also seems logical that if Tido takes the offer, their night will become extremely rich and intense and the following departure even more painful. This is a very sophisticated and macabre *pas de deux* and, according to Annelise, far more poetic than the final scene in 'Forførerens Dagbog' where Cordelia is taken by surprise by Johannes' deceit the following morning and Johannes himself returns home in triumph. First of all we find a gender inversion compared to Kierkegaard, since in 'Carnival' we find a woman in the role as the seducer, but Dinesen also wanted to invest the text with some gender equality. She was displeased with the one-sided way Cordelia was depicted in 'Forførerens Dagbog'. This she expresses in a letter to Aage Henriksen 14 October 1954, while she was working on her second Kierkegaard-tale 'Ehrengard': 'hvis hun [Cordelia] ikke er et Menneske, da er han [Johannes] hellerikke noget Menneske, hvis hun ikke er en Heltinde i en Historie, da er han hellerikke nogen Helt' (Blixen 1996b: 251) [if she is not a human being then he is not a human being either, if she is not a heroine in a story, neither is he a hero]. If the two parties on the other hand, like Annelise and Tido, are both in on it and are willing to take the risk being fully aware of the stakes (the risk of being ruined forever), no one is deceived and we have a hero *and* a heroine on equal terms.

Annelise is living entirely poetically but in Dinesen's version in a much more radical way than A's seducer. Whereas Johannes still operates within the frame of 1840s society, trying not to stick out too much, constantly being in control of the situation and being meticulously aware of not harming himself, Annelise doesn't take such petty precautions: 'She was so fresh. Hard too, and cold' (Dinesen 1977: 82). She does not care what happens to her in a physical sense, good or bad, as long as it has aesthetic and poetic value, be it the macabre love affair with Tido, or enrolling in a brothel (in order not to give up her poetry!) in Singapore.[2]

> 'Are you coming in, Annelise?' asked Julius. 'Yes,' she said. 'If you do not win the prize,' he said, 'you will have to go into a brothel, with my Pegasus — or, otherwise, give up having your poems published. Let us see now how much of an idealist you are.' 'Yes, you will see that, Julius,' said she, 'I shall go into a brothel. At Singapore. I have read of them there.' (Dinesen 1977: 93)

In a passage we also find a blow to the notion of sin and sexuality that this thoroughly treated in Kierkegaard's *Begrebet Angest*. For the non-religious smart set of the 1920s, the connection between sin and sex has lost its meaning.[3] The concept of sin, as we see it in this ironical passage, now only has aesthetic interest for the supper guests: ' "they had, upon a time, there, a very good black[4] from a terrible bad conscience, a deep guilt, you know. Sin, yes, deadly sin." "Oh, dear Rosie," lisped Soren Kierkegaard' (Dinesen 1977: 76).

Kierkegaard as a 'Macabre Dandy'

We note that the young Soren Kierkegaard, Annelise, is dressed 'as a dandy of the forties'. The dandy emerged as a new male type in the late eighteenth century and came to be associated with a certain type of intellectual or artist in the first part of the nineteenth century, with Lord Byron (1788–1824) and Charles Baudelaire (1821–1867) as the most famous examples. Dandyism is also associated with a certain type of aristocratic individualism as defined by Barbey d'Aurevilly: 'the dandy does not work; he exists' (Glick 2009: 264), and Baudelaire, for whom dandyism was a 'cult of self' characterized by 'first and foremost the burning need to create for oneself a personal originality' (Glick 2009: 27). These definitions fit very well with the young Søren Kierkegaard's burning desire to foster an image of personal originality with emphasis on artistic and individual expression — and with Dinesen's character Annelise. Dinesen rightly saw Kierkegaard as a dandy, the Copenhagen *flâneur* and free spirit of the day, but in 'Carnival' he is curiously called a 'desperate philosopher' and a 'macabre' dandy: 'the young Soren Kierkegaard — that brilliant, deep and desperate philosopher of the forties, a sort of macabre dandy of his day' (Dinesen 1977: 57). The labels 'desperate' and 'macabre', I will argue, have to do with him being a Christian virgin dandy (the discrepancy between his vital dandy-like outer appearance and his inner condition is what makes him macabre). This is separating him significantly from other famous — and sexually active — dandies from the 19th century such as Byron, Baudelaire and Barbey d'Aurevilly. This audacious suggestion I will, however, have to leave for now and return to in Chapter 11.

Polly: Seduction as a Fall

Aside from seduction presented by Annelise as a 'more honest' offer involving the consent of both parties and with equal consequences, we also find another variation of the concept of seduction in Dinesen's 'Carnival'. It also involves an offer, but operates on another level than physical seduction. It is a spiritual seduction that involves a fall — here, again, for both parties, but in different ways. In the final scene Polly reproaches herself for having manipulated and seduced Zamor to come in with them on the lottery: 'do you not understand, any of you, that I am going to make up for what I have done to Zamor? That was his virginity: that he would be like any of us. I made him sell his soul for a blank in the lottery' (Dinesen 1977: 120). She has acted like the character A from *Enten — Eller. Første Deel*. This character represents the aesthetic point of view, and is accused by Judge William in the piece 'Ligevægten':

> Du derimod, Du lever virkelig af Rov. Du lister Dig ubemærket paa Folk, stjæler deres lykkelige Øieblik, deres skjønneste Øieblik fra dem, stikker dette Skyggebillede i Din Lomme, som den lange Mand i Schlemil og tager det frem, naar Du ønsker det. (Kierkegaard 1843b: 20)

> [You, however, actually live by plundering; unnoticed, you creep up on people, steal from them their happy moment, their most beautiful moment, stick this shadow picture in your pocket as the tall man did in *Schlemihl* and take it out whenever you wish.] (Kierkegaard 1987b: 10)

Polly recognizes her role as a spiritual seducer and she does not like what she sees:

> 'It was a bad moment of my life, and Tido was right [to not ask Zamor to come in with them on the lottery]. I do not know how you, you men, have been able to carry, through all the centuries, the guilt of having seduced virgins. I cannot do it, it is to me a terrible thing to be a seducer, indeed I cannot imagine anything worse. I am giving a year to make good its loss to Zamor. Is it not strange', she went on gravely, 'that one should have to live for nineteen years to be taught, in reality, what virginity is?' (Dinesen 1977: 120).

Polly's solution to this recognition of herself being a manipulator and seducer without a conscience (her fall out of virginity) is the idea of employing Zamor as her shadow, her 'artificial conscience' to bring along for a year: 'Arlecchino [Polly] turned to old Rosendaal. ' "Shall I not take Zamor", she said, "to be my conscience for a year? Shall I not be allowed to have a conscience, Rosie? Something black in my life, a little mouche [patch] on my soul" [...] "he is to be my artificial shadow, my artificial conscience." ' (Dinesen 1977: 120). But here she — from the point of view of Judge William — makes another mistake:

> Seer man det Ethiske udenfor Personligheden og i et udvortes Forhold til denne, saa har man opgivet Alt, saa har man fortvivlet [...] Naar man derfor stundom seer Mennesker med en vis redelig Iver slide og slæbe for at realisere det Ethiske, der som en Skygge bestandig flygter, saasnart de gribe efter den, saa er det baade comisk og tragisk. (Kierkegaard 1843b: 243)

> [If the ethical is regarded as outside the personality and in an external relation to it, then one has given up everything, then one has despaired [...] That is why it is both comic and tragic to see at times people with a kind of honest zeal working their fingers to the bone in order to carry out the ethical, which like a shadow continually evades them as soon as they try to grasp it.] (Kierkegaard 1987b: 255)

Polly sees the ethical (in the sense of 'conscience') as something outside her own personality and tries to make a comical short cut by employing Zamor as her 'artificial conscience'. With that in mind Polly does appear both comic and tragic in the final scene.

Notes to Chapter 8

1. The essay was written as a series of letters to her brother Thomas Dinesen in 1923–1924, but not published until 1977 after Dinesen's death. It was translated into English in 1986 and titled *On Modern Marriage and Other Observations* (Dinesen 1986b).
2. This is also an allusion to Victor Eremita's speech in 'in vino veritas': 'Jeg for mit Vedkommende, hvis jeg var Qvinde, vilde hellere være det i Orienten, hvor jeg var Slavinde; thi at være Slavinde, hverken mere eller mindre, er dog altid Noget i Sammenligning med at være hu hei og ingen Ting. [...] Var jeg Qvinde, jeg vilde heller sælges af min Fader til den høist Bydende som i Orienten, thi en Handel er der dog Mening i' (Kierkegaard 1845: 58–59) [For my part, if I were a woman, I would rather be one in the Orient, where I would be a slave, for to be a slave — either more nor less — is still always something compared with being 'hurrah' and 'nothing'[...] If I were a woman, I would prefer being sold by my father to the highest bidder, as in the Orient, for a business transaction nevertheless does have meaning] (Kierkegaard 1988: 48–49).
3. ' "it cannot matter to us, because we do not believe in God." Pierrot nodded' (Dinesen 1977: 66).
4. At this point in the tale, Rosendaal (Rosie) is developing an argument regarding the superiority of the color black and its aesthetic qualities in relation to syphilis.

CHAPTER 9

❖

The Tragic Female Don Juan: 'The Dreamers' and A's Don Juan Essay

In this chapter I will compare Dinesen's 'The Dreamers' with A's Don Juan essay from *Enten — Eller. Første Deel* in order to demonstrate how Dinesen turns the Don Juan character and the notion of seduction in relation to gender radically upside-down. Contrary to A's idolization of Don Juan, we find Guildenstiern in 'The Dreamers' to be a comical Don Juan version. A also claims that 'the expression for Don Juan, in turn, is simply and solely music', but here Dinesen successfully utilizes Høffding's strategy of 'artistic irony' and shows that A's idea is a theoretical abstraction, since the most prominent example of the embodiment of music must be the female opera diva, who uses her body, her voice, on a very concrete level, to create music. Pellegrina is also an example of how women seduce without wanting to. She has no intention of seducing the three male characters in the tale, but the tree passionate gentlemen are actively pursuing her against her will, which in the end kills her. Thus, Dinesen here creates an original example of a tragic female Don Juan, who seduces without wanting it, which is a complete, and astute, subversion of A's Don Juan with regard to gender and seduction.

Langbaum and Brandes

Even though the American scholar Robert Langbaum was not entirely aware of how Dinesen used and inverted some of the ideas from A's Don Juan essay in 'The Dreamers', he was, however, the first to suggest that Pellegrina could be understood as a female version of Don Juan. He also establishes a direct connection between Dinesen and A's Don Juan-essay 'De umiddelbare erotiske Stadier eller det Musikalsk-Erotiske' [The immediate Stages of the Erotic, or The Musical Erotic] from *Enten — Eller. Første Deel*:

> Marcus, who carries the memory, leaves Pellegrina free to be an amoral natural force — to be Don Juan as Kierkegaard, from whom Isak Dinesen seems to derive her ideas of Don Juan, conceives him [Footnote in Langbaum's text: 'In "The immediate Stages of the Erotic, or The Musical Erotic", Either/Or, Vol. I. Isak Dinesen expressed to me her admiration for this essay'.] Kierkegaard considers the Don Juan legend specifically Christian, for only Christianity abstracts sensuousness as a principle opposed to spirit. He connects Don Juan and Faust as related medieval ideas, since Faust is the part of intellect and spirit

that Christianity excludes. Don Juan and Faust are the sensuous and spiritual demonic. Pellegrina combines Don Juan and Faust; for she overcomes not only like Don Juan through the power of the physical desire, but through the power of the erotic idea as a force that takes hold of the imagination. It is significant that she is a singer; for music, especially music with words, is, according to Kierkegaard, the art of the demonic. Kierkegaard wrote his essay to show that Mozart had in *Don Giovanni* the perfect subject for music, and that music is the only medium which could adequately express the legend of Don Juan as the life force that exists in immediacy, that is always on the point of becoming an individual but which never finally does, for if it did it would disappear in reflection and rationalization. Pellegrina, after she loses her voice, is the spirit of music let loose into life. She is demonic not only in her metamorphoses as whore and artist-revolutionary, but even in her metamorphosis as a saint. For she is a saint in the manner of Mary Magdalen, which is why every one is so attracted to her. If we consider that the three metamorphoses correspond to Dante's three realms of being, we might say that the saint is the demonic force in the realm of orthodoxy-theology-Paradise; the whore, in the realm of biology-Hell; and the artist-revolutionary, in the realm of intellect-Purgatory. (Langbaum 1964: 100–01)

In the essay A claims that 'denne sandselige erotiske Genialitet' [the sensuous in its elemental originality] can only be expressed by music and that *Don Juan* is the embodiment of music and the demonic:

> Den abstrakteste Idee, der lader sig tænke, er den sandselige Genialitet [...] Fordrer nu denne sandselige erotiske Genialitet i al sin Umiddelbarhed et Udtryk, saa spørges, hvilket Medium egner sig hertil. Det, her især maa fastholdes, er, at den fordres udtrykt og fremstillet i sin Umiddelbarhed. I sin Middelbarhed og Reflekterethed i Andet falder den ind under Sproget og kommer til at ligge under ethiske Bestemmelser. I sin Umiddelbarhed kan den kun udtrykkes i Musik [...] Udtrykket for denne Idee er *Don Juan*, og Udtrykket for *Don Juan* er igjen ene og alene Musik. (Kierkegaard 1843a: 64, 71, 90)

> [The most abstract idea conceivable is the sensuous in its elemental originality [...] If the elemental originality of the sensuous-erotic in all its immediacy insists on expression, then the question arises as to which medium is the most suitable for this. The point that particularly must be kept in mind here is that it insists on being expressed and presented in its immediacy. In its mediacy and in being reflected in another medium, it falls within language and comes under ethical categories. In its immediacy, it can be expressed only in music [...] The expression for this idea is Don Juan, and the expression for Don Juan, in turn, is simply and solely music.] (Kierkegaard 1987a: 46, 51, 64)

In 'The Dreamers' Pellegrina is, contrary to A's lofty description of Don Juan as the expression of music, depicted as a concrete embodiment of music in the shape of a female opera prima donna, *who is music in the flesh*, so to speak, when she performs. Pellegrina is Dinesen's materialistic embodiment of 'the sensuous in its elemental originality' and a realistic counter-character to A's mythical Don Juan. Dinesen must have had a hard time seeing the embodiment of music and the demonic in the shape of the compulsive, spiritless male seducer Don Juan. Again Dinesen's is strikingly in line with Brandes' critique of A's Don Juan-essay in his book about

Kierkegaard:

> Han formaaer at give det Værk, han forherliger og forklarer, en overordentlig
> Værdi for Læseren, men han bærer sig ad som en Kong Midas, der forvandler
> Alt hvad hans Haand berører til Guld, saa Værket straaler i en Gyldenglorie
> for Læserens Øie; men han formaaer ikke det fuldt saa Vanskelige at give Alt
> deri dets rette, dets naturlige Farve [...] løvrigt er Afhandlingen om 'Don
> Juan' bygget paa en nu rent forældet metafysisk Æsthetik af Hegelsk Tilsnit.
> Operaens Fortrinlighed forklares ved Sammentræffet og Overensstemmelsen
> mellem de to Abstractioner Stof og Form, hvilken Overensstemmelse efter
> Forfatterens Definition udfordres til Classiciteten, der ikke føres tilbage til
> nogen Evne hos Mozart. Det bedste musikalske Værk siges at maatte opstaa,
> hvor den abstracteste Idee traf Musikens abstracte Medium, og gjennem det
> besynderlige Postulat at 'den sandselige Genialitet' er den abstracteste Idee, der
> lader sig tænke, naaes der saa til Hovedpostulatet, at vi i Mozarts 'Don Juan'
> have den fuldendte Enhed af denne Idee og den dertil svarende Form. (Brandes
> 1877: 131, 135–36)

> [He is able to give that work he glorifies and elucidates an extraordinary value
> for the reader, but he behaves like a King Midas — everything he touches
> turns to gold — so that the work shines in a golden halo before the reader's
> eye; but he does not quite manage to give everything its due, its natural color
> [...] in addition his treatise on 'Don Juan' is based on a now purely antiquated
> metaphysical aesthetic of Hegelian nature. The opera's excellence is explained
> by the combination of and agreement between two abstractions, matter and
> form, an agreement that, according to the author's definition, is connected to
> classicism, which does not lead back to any ability in Mozart. The best musical
> work is said to arise where the most abstract idea meets the abstract medium of
> music; and through that strange postulate that 'the sensual genius' is the most
> abstract idea one can imagine, there is achieved the main postulate: that in
> Mozart's 'Don Juan' we have the complete unity of this idea and the thereby
> corresponding form.]

Pellegrina as a Tragic Female Don Juan

Pellegrina's life and identity *is* art (music) to a degree, so that when she loses her
voice and can't perform, she perceives it as her death. With regard to gender this
is opposite of what A claims about woman in the essay 'Skyggerids' [Silhouettes]
from *Enten — Eller. Første Deel*: 'Ulykkelig Kjærlighed er vel i og for sig den dybeste
Sorg for en Qvinde' (Kierkegaard 1843a: 169) [Unhappy love is in itself undoubtedly
the deepest sorrow for a woman] (Kierkegaard 1987a: 115). This does, however, not
seem to account for the female artist, Pellegrina, since her 'deepest sorrow' is when
she loses her ability to perform, her ability to create art. As a stunningly beautiful
and talented female artist, Pellegrina is a seducer in the sense that she seduces the
world, the audience, with her voice, beauty and magnetic personality. When she
loses her voice and status as a prima donna, her life changes in a rather radical way,
even though it still follows some of its previous paths. When she can't perform on
the stage any more, she has *to live her life* as if she were still an actor and singer,
which means that she constantly has to change roles in real life. She is, however,

still dedicated to helping the so-called *sinners* of the world (the poor people in the opera galleries), but now in a very hands on, practical way: the male brothel goers (when she is a whore), the revolutionaries (when she is their leader) and all the dead children and people, who are poor and have no hope left in the world (when she is the Saint in the spirit of Maria Magdalen). When being Pellegrina she seduced her audience in an abstract way through art (her voice). When she loses her voice, she seduces with her personality and actions and, in the case of Lincoln, her extraordinary skills in bed (not to forget the humorous aspect of the tale).

But the major point is that she does not seduce deliberately. She has not asked any of the men who encounter her to fall in love with her and she does nothing to seduce them deliberately. It just happens because she is what she is. Contrary to the Baron, who is the Don Juan parody of the tale, Pellegrina seduces without effort, but with such an irresistible effect that her lovers desperately chase her across Europe and in the end, this kills her. We are here dealing with a woman, Pellegrina, who is not able to escape her own seductiveness, thus we are dealing with a tragic figure, a tragic female Don Juan, who attracts and seduces without wanting it and at the same time is forced to flee the relationship after a few years to cover up her identity and keep her roles in flux.

I, however, see no reason to characterize Pellegrina as 'demonic' as Langbaum does. She may *appear* that way in the mind of Langbaum (and the three unhappy lovers) and she might very well look like Kierkegaard's Don Juan with regard to how she transforms herself and disappears in front of her lover's eyes like music: 'Her viser det sig ret, hvad det vil sige, at Don Juans Væsen er Musik. Han opløser sig ligesom for os i Musik, han udfolder sig til en Verden af Toner' (Kierkegaard 1843a: 136) [What it means to say — that Don Giovanni's essential nature is music — is clearly apparent here. He dissolves, as it were, in music for us; he unfurls in a world of sounds] (Kierkegaard 1987a: 94), but here the similarities stop. Pellegrina is, on the contrary, described as an extraordinary woman, who, in the words of Lincoln, has 'so much life in her, and that great strength' (Dinesen 1934: 283),[1] '[t]here was nothing black or sad in her nearness' (Dinesen 1934: 287)[2] and he concludes: 'To this woman I owe it that I have ever understood, and still remember, the meaning of such words as tears, heart, longing, stars' (Dinesen 1935: 270).[3] In her post opera-singer life Pellegrina is not demonic but 'et skikkeligt Menneske' [a good-natured person] as Dinesen also calls Lady Flora in 'Kardinalens tredje Historie' in her response to Bjørn Poulsen's characterization of her as being demonic in the Kierkegaardian sense (Blixen 1996b: 13).[4]

Dinesen seems to suggest that women (or some women) seduce without effort and without necessarily wanting it (like Pellegrina and her alter egos).[5] Woman automatically seduces because she is *woman*, thus, *eo ipso*, the object of male adornment ('attraa'). And what are the four most seductive archetypical female characters that have always had the most power to seduce and enchant men? The answer in 'The Dreamers' is: *the Diva* (Pellegrina), *the Whore* (Olalla), *the Saint* (Rosalba) and the *Artist-Revolutionary* Jeanne d'Arc-type (Madame Lola).

Baron Guildenstern as a Comical Don Juan

> Som bekjendt har nemlig *Don Juan* existeret langt tilbage i Tiden som et
> Fjellebodsstykke, ja dette er vel egentlig dets første Existens. Men her er
> Ideen bleven opfattet comisk, som det overhovedet er mærkeligt, at saa dygtig
> Middelalderen var i at udruste Idealer, ligesaa sikker var den i at see det
> Comiske, der laae i Idealets overnaturlige Størrelse. At gjøre *Don Juan* til en
> Pralhans, der bildte sig ind at have forført alle Piger, at lade *Leporello* troe hans
> Løgne, var vel ikke et aldeles uheldigt comisk Anlæg. (Kierkegaard 1843a: 96)

> [As is known, *Don Juan* existed long ago as melodrama; indeed, this was probably
> its first existence. But here the idea was conceived comically; moreover, it is
> noteworthy that just as the Middle Ages was very proficient in fitting out ideals,
> it was equally sure to see the comic in the preternatural magnitude of the ideal.
> To make *Don Juan* a braggart who imagined he had seduced all the girls and to
> have *Leporello* believe his lies certainly was not an altogether bad comic design.]
> (Kierkegaard 1987a: 68)

In 'The Dreamers' Dinesen is clearly in line with this medieval comical interpretation
of Don Juan and Leporello, when we take a closer look on her depiction of Baron
Guildenstern and Pilot. In the tale Dinesen lets Lincoln Forsner paint this less
flattering and comical portrait of the Baron (Don Juan) and Pilot (Leporello):

> He presented his friend to me as baron Guildenstern of Sweden. I had not
> had the pleasure of their company for ten minutes before I had been informed
> by booth of them that the Baron in his own country held the reputation of
> a great seducer of women. This made me meditate — although all the time
> my intercourse with other people was carried on only upon the surface of my
> mind — on what kind of women they have in Sweden. The ladies who have
> done me the honor of letting me seduce them have, all of them, insisted upon
> deciding themselves which was to be the central point in the picture. I have
> liked them for it, for therein lay what was to me a variety of an otherwise
> monotonous performance. But in the case of the Baron it was clear that the
> point of gravity had always been entirely with him. You would suppose him
> to be of an unenthusiastic nature, even while he was talking of the beauties
> whom he had pursued, but you would not find him lacking in enthusiasm when
> he had once turned your eyes toward what he wanted you really to admire. It
> appeared from his talk that all his ladies had been of exactly the same kind, and
> that kind of woman I have never met. With himself so absolutely the hero of
> each single exploit, I wondered why he should have taken so much trouble —
> and he was obviously prepared to go any length of trouble in these affairs — to
> obtain, time after time, a repetition of exactly the same trick. To begin with I
> was, being a young man myself, highly impressed by such a superabundance of
> appetite. Still I got, after a while, from his conversation, which was very lively
> and became more so after we had emptied a few bottles together, the key to
> the existence of the young Swede, which lay in the single word 'competition'.
> [...] His past life, I found from his talk, he saw as a row of triumphs over a row
> of rivals, and as nothing else whatever, although he was a little older than I.
> Neither in his rivals nor in his victims had he any interest at all. He had in him
> neither admiration nor pity, no feeling that was not either envy or contempt.
> [...] The two got on very well together, Pilot being flattered into existence by

the cute young Swede — I have got, Pilot thought, a friend who is a terrible seducer of women; consequently I exist — and the Baron quite pleased to have outshone all former friends of the rich young German, and to be admired by him. (Dinesen 1934: 294–96)[6]

In another passage Pellegrina, in the role of Madame Rosalba (the Saint), makes a clear connection between Baron Arvid Guildenstern and Don Juan:

'"Arvid," she said, "have you ever heard the story of Don Giovanni?" She looked at me so intently that I had to answer that I had even heard that opera about him. "Do you remember, then," she said, "the scene in which the statue of the Commandante comes for him? Such a statue there is on the tomb of General Zumala, in Spain." I said, "Oh, let it keep him down in it, then." "Wait," said Rosalba. "Rosalba belonged to General Zumala Carregui. When she betrays him, poor Rosalba must disappear. But then, an opera must have a fifth act to it sooner or later. And you, my star of the north, are to be the hero of it." [...] "For you, Arvid, I am worried, I am terribly sorry. An awful future awaits you — waste, a desert — oh, tortures!" [...] "For soon [...] it may be too late, and we shall hear the fatal step on the stair, marble upon marble".' (Dinesen 1934: 311–12)[7]

As we understand from this passage, Pellegrina feels pity for Arvid (Guildenstern) because she is convinced that their one-night stand (which will enable Guildenstern to win the competition with his two fellow rivals and get the award; the fine Andalusian horses) will lead to his demise just like Donna Anna's dead father, the Commendatore, became Don Juan's nemesis in the opera. Here Rosalba clearly overestimates her own powers with regard to Guildenstern. Seven years have passed when they finally meet again for one last showdown in the mountains, and the Baron has not been judged by any Commendatore (conscience) but is in great shape and has not changed the least. His reaction is very different from Pilot and Lincoln's love-struck, desperate outcries:

'Hullo,' he cried, 'the chase is up and the Englishman has won. He has improved the occasion at once, and that at ten degrees of frost. We ought not to have told him of so many attractions. He has seen only the women of his own country till now, and we drove him mad straight away. Let us have a look at the lady now ourselves, Fritz.' [...] The Baron starred at her. So did Pilot. 'So it is you, indeed, my sainted Rosalba,' said the former, 'pausing a moment on your way to heaven. I wish you luck in the more pleasant career.' I could see that at his words Ollala could with difficulty keep from laughing. In fact every time she looked at the Swede she was tempted to laugh. But she was very pale, and with every minute she grew paler. (Dinesen 1934: 325)[8]

Pellegrina, now playing the role of Hofraad Hersbrandt's wife, can't help laughing at Guildenstern, the comical, compulsive Don Juan, even though she is herself mortally wounded. To conclude: in Dinesen's version Don Juan is not the embodiment of a natural force (the sensuous) expressed in music, but a real, rather simple — yet cunning — narcissistic man, Baron Guildenstern, who, driven by a desire to outshine other men, uses his countless love affairs as a means to obtain the bragging rights and to feel better about himself. According to A in Kierkegaard's essay, Mozart's Don Juan is not a reflected seducer (as is the case of Johannes). He is only a seducer insofar as his adornments enchant and spellbind the women to a degree, so that they are eventually seduced by his compliments, effort and enthusiasm:

> Til at være Forfører hører der altid en vis Reflexion og Bevidsthed, og saasnart denne er tilstede, da kan det være paa sit Sted at tale om List og Rænker og snedige Anløb. Denne Bevidsthed mangler *Don Juan*. Han forfører derfor ikke. Han attraar, denne Attraa virker forførende; forsaavidt forfører han. Han nyder Attraaens Tilfredsstillelse; saasnart han har nydt den, da søger han en ny Gjenstand og saaledes i det Uendelige. (Kierkegaard 1843a: 102)

> [To be a seducer always takes a certain reflection and consciousness, and as soon as this is present, it can be appropriate to speak of craftiness and machinations and subtle wiles. Don Giovanni lacks this consciousness. Therefore, he does not seduce. He desires, and this desire acts seductively. To this extent he does seduce. He enjoys the satisfaction of desire; as soon as he has enjoyed it, he seeks a new object, and so it goes on indefinitely.] (Kierkegaard 1987a: 72)

Based on this passage one could even argue that it is actually the un-reflected Don Juan who is seduced over and over again by the sheer appearance of women that he just can't resist. This makes Don Juan even more comical since he is not the one, who is in charge, even though he himself believes so, but is instead pulled around by the nose of a bigger force; *woman* that seduces *him* over and over again, while his assistant is keeping count of the numbers.

The Male Characters: Don Juan's Women Inverted

Following in the trail of Langbaum, Nilsson has suggested that the three male characters in 'The Dreamers' could be interpreted as gender inversions of the three female antagonists in *Don Juan*:

> For mig at se imødekommer Pellegrina efter branden sine elskeres maskuline forventninger, de oplever med hende en enestående livsintensitet, men efter hendes løftelse af dem til højder hinsides hvad de før kendte til, forlader hun dem pludselig uden forklaring, hvorpå de falder tilbage til dagliglivets sfinxforladte realiteter. Og efter dette tab og tilbagefald har de det mildt sagt ikke godt. De føler sig snydt og reagerer nøjagtigt som operaens tre forurettede kvinder i forhold til Don Juan, som de enten vil fastholde eller omvende, skønt en fastholdelse og omvendelse af ham ville udelukke den løftelsens entusiasme de ønsker tilbage, eller de vil som Donna Anna og Baronen have hævn. (Nilsson 2004: 212)

> [In my view, after the fire, Pellegrina meets her lovers' masculine expectations; with her they experience a singular intensity of life. But after she elevates them to heights beyond what they have ever known, she leaves them suddenly and without explanation, whereon they fall back to the sphinx-abandoned realities of everyday living. And after this loss and relapse, they are, to put it mildly, not doing so well. They feel cheated and react exactly like the opera's three wronged women in relation to Don Juan, whom they will either hold on to or convert, although a retention or conversion of him would preclude the

elevating enthusiasm they want back. Or, like Donna Anna and the Baron, they want revenge.]

Returning to Kierkegaard's original text, we can see that the three male characters in 'The Dreamers' do seem to fit the three spiteful women and their relation to Don Juan after they have been seduced by him as we find it described by A:

> Med Undtagelse af Commandanten staar alle Personer i en Art erotisk forhold til Don Juan. Over Commandanten kan han ingen Magt udøve, han er Bevidsthed; de Andre ere i hans Magt. *Elvire* [Lincoln] elsker ham [hende], derved er hun i hans magt, *Anna* [Baron Guildenstern] hader ham [hende], derved er hun i hans Magt, *Zerline* [Pilot] frygter ham [hende], derved er hun [han] i hans [hendes] Magt. (Kierkegaard 1843a: 127, author's insertions in square brackets)

> [With the exception of the Commendatore, all the characters stand in a kind of erotic relation to Don Giovanni. He cannot exercise any power over the Commendatore, who is consciousness; the others are in his power. Elvira [Lincoln] loves him [her], and thereby she is in his power; Anna [Baron Guildenstern] hates him [her], and thereby she is in his power; Zerlina [Pilot] fears him [her], and thereby she [he] is in his [her] power.] (Kierkegaard 1987a: 88)

When taking in the gender inversions that occur on more levels in 'The Dreamers' into account, Nilsson's interpretation is very plausible and fits the general outline of 'The Dreamers' as a counter-story to A's ideas presented in the Don Juan-essay in *Enten — Eller. Første Deel* with regard to gender and seduction.

'The Dreamers' and Don Juan: Tradition and Repetition

In 'The Dreamers' Dinesen picks up and repeats the Don Juan motif that was one of the preferred motifs in literature during Romanticism, which Brandes points out in the passage below humorously hinting at Kierkegaard:

> — Saa bliver han [Kierkegaard] da selv i Forholdet Don Juan. Som den hele Generation af unge Digtere i Frankrig, Tydskland og Rusland havde han med sin Tanke bestandig kredset om dette Ideal. Mussets berømte Stanzer, Gautiers Ungdomspoesier, Grabbes Drama, Lenau's [sic] Fragment, Lermontow's [sic] 'Vor Tids Helt' fremstillede i Byrons Spor Typen i moderne Skikkelse. I vor egen Literatur havde Heiberg og Paludan-Müller syslet med denne Opgave. Poeterne drømte dengang om Don Juan som Politikerne nutildags beskjæftige sig med Bismarck. (Brandes 1877: 85)

> [— Thus, it is the same relationship he [Kierkegaard] has to Don Juan. Like the entire generation of young poets in France, Germany, and Russia, his thoughts had constantly circled around this ideal. Musset's famous stanzas, Gautier's youthful poetry, Grabbe's drama, Lenau's fragment, Lermontov's *Hero of Our Time,* all produced the type, à la Byron, in modern form. Heiberg and Paludan-Müller had fiddled with this task in our own literature. At that time, the poets dreamed about Don Juan the way politicians nowadays concern themselves with Bismarck.]

Heiberg's marionette comedy *Don Juan* (1814) is also mentioned in A's essay together with Molière's play as two examples of epic narratives that treat the Don Juan character from a comical perspective:

> En fuldent Opfattelse, der har ført ham ind under det Interessante, har jeg ikke seet; derimod gjælder det om de fleste Opfattelser af *Don Juan*, at de nærme sig til det Comiske. Dette lader sig let forklare deraf, at de knytte sig til *Moliere* [sic], i hvis Opfattelse det Comiske slumrer, og det er *Heibergs* Fortjeneste, at han er bleven sig dette tydeligt bevidst og derfor ikke blot kalder sit Stykke Et Marionetspil, men paa saa mange andre Maader lader det Comiske skinne frem. (Kierkegaard 1843a: 112)

> [A consummate interpretation that has drawn him under the rubric of the interesting, I have not seen; it holds true, however, of most versions of Don Juan that they approach the comic. This is easily explained by their attachment to Molière, in whose interpretation the comic is dormant, and it is to Heiberg's credit that he was clearly aware of this and therefore not only calls his play a marionette show but in so many other ways has the comic shine forth.] (Kierkegaard 1987a: 78)

Dinesen's 'The Dreamers' obviously belongs to this literary tradition of comical Don Juan depictions with regard to Baron Guildenstern, but the way she portrays the Pellegrina character as a tragic female Don Juan and how she inverts common ideas about gender and seduction in the tale are completely original. One could even rightly claim that Pellegrina as a female Don Juan does indeed belong to the category of 'det Interessante' [the interesting], which means that Dinesen is giving us the example that A claims in the previous quote that he has never seen: 'En fuldent Opfattelse, der har ført ham [hende] ind under det Interessante' (author's insertion in square brackets) [A consummate interpretation that has drawn him [her] under the rubric of the interesting].

The major inversions in 'The Dreamers' of the ideas presented in A's Don Juan essay can be broken down like this: 1) Pellegrina as a female counter-version of Don Juan — a very attractive woman who seduces involuntarily and an example of the true embodiment of music in the shape of an opera diva. 2) Don Juan as a cunning and narcissist man who only seduces to outshine his rivals (as a more realistic counter-version of A's unreflected seducer), and, finally 3) the three men — Lincoln (Elvira), Baron Guildenstern (Anna) and Pilot (Elvira) — cast in the roles of Don Juan's unhappy female lovers, who keeps pursuing Pellegrina. In 'The Dreamers' Dinesen furthermore casts the wealthy Jew Marcus Cocoza in the role of the Commendatore, but instead of the cold stone figure of the Commendatore that approaches Don Juan in the final scene, Marcus and Pellegrina are glowing with heat in the last minutes before Pellegrina takes her last breath upon uttering a line from Mozart's *Don Juan*:

> As she spoke these words of the old opera a wave of deep dark color, like that of a bride, like that in the face of the old Jew, washed over her white and bruised face. It spread from her bosom to the roots of her hair. The three of us who were lookers-on were, I believe, pale faced; but those two, looking at each other, glowed in a mute, increasing ecstasy. (Dinesen 1934: 351)[9]

Pellegrina is not escorted down to Hell by any demons, which is the fate of Don Juan in Mozart's opera, when he is judged a sinner: 'Questo è il fin di chi fa mal, e de' perfidi la morte alla vita è sempre ugual' [Such is the end of the evildoer: the death of a sinner always reflects his life]. Pellegrina is not a sinner, and Dinesen lets her die with great dignity, glowing with heat and ecstasy. This reversal underlines the moral of the tale that Pellegrina, unlike Don Juan, has done nothing wrong and that her (noble) death reflects *her* life.

Notes to Chapter 9

1. Dinesen 1935: 270.
2. Dinesen 1935: 274.
3. Dinesen 1934: 282.
4. In a letter from 7 February 1951, Bjørn Poulsen uses Kierkegaard's notion of the demonic in his analysis of 'Kardinalens Tredje Historie' ('The Cardinal's First Tale') to claim that Lady Flora is a demonic character (Blixen 1996b: 10). In a letter to Thorkild Bjørnvig sent the following day, Dinesen strongly disagreed with this interpretation: 'Men Lady Flora var ikke dæmonisk, hun var et skikkeligt menneske' (Blixen 1996b: 10) [But Lady Flora was not demonic, she was a good-natured person]. Bjørnvig's answer came back on 10 February 1951. Here he agreed with Dinesen and tried to explain how Poulsen has misunderstood Kierkegaard's notion of the demonic in connection to his understanding of Lady Flora, which, I would argue, could account for Pellegrina as well: 'Kierkegaard definerer ganske rigtigt det dæmoniske som Angsten for det gode — men paa ingen Maade som Angsten for menneskelig berøring. Det er en lovlig haatrukken Parallel for at faa det Regnestykke til at gaa op, at Lady Flora skulde være dæmonisk. Yderligere definerer Kierkegaard det dæmoniske som Angsten for det sande og skønne — og intet kunde jo passe daarligere paa Lady Flora, som just *elskede*, mener jeg, det sande og det skønne' (Blixen 1996b: 13) [Kierkegaard quite accurately describes the demonic as fear of the good — but in no way as fear of human touch. It is a somewhat far-fetched analogy to justify the assessment that Lady Flora is demonic. Kierkegaard further defines the demonic as fear of the true and the beautiful — and I think nothing would apply worse to Lady Flora, who only loved the true and the beautiful].
5. Other example of women who seduce by their sheer appearance and without wanting to are the two beautiful but virtuous virgin sisters Martine and Phillippa in 'Babette's Feast': 'They were never to be seen at balls or parties, but people turned when they passed in the streets, and the young men of Berlevaag went to church to watch them walk up the aisle' (Dinesen 1958: 22).
6. Dinesen 1935: 280–82.
7. Dinesen 1935: 296–97.
8. Dinesen 1935: 308–09.
9. Dinesen 1935: 332.

CHAPTER 10

❖

The Seducer Seduced:
'Ehrengard' and 'Forførerens Dagbog'

In this chapter, I will analyze Dinesen's novella 'Ehrengard', which is her longest and most elaborate counter-story to Kierkegaard's 'Forførerens Dagbog'. Contrary to Kierkegaard's Johannes Forføreren, Johann W. Cazotte is only trying to seduce the young maiden Ehrengard spiritually without the slightest touch so that she becomes aware of sexuality in spirit only. It is a purely intellectual undertaking, but in Cazotte's mind loaded with erotic energy. The plan, however, collapses when Ehrengard discovers his intention and decides to teach him a lesson. In the concluding scene she manages to seduce him when she makes him blush in public by claiming that Cazotte is the father of the kidnapped child and she the mother (even though it is a lie). Up until then everyone has been talking about the middle-aged artist Cazotte as the great seducer, eroticist and Don Juan of the day, but Ehrengard has figured out that he is in fact a virgin, and only engages in erotic situations as long as it feeds his creativity and sense of spiritual omnipotence. This is why she can make him blush, because he suddenly understands that she knows his secret. Thus, Ehrengard wins this intellectual duel with Cazotte, which is a subversion of the intellectual power balance between Johannes and Cordelia in 'Forførerens Dagbog'. But while Cazotte subsequently experiences a fall into sexuality, when he, after the blush, goes to Italy and indulges in physical love, Ehrengard experiences her intellectual fall as troublesome and painful, just like Polly in 'Carnival'. The name of the character, Johann W. Cazotte, and his being a forty-year-old virgin is an allusion to Goethe, who was probably a virgin up until his second sojourn to Italy. This, I argue, is the secret note outside the text that the reader has to know in order to fully understand the tale. Dinesen's last tale, her swan song 'Ehrengard', is the most poignant, elaborate and striking example of her counter-story strategy, and bears testament to her lifelong interest in — and disagreements with — Kierkegaard when it comes to gender and seduction.

'You might call it "The Seducer's Diary"'

The novella 'Ehrengard' from 1963 has commonly been regarded, and rightly so, as Isak Dinesen's answer to Søren Kierkegaard's 'Forførerens Dagbog' from *Enten — Eller. Første Deel* (1843). Shortly after the publication, Robert Langbaum was the first scholar to point out the connections between 'Ehrengard' and 'Forførerens Dagbog' in his book *The Gayety of Vision* (1964). Here he quotes a letter Dinesen wrote to *Ladies' Home Journal* in June 1962 when she submitted the final version (that was, however, later cut, and the title changed — see page 91). In the passage Dinesen links the novella directly to Kierkegaard's 'Forførerens Dagbog' and emphasizes the irony:

> 'You might call it,' she wrote to the Ladies' Home Journal on June 25 1962, 'The Seducer's Diary' — which is, of course, a quotation from Kierkegaard, but which is here to be taken ironically and might give the reader an idea of the nature of the story (Langbaum 1964: 274)

Since the publication of Langbaum's work, at least twenty articles or separate book chapters discussing the novella have been published, for the most part focusing on the notion of gender, art, and seduction (for a full list see Bunch 2013a). A visit to the Royal Danish Library (December 2010), where seven different manuscript versions of the novella were to be found in the Karen Blixen Archive, confirmed that even though 'Ehrengard' has received renewed scholarly attention the past fifteen years, important information crucial to our understanding of the novella has so far been overlooked (until Bunch 2013a). In order to review and enrich our understanding of this significant work, Dinesen's last tale, I will focus on the following: 1) I will point out new meta-narrative connections to 'Forførerens Dagbog', significant for the interpretation and understanding of both the novella and the diary, 2) I will show how deleted passages in the earlier drafts carry new information crucial for our understanding of Johann W. Cazotte's blush in the final scene, and 3) I will show how hidden homophonic puns add to the understanding of the novella as an ironical counter-story to Kierkegaard.

Dinesen, Kierkegaard, and 'Ehrengard'

Dinesen's interest in Kierkegaard peaked for the second time in the 1950s and she returned to 'Forførerens Dagbog', which she had also treated in the — yet still unpublished — tale 'Carnival' thirty years earlier. We know from the letters that she eagerly discussed Kierkegaard with the new young poets and scholars of the day that she came to meet in the late 1940s (Thorkild Bjørnvig) and the first part of the 1950s (Aage Henriksen). Kierkegaard is in fact mentioned eighteen times in her letter correspondences from January 1951 to August 1955, while she was working on 'Ehrengard' at Rungstedlund. As I have already mentioned in Chapter 4, Dinesen took up studies of the latest secondary literature about Kierkegaard (Brandt, Bruun Andersen and Rohde), following her intense Kierkegaard discussions with Aage Henriksen, which informed her view on Kierkegaard in new ways during the long working process with 'Ehrengard'.

The process from the first draft written in the late winter and spring of 1952 to the final manuscript, which was published posthumously in 1963, was long and challenging. In April and May 1952, while working on the first draft, Dinesen and her secretary Clara Selborn had problems collaborating. Selborn did not like the novella and was not able to hide it when she took dictation (Selborn 1974: 77). Selborn, who was a Catholic, had problems with the humorous sexual content in the novella and felt that Dinesen went too far. This made Dinesen furious (Selborn 1974: 83). The outcome of their dispute was that Dinesen sent Selborn away on a mandatory leave to France and Italy in May 1952, so she could continue working on 'Ehrengard' without Selborn meddling (Selborn 1974: 76–77 and Blixen 1996b: 85–87). In the summer and fall of 1952, she sent the first draft to Erik Clemmesen (he answered 14 July) and Ellen Dahl (she answered 18 July) for comments, and later in the fall to Jørgen Gustava Brandt (he answered 10 October) (Blixen 1996b: 92–96). They were all very appreciative but Dinesen was, however, not satisfied with the novella and stored it away. Nine years later she took it up again and rewrote it several times in 1961 and 1962, until she finally submitted it to the *Ladies' Home Journal* in June 1962 (Langbaum 1964: 274). The journal, however, thought that the novella was too long for a magazine story and asked for the number of pages to be significantly reduced. This was very hard for Dinesen to accept after having worked on it for more than ten years. She mentioned that it felt to her 'som at skære i mit hjerte' (Lasson 2008: 481) [like cutting my heart], but she needed the money and had to accept the changes. The shortened version was published in *Ladies' Home Journal* in December 1962 under the title 'The Secret of Rosenbad' just a few months after Dinesen died (Langbaum 1964: 274). The year after in 1963 'Ehrengard' was published in full length in both the original, uncut English version and in Clara Selborn's Danish translation. The narrative complexity, the subtle intrigue, and the profound insights into the anatomy of art and seduction are products of this long and complex process through which it came into being. The end result is a novella of great depth and complexity.

Johann and Johannes

The male protagonist in 'Ehrengard' is a composite of three characters, but only two of them will be included in this examination of the novella.[1] As the name suggests, the character of Johann Wolfgang Cazotte is based on German writer and painter Johann Wolfgang Goethe: 'that great artist Geheimrat Wolfgang Cazotte' (Dinesen 1963: 218) and the character in the tale is well aware of the name similarity: 'The world did not grudge sweet Gretchen — the heroine of my gigantic namesake — her guilt, it admitted her crime of infanticide and her debt to the sword of justice' (Dinesen 1963: 245). The depiction of the psychological make-up of Cazotte is, however, closer to Søren Kierkegaard's character Johannes Forføreren (Johannes the Seducer) from 'Forførerens Dagbog'. They have very similar names (Johann and Johannes) and Cazotte's approach to seduction closely follows what Johannes expresses in 'Forførerens Dagbog'. As readers, we do not know much about Johannes, only that he is some kind of intellectual and a devotee of living aesthetically. He is a seducer, but not in an ordinary sense as A correctly notices in the foreword: 'Han levede altfor meget aandeligt til at være en Forfører i almindelig Forstand' (Kierkegaard 1843a: 297) [He was much too endowed intellectually to be a seducer in the ordinary sense] (Kierkegaard 1987a: 193) and this passage in the diary explains why: 'Det er mig slet ikke om at gjøre i udvortes Forstand at besidde Pigen, men kunstnerisk at nyde Hende' (Kierkegaard 1843a: 360) [I do not care at all to possess the girl in the external sense but wish to enjoy her artistically] (Kierkegaard 1987a: 232).

Dinesen elaborates on this connection between art and seduction in 'Ehrengard' in the letters Cazotte writes to his confidante and former beneficiary Countess von Gassner (this character is the novella's equivalent to Goethe's Charlotte von Stein). Through the voice of Cazotte, Dinesen implicitly answers the question Johannes poses in 'Forførerens Dagbog', but never answers himself: 'Men hvor træffer man slige systematiske Forførere, hvor slige Psychologer' (Kierkegaard 1843a: 351) [But where does one meet such systematic seducers, such psychologists?] (Kierkegaard 1987a: 227). The answer in 'Ehrengard' is of course the artist:

> You call an artist a seducer and are not aware that you are paying him the highest of compliments. The whole attitude of the artist towards the Universe is that of a seducer. For what does seduction mean but the ability to make, with infinite trouble, patience and perseverance, the object upon which you concentrate your mind give forth, voluntarily and enraptured, its very core and essence. (Dinesen 1963: 219, italics original)

The juxtaposition between seduction and art, seducer and artist, Johannes and Cazotte, is a dominant structure that runs all through the novella. Both Cazotte and Johannes see the whole process of seducing a young girl first and foremost as a process of personal inspiration and artistic stimulation. As the narrator describes Cazotte: 'The course of things was inspiring, and of all things in the world Herr Cazotte really with his whole heart wanted only one: inspiration' (Dinesen 1963: 266) and as A notes about Johannes in the preface to 'Forførerens Dagbog': 'Individerne have for ham blot været Incitament, han kastede dem af sig, ligesom Træerne ryste Blade af — han foryngedes, Løvet visnede' (Kierkegaard 1843a: 297) [For him individuals were merely for stimulation; he discarded them as trees shake off their leaves — he was rejuvenated, the foliage withered] (Kierkegaard 1987a: 194). Aside from the personal stimulation and inspiration the seduction process bring them, Johannes and Cazotte are also addicted to the intoxicating feeling of omnipotence that emerges from being a sovereign creator; that being of a seduction story with a young girl or the creator of a work of art. Johannes: 'Jeg er beruset ved Tanken om, at hun er i min Magt' (Kierkegaard 1843a: 365) [I am intoxicated with the thought that she is in my power] (Kierkegaard 1987a: 236). The narrator about Cazotte: 'He is at this moment an artist absorbed in and intoxicated by the creation of his chef d'oeuvre. Food and rest are nothing to him, he is fed by winged inspiration' (Dinesen 1963: 244). In *Shadows on the Grass* Dinesen compares the hunter with the seducer and mentions Kierkegaard's work:

> The hunter must take wind and terrain into account and sneak close to them slowly and silently without their realizing the danger. It is a fine and fascinating art, in the spirit of that masterpiece of my countryman Sören [sic] Kierkegaard, The Seducer's Diary, and it may, in the same way, provide the hunter with moments of great drama and with opportunity for skill and cunning, and for

self-gratulations. Yet to me this pursuit was never the real thing. And even the big game, in the hunting of which there is danger, the buffalo or the rhino, very rarely attack without being attacked, or believing that they are being attacked. (Dinesen 1960: 54)[2]

Cazotte and Johannes also agree that one must break off the relationship as soon as the desired reaction, the objects complete fall into surrender and devotion has been achieved. Johannes: 'Naar en Pige først har hengivet sig aldeles, saa er det Hele forbi' (Kierkegaard 1843a: 422) [As soon as a girl has devoted herself completely, the whole thing is finished] (Kierkegaard 1987a: 272) and Cazotte: 'The honest and loyal seducer, when he has obtained the smile, the side glance, the waltz or the tears, will uncover his head to the lady, his heart filled with gratitude, and will be dreading only one thing: that he may ever meet her again' (Dinesen 1963: 220). For Cazotte and Johannes the 'breaking off' is the only way the love affair can be preserved as an infinite source of spiritual recollection and also the only way for them to keep full control over it, since they can recollect, shape and narrate it as they please, without any interference from reality. If not broken off, the future fiancé or wife will have something to say too; compromises have to be made, reality takes over and the omnipotent, spiritual aspect of the love affair is annulled.

Life versus Art

Even though Johannes and Cazotte are similar in many ways, we do find a couple of fundamental differences. Johannes' mission in life is to *live artistically*, whereas Cazotte's mission is to *be an artist*. Johannes wants to *live poetically*, in the moment, in full presence and enjoyment: 'Hans Liv har været et Forsøg paa at realisere den Opgave at leve poetisk' (Kierkegaard 1843a: 294) [His life has been an attempt to accomplish the task of living poetically] (Kierkegaard 1987a: 192). Conversely, Cazotte wants to *create art* that is infinite and immortal. Johannes shapes, stages and creates poetic situations in life with his intellectual power and ability to manipulate and seduce. This makes Johannes a *poet of life*, but not a poet or an artist, since the diary is strictly reserved for his private observations. As the narrator A correctly observes in the preface with regard to the diary: 'at den i strængeste Forstand blot har havt personlig Betydning for ham, er iøinefaldende; og at ville antage, at jeg har et Digterværk for mig, maaskee endog bestemt til at trykkes, forbyder saavel det Hele som det Enkelte' (Kierkegaard 1843a: 295) [it is obvious that in the strictest sense it had only personal importance for him, and to assume that I have before me a poetic work, perhaps even intended for publication, is excluded by the whole as well as by its parts] (Kierkegaard 1987a: 192). In 'Forførerens Dagbog' Johannes proudly proclaims that 'Hendes Udvikling det var mit Værk' (Kierkegaard 1843a: 431) [Her development — that was my work] (Kierkegaard 1987a: 277), but this *work of life* of his, Cordelia and her love, will die (and so will he) and the infinite aspect of their love will eventually be annulled. Cazotte on the contrary is obsessed with the idea of eternity because he is an artist. His main aim is to immortalize his relationship with Ehrengard in a work of art:

In what possible way could he more fully and thoroughly make the girl his own than by capturing, fastening and fixing upon his canvas every line and hue of her young body [...] and immortalizing it, so that nobody in the world could ever again separate the two of them. It would be, unmistakably and for all eternity, Ehrengard, the maid from the mountains, and it would be, unmistakably and for all eternity, a Cazotte. In the picture the face of the bather would be turned away. By no means would he betray or give away his maid-of-honor. He might show his masterpiece to Princes and Princesses, art critics and enraptured lookers-on, and the girl herself at the same moment, and no one but he and she would know the truth. (Dinesen 1963: 251)

Physical versus Spiritual Seduction

Another fundamental difference exists between Dinesen's Cazotte and Kierkegaard's Johannes, which is probably also the most important one. It concerns the nature of the seduction. Contrary to Johannes, Cazotte intends to carry out his final seduction of Ehrengard exclusively as a spiritual seduction, and not an actual physical one involving sexual intercourse. He explains why, in this passage:

I might, upon your friendly advice, undertake to seduce the girl in the orthodox and old-fashioned manner, and the task might not be as difficult as it looks [...] I might seduce her, for she is impulsive and unreflecting, in a particularly impetuous moment of hers. And, Madame, it would mean nothing. For her ruin in such a case, would be fact and reality. (Dinesen 1963: 244)

Cazotte continues and imagines the implications of this type of spiritual seduction of Ehrengard:

Alas, Madame, she will not catch me up, for I shall be away painting other fair ladies, having handed her over, intact but annihilated, to the fond cares of a young husband who will never have the faintest notion that he is drinking up my remains. And will not then, you ask me, her ruin be a fact and a reality? Verily, my friend, it will be so, inasmuch as the reality of art be superior to that of the material world. Inasmuch as the artist be, everywhere and at all times, the arbiter of reality. (Dinesen 1963: 246)

Dinesen is here delivering a clever response to Kierkegaard's plot in 'Forførerens Dagbog' with regard to the humiliating situation in which Johannes eventually leaves Cordelia. After their pre-marital sexual intercourse Johannes abandons Cordelia for good. He leaves her a fallen woman, and from an eighteen-forties societal point of view, her life is in fact forever ruined. Thus, in Dinesen's eyes Johannes has deceived his own idea of having created 'et skjønnere og betydningsfuldere Forhold til Cordelia' (Kierkegaard 1843a: 365) [a more beautiful and significant relationship to Cordelia] (Kierkegaard 1987a: 236). In 'Forførerens Dagbog' Cordelia's ruin is 'fact and reality', which is exactly what Cazotte wants to avoid in his dealings with Ehrengard. This is Dinesen's critique of the character Johannes in 'Forførerens Dagbog' and also the background for one of the major changes she makes in her version of the story, namely that Cazotte will seduce Ehrengard only insofar as he is not compromising her virginal honour and social position: 'I insist on obtaining full surrender without any physical touch' (Dinesen 1963: 244). This means that Cazotte will leave Ehrengard 'intact' from a societal point of view, even though he does succeed in annihilating her on a private and spiritual level. This is also a significant blow to the guarantee Johannes issues in 'Forførerens Dagbog': 'Overhovedet kan jeg tilsikre enhver Pige, der vil betroe sig til mig, en fuldkommen æsthetisk Behandling' (Kierkegaard 1843a: 368) [I can guarantee perfect aesthetic treatment to any girl who entrusts herself to me] (Kierkegaard 1987a: 238). Dinesen's 'Ehrengard' thus becomes the *true version* of how to apply 'perfect aesthetic treatment' in the discipline of seducing a young girl. This inversion of the seduction strategy and its implications stand out as a prominent and significant meta-narrative counter-comment to 'Forførerens Dagbog'.

Cordelia versus Ehrengard

Dinesen also thought that the character of Cordelia was too simple and one-sided and that Kierkegaard's 'Forførerens Dagbog' underestimates the female intellect and a young woman's ability to understand men and the subtle game of love and seduction. This is also expressed by Lincoln Forsner in 'The Dreamers' (Dinesen 1935) where he states that a woman in a love affair is very well aware of her seducer's intention and in the end is the one who is deciding whether her seducer is going to be successful or not (see quote in Chapter 9, pp. 83–84). We also find Cordelia's point of view to be almost absent in the story. The only passages representing her point of view are the two short letters to Johannes we find in the foreword.[3] Here we, surprisingly, discover that she is still hopelessly in love with him, even though he has annihilated her and left her a social outcast. Cordelia's one-sided role in the story has implications for Dinesen's view on Johannes as she expresses in this letter to Aage Henriksen on 14 October 1954: 'hvis hun ikke er et Menneske, da er han hellerikke noget Menneske, hvis hun ikke er en Heltinde i en Historie, da er han hellerikke nogen Helt' (Blixen 1996a: 251) [if she is not a human being then he is not a human being either, if she is not a heroine in a story, he too is not a hero]. In 'Ehrengard' Dinesen creates a scenario that follows a more equal situation when she gives Ehrengard a voice and an intellect of her own. She basically grants Cazotte what Victor Eremita in the foreword to *Enten — Eller. Første Deel* thinks would be Johannes' wish, if he had known about the publication of 'Forførerens Dagbog':

> Giv mig et halvt Aar, og jeg tilveiebringer en Historie, der skal være interessantere end Alt hvad jeg hidtil har oplevet. Jeg tænker mig en ung, kraftfuld, genial Pige faae den ualmindelige Idee at ville hævne Kjønnet paa mig. Hun mener at skulle kunne tvinge mig, at lade mig smage ulykkelig Kjærligheds Smerter. See det er en Pige for mig. Hitter hun ikke selv dybt nok derpaa, saa skal jeg komme hende til Hjælp. Jeg skal vride mig som Molboernes Aal. Og naar jeg da har bragt hende paa det Punkt, jeg vil, saa er hun min. (Kierkegaard 1843a: 17)

> [Give me half a year, and I will produce a story that will be ever so much more interesting than everything I have so far experienced. I picture to myself a young, energetic girl of genius having the extraordinary idea of wanting to

avenge her sex on me. She thinks she will be able to coerce me, to make me taste the pains of unhappy love. That, you see, is a girl for me. If she herself does not think of it profoundly enough, I shall come to her assistance. I shall writhe like the Molbo's eel. And when I have brought her to the point where I want her, then she is mine.] (Kierkegaard 1987a: 21)

This meta-narrative connection has already been pointed out by Selboe 1996 (145–46) and Kondrup 2011 (90) but this re-match between Johannes and Cordelia in 'Ehrengard', I will argue, ends in a tie and not with Ehrengard's triumph and Cazotte's demise as previous scholars have so far agreed upon.

Johann W. Cazotte as the Puppet Master

In 'Forførerens Dagbog' Johannes develops a master plan for the seduction of Cordelia that he follows meticulously and succeeds in realizing without any missteps. In 'Ehrengard' we slowly discover that Cazotte's plan to seduce Ehrengard was in fact also in place from the very beginning of the narrative. When unraveling the plot, it becomes clear that Cazotte, meticulously as a chess player and with the strategic skills of a Napoleon, has been the master puppeteer of the whole affair: Lothar's falling in love with Ludmilla and their pre-marital physical love-relationship have just been a firing ramp for Cazotte to launch the setup at Schloss Rosenbad and involve Ehrengard as Ludmilla's maid-of-honour (also pointed out by Heede 2001: 88 and Sørensen 2002: 120). Up until his first meeting with Ehrengard at the Leda Fountain, Cazotte has cleverly managed to put himself in a position where he has been able to direct and manipulate the course of events. The key passage revealing that Cazotte has had his eyes on Ehrengard, and a desire to seduce her long before he brings Lothar to the court of Leuchtenstein to fall in love with Ludmilla, is first disclosed well into the story:

> I saw, at a court ball, a girl in a white frock, the daughter of warriors, in whose universe art, or the artist, have never existed. And I cried with Michelangelo: 'My greatest triumph hides within that block of marble.' Since then I have at times ventured to believe that it be this vision of mine which has caused our entire course of events, and has, in the end, lifted my young eaglet off her native mountain peak to drop her in the flower Garden of Rosenbad. (Dinesen 1963: 232–33)

Other crucial passages in the novella support this interpretation of Cazotte as being responsible for the whole chain of events: 'Herr Cazotte from the beginning had had his eyes on a particular court [...] He led his steps, and those of Prince Lothar, to Leuchtenstein' (Dinesen 1963: 222), 'He developed to the Grand Duchess a plan, which, although it must have been conceived on the spot, seemed well thought through' (225), 'The choice of residence itself was entrusted to Herr Cazotte' (227) and finally: 'A problem presented itself with the nomination of a maid-of-honour to the Princess [...] Herr Cazotte sat for some time in silence with a thoughtful face. Possibly he had already made his choice, but was taking pleasure in letting the highborn maidens of Babenhausen pass muster before his inner eye' (227–28).

Cazotte's relationship to the Grand Duchess and his ability to manipulate her is similar to the way Johannes manages to manipulate Cordelia's aunt in 'Forførerens Dagbog', which eventually clears the way for her giving him her consent to his engagement to Cordelia: 'jeg gjør ingen Hemmelighed af mine Udgydelser for Tanten, Torvepriser, en Beregning over, hvor mange Potter Mælk der skal til eet Pund Smør, igjennem Flødens Medium og Smørkjernens Dialektik...jeg sværmer med Tanten' (Kierkegaard 1843a: 339) [I make no secret of my effusions to the aunt — market prices, an estimate of how many quarts of milk it takes for one pound of butter through the medium of cream and the dialectic of the butter churn...I romance with the aunt] (Kierkegaard 1987a: 219) and 'Tanten overbyder sig selv ved min kraftige Bistand i denne Retning. Hun er næsten bleven fanatisk, Noget, hun da kan takke mig for' (Kierkegaard 1843a: 343) [With my powerful assistance on this score, the aunt is outdoing herself. She has become almost a fanatic — something she can thank me for] (Kierkegaard 1987a: 221). Cazotte is equally capable of manipulating the Grand Duchess in order to get what he wants: 'The slightest of hints was sufficient, the painter read the Grand Ducal mind like a book, and like an Aeolian harp responded to its inaudible sigh' (Dinesen 1963: 221). We see from Cazotte's role in the narrative that the only step with regard to the seduction of Ehrengard that was *not* planned in detail before he arranged the affair between Lothar and Ludmilla was the actual seduction method (the nude painting), but the idea of the outcome — the blush — was there from the very beginning.

The Seduction Set-up and the Blush

The surroundings and the set-up for Cazotte's spiritual seduction of the young virgin Ehrengard follow the basic ideas of Johannes, when he meticulously prepares the love nest for the final seduction of Cordelia in 'Forførerens Dagbog:'

> Intet er glemt, der kunde have nogen Betydning for hende, og derimod er der Intet anbragt, der slet og ret kunde erindre om mig; medens jeg dog overalt er usynligt tilstede [...] Beliggenheden er som hun kunde ønske sig den [...] Illusionen er fuldstændig. (Kierkegaard 1843a: 429–30)

> [Nothing has been forgotten that could have any significance for her; on the other hand, nothing has been forgotten that could directly remind her of me, although I am nevertheless invisibly present everywhere [...] The location is just as she would like it [...] The illusion is perfect.] (Kierkegaard 1987a: 275–76)

Cazotte uses a similar strategy when he decorates his love nest 'Schloss Rosenbad':

> You may mount the stairs at liberty and walk undisturbed from room to room: an artist and poet, you will then admit, has gone through the house before you and has made it speak [...] Look up and down, right and left, with your most critical eye — you will not find a single tone which be not harmoniously tuned into the harmony of the whole. (Dinesen 1963: 231)

Until Cazotte discovers that Ehrengard swims naked in a nearby lake every morning, it has been unclear to himself — as well as the reader — how he would actually execute the final seduction. So far he has only contrived the desired outcome of the seduction: Ehrengard's final and fatal 'blush', but he has so far been unable to come up with an actual method to provoke it. After seeing her naked at the lake, a diabolic plan finally emerges. From a hiding place on the bank he will paint Ehrengard when she is taking her morning bath, and when the work is finished, he will show the painting to her in order to trigger the desired reaction:

> Her mind never worked quickly, it would take her two or three minutes to grasp her position. Three facts she would at the end of them have made her own. That she was beautiful. That she was naked — and already in the third chapter of Genesis such a recognition is reported to be fatal. And, lastly, that in being thus beautiful and naked she had given herself over to the Venusberg. And to him [...] her blood is to rise, in pride and amour-propre, in unconditional surrender to those perils, in the enraptured flinging over of her entire being to the powers which, till this hour, with her entire being she has rejected and denied, in full, triumphant consent to her own perdition. In this blush her past, present, and future will be thrown before my feet. (Dinesen 1963: 234, 252)

When seeing the painting Ehrengard will understand that Cazotte has enjoyed her many mornings and she will never be able to tell anybody. The painting will be admired at the courts of Europe but Ehrengard's face will not be visible: 'In the picture the face of the bather will be turned away. By no means would he betray or give away his maid-of-honour' (Dinesen 1963: 251). Since Ehrengard cannot be recognized she will keep her social honour, but through self-reflection she will discover sexuality (her naked body as a desirable sexual object), love (in the deep and secret connection with Cazotte) and eternity (the immortal artwork by the famous Cazotte) in one and the same moment, and in the blush she will throw her past (her as a naïve being, a spiritual virgin so to speak), her present (her fall into reflection and self-consciousness) and future (her new level of consciousness and the infinite implications of the painting) before his feet. He and she will forever be united in this secret spiritual — yet highly erotic — relation, and no matter whom Ehrengard will marry later in life, her husband will forever be a spiritual cuckold, since she will never be able to tell him about the painting and the piquant, pre-marital affair with Cazotte. Contrary to Johannes' 'priceless' and 'delicate' blush in 'Forførerens Dagbog':

> Der er forskjellige Arter af qvindelig Rødme. Der er den grove Rødsteens-Rødme. Det er den, Romanskriverne altid have nok af, naar de lader deres Heltinder rødme über und über. Der er den fine Rødme; det er Aandens Morgenrøde. Hos en ung Pige er den ubetalelig. (Kierkegaard 1843a: 352)

> [There are various kinds of womanly blushes. There is the dense brick-red blush. This is the one novelists always have in good supply when they have their heroines blush über und über. There is the delicate blush; it is the spirit's sunrise-red. In a young girl it is priceless.] (Kierkegaard 1987a: 227)

Cazotte has another type of blush in mind for Ehrengard, which also counts in the aftermath of the spiritual fall, and here we arrive at another crucial difference. The type of blush Cazotte wants to provoke in Ehrengard is not a delicate *sunrise*-red blush, but instead an intense and fatal *sunset*-red — a last desperate glow of daylight, whereupon black night will follow upon the recognition that she will forever be Cazotte's bride in spirit. His example is the phenomenon of the 'Alpen-Glühen':

> She is to be the rose which drops every one of her petals to one single breath of the wind and stands bared. In high mountains, as you will know, there is a phenomenon of nature called Alpen-Glühen [...] After the sun has set, and as the whole majestic mountain landscape is already withdrawing into itself, suddenly the row of summits, all on their own, radiate a divine fire, a celestial, deep rose flame, as if they were giving up a long kept secret. After that they disappear, nothing more dramatic can be imagined: they have betrayed their inmost substance and can now only annihilate themselves. Black night follows [...] what void afterwards. (Dinesen 1963: 234)

Again we see how Dinesen creates another astute meta-narrative counter comment to 'Forførerens Dagbog'. She develops the plot so it also counts in the tragic aftermath of the seduction, the spiritual fall, which is an element that is completely absent in 'Forførerens Dagbog' where Johannes is only able to see Cordelia's fall as a positive development, since he is only able to evaluate it from an aesthetic point of view.

The Turning Point: The Leda Fountain

Cazotte never gets the final and fatal blush from Ehrengard that he had hoped for, but it is important to remember that Ehrengard actually *does* blush at their first meeting at the Leda fountain. The significance of this slight blush is, however, downplayed and obfuscated by the narrator, which makes it tempting for the reader, in accordance with Cazotte, to misunderstand the situation:

> On a very lovely evening he had been reading to her in the garden and was slowly accompanying her back to the house, when he stopped and made her stop with him by a fountain representing Leda and the swan and repeated a stanza from the poem they had last read together. He was silent for a while, the girl was silent with him, and as he turned toward her he found her young face very still. 'A penny for your thoughts, my Lady Ehrengard,' he said. She looked at him, and for a moment a very slight blush slid over her face. 'I was not,' after a pause she answered him slowly and gravely, 'really thinking of anything at all.' He had no doubt that here, she was speaking the truth. (Dinesen 1963: 243)

The stanza that Cazotte recites for Ehrengard must be the passage with Leda and the swan from Goethe's *Faust. Der Tragödie zweiter Teil* (1832):

> HOMUNCULUS:
>
> Bedeutend!
>
> Schön umgeben! — Klar Gewässer
> Im dichten Haine! Fraun, die sich entkleiden,
> Die allerliebsten! — Das wird immer besser.
> Doch eine läßt sich glänzend unterscheiden,
> Aus höchstem Helden-, wohl aus Götterstamme.
> Sie setzt den Fuß in das durchsichtige Helle;

Des edlen Körpers holde Lebensflamme
Kühlt sich im schmiegsamen Kristall der Welle. —
Doch welch Getöse rasch bewegter Flügel,
Welch Sausen, Plätschern wühlt im glatten Spiegel?
Die Mädchen fliehn verschüchtert; doch allein
Die Königin, sie blickt gelassen drein
Und sieht mit stolzem weiblichem Vergnügen
Der Schwäne Fürsten ihrem Knie sich schmiegen,
Zudringlich-zahm. Er scheint sich zu gewöhnen. —
Auf einmal aber steigt ein Dunst empor
Und deckt mit dichtgewebtem Flor
Die lieblichste von allen Szenen.

(Goethe 1832: n. pag.)[4]

[HOMUNCULUS: (*Astonished.*)

Interesting!

(*The phial slips out of Wagner's hands, hovers over Faust, and shines on him.*)

Lovely surroundings! — Clear water
In thick forest! Women there: undressing.
The loveliest of all! — It's getting clearer.
One's left, different from the rest, gleaming:
Of highest race, for sure, a heavenly name.
She places her foot in the transparent glow,
Her noble body's sweetly living flame
Cools itself in the yielding crystal flow. —
But what's that rush of beating wings for:
That thrashing, splashing, in the mirror?
The lovely girls, intimidated, flee:
Their queen, alone, looks on, composedly,
To see, with a proud feminine pleasure,
The Swan-Prince press against her knee, there,
Forward yet tame. Familiar, he seems. —
But suddenly a vapour heaves,
And covers, with the veil it weaves,
The loveliest of scenes.][5]

Sørensen, however, relates the stanza that Cazotte is quoting to Ovid's *Metamorphoses* (Sørensen 2002: 131) but there are good reasons to believe that Dinesen is instead aiming at the scene in Goethe's *Faust,* Part II. Firstly, *Faust* is written by Johann W. Cazotte's great 'namesake' Johann W. Goethe, who is playing such a big part in the novella as a background figure. Secondly, the Leda and swan scene in *Faust* fits the scenery of Ehrengard's morning bath much better than the shorter and much less descriptive scene in Ovid's *Metamorphoses* (quoted in Sørensen 2002: 132). Thirdly, the description of Leda in the passage from Goethe's *Faust* also fits with the ways Cazotte describes Ehrengard elsewhere in the novella as a 'white-hot young angel' of the highest race, stern and proud (Dinesen 1963: 228–29). The purpose of reading the stanza is to see how Ehrengard responds to Cazotte quoting this highly erotic passage from Goethe's poem that obviously put her in the role of Leda and him in the role of Zeus (the swan). To enhance the effect of his words, he does it in front of a fountain that is displaying the exact same scene. With this setup Cazotte hopes to provoke the crimson-red fatal blush that he has longed for so long, but when he asks Ehrengard about her thoughts only 'a very slight blush slid over her face' (Dinesen 1963: 243). Shortly after she 'slowly and gravely' claims that she was 'really thinking of nothing at all' and Cazotte believes her: 'He had no doubt that here, as ever, she was speaking the truth' (243). But Ehrengard is far less naïve than Cazotte thinks, and in this situation she *does* actually see the connection between Leda (herself) and the swan (Cazotte) and what this connection implies. The 'very slight blush' stems from the fact that she is now aware that *this is the way Cazotte is seeing* their relationship — not because she discovers her own sexuality, since: 'She is a country-bred girl and familiar with the facts of life. She knows at what date after the wedding a child should be born' (237). On the contrary, she blushes in discontent and anger, since she realizes that her friend and confidante, whom she up until now has perceived as a loyal father figure, is thinking about their relationship in a completely different way and has so far been doing everything he could to manipulate her. Ehrengard's newly gained knowledge is detrimental for Cazotte's plan, since she is now aware that he has a hidden agenda and this means that he will not be able to take her by surprise anymore. In fact she is turning against him from now on in an attempt to change the power dynamics and reverse the roles. When analyzing the events following this first meeting at the Leda fountain, it is striking that Cazotte only a few days after reciting the stanza to Ehrengard finds her nude bathing at the lake in the forest, which is a repetition of the passage he just read to her. Thus, the morning bath sessions are the first step in the reversal of the roles and mark the beginning of Ehrengard's seduction of Cazotte, even though he is completely unaware of it. This interpretation is supported by the following chain of events: the very same evening when Ehrengard's maid discovers Cazotte at the lake (13 July), Ehrengard presents Lothar and Ludmilla's child to him, while looking him straight in the eyes. He avoids her gaze, completely unaware of the subtle subtext, and continues to view Ehrengard as a work of art and not as young woman of flesh and blood:

> At her request Ehrengard lifted the basket and the child from the Princess' knee, and on her strong arms presented them to Herr Cazotte. The painter, still reluctant to look her in the face, let his eyes rest on the baby. But the pose of her figure recalled to him a group by the great sculptor Thorvaldsen, 'Psyche selling amorini'. (Dinesen 1963: 256)

The very same evening they stroll in the garden with Countess Poggendorff, but when the Countess withdraws, Ehrengard deliberately stops at the Leda fountain to use it as a backdrop for their second meeting. Again Cazotte underestimates her completely: 'Herr Cazotte wondered whether Ehrengard, as upon an earlier evening, was thinking of nothing at all' (257), but she is indeed thinking and this is what she has prepared for him:

> As upon that earlier evening they passed the Leda fountain, Ehrengard slowed

her steps, stopped and stood for a moment with the tips of her fingers in the clear water of the basin from which the breast and the proud neck of the swan rose toward's [sic] Leda's knees. As she lifted her head, turned and faced Herr Cazotte, she was a little pale, but she spoke in a clear voice. 'My maid tells me,' she said, 'that you want to paint a picture. Out by the east of the house. I wish to tell you that I shall be there every morning, at six o'clock'. (Dinesen 1963: 257)

In this scene Ehrengard cleverly destroys Cazotte's master plan. When she has the nerve and audacity to voluntarily invite him to come and paint her naked at the lake, he of course cannot expect her to blush when showing her the painting. Cazotte, understandably, spends a sleepless and troubled night upon this disturbing second meeting that has forever ruined his plan. The day after, the little Prince is kidnapped from Schloss Rosenbad, and when the situation at the loft of Black Boar Inn develops, Ehrengard cleverly seizes the moment and teaches Cazotte the final lesson. Here she eventually succeeds in making Cazotte look at her as a sexual object of flesh and blood, when she announces their pre-marital sexual intercourse, which ultimately leads to his fall into physical sexuality. This has been Ehrengard's plan since their first Leda fountain meeting without Cazotte having had the faintest idea of it.

Nemesis Strikes

As A writes about Johannes in the preface to 'Forførerens Dagbog':

> Som han har ledet Andre vild, saa tænker jeg, han ender med selv med at løbe vild. De Andre har han ledet vild ikke i udvortes Henseende, men i indvortes dem selv betræffende [...] Saaledes tænker jeg det vil gaae ham selv efter en endnu langt forfærdeligere Maalestok. (Kierkegaard 1843a: 297–98)

> [Just as he has led others astray, so he, I think, will end by going astray himself. He has led others astray not in the external sense but the interior sense with respect to themselves [...] I think he himself will have the same experience on an even more terrible scale.] (Kierkegaard 1987a: 194)

This is a very precise description of the scenario Dinesen has prepared for Cazotte in 'Ehrengard', as well as another meta-narrative blow to Johannes' omnipotent status in 'Forførerens Dagbog' and the fact that Johannes actually gets away with playing with the Gods: 'jeg som kan ansee mig for Gudernes Yndling' (Kierkegaard 1843a: 324) [I, who can regard myself as a favorite of the gods] (Kierkegaard 1987a: 210). But it is dangerous to play with the Gods as Cazotte correctly observes in 'Ehrengard': 'But the generosity of the Gods was more alarming and astounding still [...] and dangerous for a mortal, even for an artist, to associate with' (Dinesen 1963: 250–51). And this time Nemesis *does* strike, as we have seen it many times before in Dinesen's works. Towards the end of the story, the baby child of Prince Lothar and Ludmilla is kidnapped by Matthias. He is the husband of the Lispeth who is also the child's nurse. Ehrengard immediately sets out to find the kidnapper and eventually finds Matthias, Lispeth and the little Prince at the loft of The Blue

Boar Inn and Cazotte soon joins her. It is of course paramount that the child's identity is kept secret, so when questions arise about the nature of the conflict and the identity of the child, Ehrengard tells the party (even though her fiancé Kurt von Blittersdorff is standing right next to her) that the child is hers and Cazotte's. When uttering these crucial words she is looking Cazotte straight in the eyes and, seconds after, his head turns crimson-red in a heavy blush. He is now himself becoming the victim of the emotional reaction he had planned for Ehrengard:

> At these words Herr Cazotte's blood was drawn upwards, as from the profoundest wells of his being, till it colored him all over like a transparent crimson veil. His brow and cheeks, all on their own, radiated a divine fire, a celestial, deep rose flame, as if they were giving away a long kept secret. And it was a strange thing that he should blush. For normally an onlooker in a fauteuil d'orchestre would grow pale at seeing the irate hero of the stage suddenly turn upon him. (Dinesen 1963: 276)

The big question is of course: why does the powerful and always composed Cazotte blush at the idea that he should be the father of Ehrengard's child? Why does he not grow pale? Or why does he not laugh off Ehrengard's farfetched suggestion? The answer is: through the idea that he should be the father of an actual child, Cazotte becomes aware of physical sexuality, or rather the lack of it in his own life, since children don't come — as we all know — with the stork. Up until this crucial moment the artist Cazotte has not been a sexually active human being, but has instead been sublimating all his sexual energy into the creation of divine and spiritual art with the nude painting of Ehrengard as the diamond he was to set in his crown. Cazotte blushes because he now knows that Ehrengard knows that he is a virgin, and that is — for a man of forty-five — a rather embarrassing revelation. This is exactly the 'long kept secret' the blush gives away: 'brow and cheeks [...] radiated a divine fire [...] as if they were giving away a long kept secret' (Dinesen 1963: 276). The closing lines of the novella that describe Cazotte's love affair in Rome succeeding the events at Schloss Rosenbad, supports the idea that a significant transformation of his nature has indeed taken place:

> A week later the betrothed couple were present at the baptism of the new-born Prince in Dom of Babenhausen [...] Herr Cazotte to the surprise of the court was not present at the ceremony. He had been called back to Rome to paint a portrait of the Pope. It was here, now, that he had that famous liaison with a cantatrice of the Opera which caused much talk and made his acquaintances smilingly alter his name to that of Casanova. (Dinesen 1963: 276–77)

Cazotte's blush in the final scene, in combination with the love affair in Rome, which causes his acquaintances to alter his name to that of Casanova, supports the interpretation that Cazotte undergoes a crucial transformation succeeding his fatal blush at the loft at the Blue Boar Inn: from a spiritual seducer (an artist) to a physical seducer of flesh and blood (a Casanova).

'The Secret Note': The Key to the Final Interpretation

A certain piece of biographical information about Johann Wolfgang Goethe is crucial for the validation of this interpretation. Goethe most likely did not have a physical love relationship with a woman until his second journey to Italy 1786–1788 when he was thirty-nine years old. Goethe scholars have commonly acknowledged this since the publication of K.R. Eissler's *Goethe, A Psychoanalytic Study 1775–1786* in 1963, where Eissler states that:

> It seems — as I observed previously — that Goethe had sexual intercourse for the first time in his life during his second sojourn in Rome, after his return from Sicily. That he had intercourse in Rome can be proved; that it was for the first time is, of course, beyond proof, but nevertheless an assumption of such high probability that I tend to consider it a certainty. (Eissler 1963: 1019)

Eissler assesses the event to have taken place close to the date of a decisive letter Goethe sends to Duke Karl August on 16 February 1788, describing his new experiences in the erotic (Eissler 1963: 1027–28) and Eissler concludes: 'first intercourse at the age of thirty-nine' (Eissler 1963: 1031). Danish Goethe scholar, Per Øhrgaard (1999: 73), and Danish Dinesen and Goethe scholar, Aage Henriksen, both agree with Eissler. In the passage below Aage Henriksen explains why Goethe denied himself a sexual relationship until he was almost forty years old. Henriksen's explanation fits very well with the psychological constitution of the artist Cazotte and the hidden plot in 'Ehrengard':

> Der er tale om en erotisk karriere, som nok havde været umulig, hvis han ikke som adskillige kunstnere havde været sådan indrettet, at den letvakte, uforløste seksualitet steg op igennem ham og frigjorde syner og kunstneriske erkendelser. Dette forsagelses- program, i tiltagende grad utåleligt, holdt indtil midten af 1780'erne, hvor han flygtede fra sit gamle liv til sine længslers land, Italien [...] i sit praktiske liv foretog han en ændring, som under omstændighederne må kaldes radikal, idet han endelig frigav sin så længe bundne seksualitet. (Henriksen 2004: 103–04)

> [We are dealing with an erotic career, which would most likely have been impossible if he had not, like most artists, had a psychological makeup that allowed the easily awoken, yet unresolved sexuality, to rise through him and release visions and artistic recognitions. This type of renunciation, increasingly unbearable, prevailed until the mid-1780s when he escaped to the land of his longings, Italy [...] in his day-to-day life he underwent a change, which under the circumstances must be called radical since he finally released his latent sexuality.]

Shortly after returning from Rome, Goethe decided to follow the newfound path of physical sexuality he discovered in Italy, and — head over heels — began a sexual relationship with the twenty-three year old Christiane Vulpius. Shortly after their first meeting she moved in with him (Øhrgaard 1999: 115). The role this small piece of biographical information about Goethe plays in 'Ehrengard' is what Danish Dinesen-scholar Poul Behrendt calls 'den hemmelige note' [the secret note]. The secret note is a crucial piece of information that is impossible to detect in the text itself, but when (or rather if) the reader discovers it, it changes the whole interpretation: 'Den forandrer begivenheder radikalt, ikke ved at gribe ind i dem, men ved at ændre synspunktet på dem' (Behrendt 2007: 8) [it changes the events radically, not through direct interference, but because the view on the events is changed].

The above interpretation of the story propagating Goethe's sexual development as the key to the final interpretation of Cazotte's blush was validated during a visit to the Royal Library in Copenhagen in December 2010. In Capsule 133 in the Karen Blixen Archive, we find seven different versions of the Ehrengard-novella: the first draft is most likely from the late summer or fall of 1952. It is titled 'Forskrift' with Dinesen's handwriting, but with no date,[6] two different re-writings from 1961 (one titled 'Arbejdseksemplar' with a calendar sheet dating the draft to 28 April 1961), three different re-writings possibly from 1962 (at least two of them)[7] and the final manuscript with a few minor corrections made by Clara Selborn from 1963. In all of the versions up until the re-writings in 1962, the tale ends with this passage:

> He stayed in Rome for the same length of time as — fifty years earlier — his great namesake Johann Wolfgang Goethe. And at his return to Babenhausen he declared that the Eternal City had had exactly the same effect on his own genius as upon that of the poet. 'But,' the old lady concluded, 'as unfortunately I am not an expert on Goethe, I cannot tell you exactly what that effect was.' ('Ehrengard', first four drafts 1952–1961, Capsule 133, Royal Library in Copenhagen)

The above passage has, however, been crossed out in the first revision from 1962. But in the second revision, from the same year, we find another, albeit very short, ending: 'If I had really known,' she said, 'what kind of man Cazotte was'. Dinesen probably thought that the ending from before 1962 made the connections to Goethe and the events in Italy too obvious, but too obscure when completely left out in the very short second version. Thus, she decided on a third and final version that was a compromise between the ending from before 1962 and the very short second revision from 1962, which is the ending we know from the tale today:[8]

> It was here, now, that he had that famous liaison with a cantatrice of the Opera which caused much talk and made his acquaintances smilingly alter his name to that of Casanova. When the Grand Duchess heard of it she was upset. 'I had really,' she said, 'during that time at Rosenbad, come to have such faith in Geheimrat Cazotte.' (Dinesen 1963: 277)

When reading the earliest, and now presumably lost, July 1952 version, Ellen Dahl is not sure what the Goethe allusion means, but the allusion in this early draft must have been rather clear (close to the ending we find in the drafts up until 1962) as we understand from her letter to Dinesen from 18 July 1952:

> Også for mig har den dunkle Punkter. Saaledes ved jeg ikke, skønt jeg netop er i færd med at læse en Bog om Goethe, hvor ogsaa den italienske Rejse og dens Indflydelse paa hans Produktion behandles, hvori denne falder sammen med Hr. Cazottes? (Blixen 1996b: 94)

[Also for me it has dim points. Thus, I don't know, even though I am just reading a book about Goethe where his journey to Italy and its influence on his production is also treated, how this coincides with Cazotte's?]

We do not know where Dinesen got the idea of Goethe's arrested love life from in 1952, eleven years before Eissler's book came out. Georg Brandes does not mention anything about Goethe's sexuality in his Goethe biography from 1920. Ole Meyer, Poul Behrendt, and others, however, believe it was common knowledge among scholars and writers with particular interest in Goethe at the time when Dinesen wrote 'Ehrengard' that Goethe was a virgin until his second trip to Italy. Eissler was just the first scholar to indiscreetly spell it out in 1963. Still, it is puzzling why Dinesen scholars, up until now, have not managed to see how crucial a role this biographical knowledge of Goethe plays in 'Ehrengard'.

Johann W. Cazotte and the Comic

With the secret note in mind, we discover the irony in the title 'The Seducer's Diary' that Dinesen proposes in the letter to *Ladies' Home Journal* (quoted in the beginning of this chapter) and we suddenly understand 'the nature of the story' as deeply comical on the part of Johannes Forføreren disguised in the narrative as Johann W. Cazotte. The comical lies in the inversion of common sexual practice for a middle-aged man and the great artist and seducer, who has not yet experienced physical love at the age of forty-five and blushes like a young schoolboy when Ehrengard points him out as the father of her child. The inverted power roles between Ehrengard and Cazotte also contribute to the comic since the supposedly weak character (Ehrengard), which we up until the final scene have thought to be in the hands of the great artist, suddenly outwits him, thus transforming the most powerful character of the story into the underdog. Another comical element in this final scene lies in the involuntariness of the blush. As Kierkegaard's character 'Det Unge Menneske' [The young man] correctly observes in 'in vino veritas':

> I Henseende til det Uvilkaarlige er Modsigelsen oprindelig tilstede, som den: at man af et frit Fornuftvæsen ikke venter det Uvilkaarlige. Naar man saaledes antog, at Paven i det Øieblik han skulde sætte Kronen paa Napoleons Hoved kom til at hoste, eller at Brud og Brudgom i Vielsens høitidelige Øieblik kom til at nyse, saa viser det Comiske sig. Jo mere den givne Leilighed accentuerer det frie Fornuftsvæsen, desto mere comisk bliver det Uvilkaarlige. (Kierkegaard 1845: 44)

> [As for the involuntary, the contradiction is initially present: that we do not expect the involuntary from a free rational being. Suppose, for instance, that the pope started coughing the very moment he was about to place the crown on Napoleon's head or that in the solemn moment of exchanging vows the bride and bridegroom began to sneeze — the comic would be apparent. The more the given occasion emphasizes the free rational being, the more comic the involuntarily becomes.] (Kierkegaard 1988: 39)

In this case we see the older, rational, powerful artist, who has so far controlled the events, involuntarily lose control over the color of his face. Together with the sudden inversion of the power roles it arguably places him in the category of the comical.

Turning Pale: Ehrengard and the Tragic

Cazotte is obviously playing the comical role in the novella, but another fall that carries a tragic dimension also takes place in the final scene, even though it has so far been overlooked by scholars:

> To Ehrengard, too, something was happening as here she stood up straight, face to face with Kurt's straight figure. She too felt, in a new way, the depth of life. There was a sweetness in it which she till now had never known of, there was a terrible sadness as well. She would never have believed, had anybody told her, that to meet and part with Kurt von Blittersdorff could mean so much. The recognition at this moment was, she felt, the outcome of her stay at Rosenbad. (Dinesen 1963: 274–75)

What Ehrengard in this moment discovers is the implications of Cazotte's plan that despite marrying Kurt von Blittersdorff, she will forever be isolated and alienated in this relationship, since, due to the machinations of Cazotte, she now possesses a deeper knowledge of the world (about how to manipulate and seduce) that she will never be able to communicate to Kurt. As the Plutarch quote, which is the motto for Kierkegaard's essay 'Adskilligt om Ægteskabet mod Indsigelser' [Some Reflections on Marriage in Answer to Objections] in 'in vino veritas' rightly states: 'den Bedragne [er] visere end den Ikke-Bedragne' (Kierkegaard 1845: 113) [The deceived is wiser than one not deceived] (Kierkegaard 1988: 68). This also means that Cazotte eventually gets from Ehrengard what he wants (her spiritual fall), but the physical manifestation turns out to be the opposite of what he had hoped for (the blush); when all the blood leaves her face and she turns deadly pale:

> Ehrengard had grown pale [...] So colorless did her face become that the light in her eyes seemed dark in it, like two cavities. Then she turned and looked straight at Herr Cazotte. Under her glance the gentleman[9] rose from the bed. The girl's glance was strong and direct, like an arrow's course from the bowstring to the target. In it she flung her past, present and future at his feet [...] 'It is he,' she said. 'Herr Cazotte is the father of my child'. (Dinesen 1963: 275–76)

Both Kierkegaard and Dinesen worked consciously with the physical reactions of 'blushing' and turning 'pale' as significant outer symbols of inner emotions. In 'Ehrengard' the notion of 'pale' is connected to intellectual and spiritual recognitions with tragic implications (which seem to be the case for most of her tales). Ehrengard turns pale, when she invites Cazotte to come and paint her naked at the lake: 'As she lifted her head [...] she was a little pale, but she spoke in a clear voice' (Dinesen 1963: 257), which is also the case when she finally succeeds in seducing Cazotte at the loft: 'Ehrengard had grown pale' (275). Kurt also turns 'very pale' in the final scene when Ehrengard asks him to give up his love for her forever (274). It is, however, the description of Ehrengard's face: 'So colorless did her face become that the light in her eyes seemed dark in it, like two cavities' (275) resembling the skull of a dead human being that most directly points to the tragic implications of her newborn recognition and 'the terrible sadness' that follows this fall; that when this higher level of reflection is born, something else in her dies. She will now forever be disconnected from her former naïve self and more devastatingly, from her future husband Kurt. At the beginning of the novella, Ludmilla encourages Ehrengard to have a secret. She eventually gets it, but unfortunately with the wrong man:

> 'Have you two ever had a secret together?' 'Yes,' Ehrengard again answered. 'When the boys had done something bad, and I helped them to keep it from Papa.' The Princess was silent, then suddenly exclaimed in a low voice: 'Try to have a secret with him [Kurt]. Something that, in the whole world, only you and he know of. You will be feeling, then, that he is you and you are he'. (Dinesen 1963: 236–37)

Through the secrets that Ehrengard and Cazotte share, that he has painted her naked at the lake every morning for a full week, that she invited him to do it and that he — the great seducer — is a virgin, he and she will forever be united because they will never be able to share these secrets with anyone else within the frame of this nineteenth-century environment. This is an ironic fulfillment of Ludmilla's description that 'he is you and you are he', since it happened with the wrong man. This is also the nemesis of Ehrengard for her 'playing with Gods' (manipulating in real life).

Tragedy, Irony, and Gender

In a bold statement about woman and tragedy in Kierkegaard's 'in vino veritas', Constantin Constantius concludes: 'Gjører ligesaa kjære Drikkebrødre, og forstaaer nu Aristoteles. Han bemærker rigtigt, at Qvinden ikke ret er brugbar i Tragoedien' (Kierkegaard 1845: 56) [Do likewise, dear drinking companions, and then understand Aristotle. He makes the correct observation that woman is really not usable in tragedy] (Kierkegaard 1988: 47). In the final scene Dinesen seems to think the opposite of Constantin, when she lets Cazotte blush and Ehrengard grow pale. Comedy, not tragedy, is the privilege of *man*, in this case Cazotte, and tragedy the privilege of *woman*, in this case Ehrengard. This brings us back to a crucial sentence in the beginning of the novella where a double movement of the story is indicated, but never taken up again: 'So to begin with, my dearest, I shall inform you that the stage of our little comedy or tragedy was the lovely country and the fine city of Babenhausen' (Dinesen 1963: 215–16). The Old Lady never elaborates on the story as being either 'a comedy or a tragedy', but the logical answer to this question is, as we understand from the final scene, that the story is *both*, depending on which one of the main protagonists we are considering.

In Dinesen's world comedy is viewed as the divine poetic contradiction of life, and tragedy is the only way to achieve a deeper and more profound relation to life. Dinesen reserves comedy for the 'Gods', in this case the God-like figures in her tales, which in almost all cases are men: the Councilor in 'The Poet', Prince Potenziani in 'The Roads Round Pisa', the Uncle in 'Sorrow-Acre', Mr. Clay in 'The Immortal

Story', and Cazotte here in 'Ehrengard'. These seemingly omnipotent lords, artists and businessmen are often sexually impotent, which is exactly the comic contradiction. In Dinesen's world, tragedy on the other hand is the exclusive privilege of common people and women. Examples are plenty: Pellegrina in 'The Dreamers' and Agnese in 'The Roads Round Pisa', Anne-Marie in 'Sorrow-Acre', Malli in 'Tempests' and of course Ehrengard in 'Ehrengard' just to mention a few. Both comedy and tragedy are closely connected to Dinesen's idea of nemesis. Comedy is the nemesis of the privileged (which includes men) and tragedy is the nemesis of the common people (which includes women). This is a consistent juxtaposition throughout Dinesen's production.

This interpretation of the two roles concerning the comic and the tragic is supported when examining the developments of the two characters in the various drafts of 'Ehrengard' at The Royal Library in Copenhagen. Cazotte's birthday is changed from the 'twenty-first of May' to 'first of April, a 'true fool' in the revisions following the first draft, sharpening the comical aspect of his character. In the first draft we also find the crucial passage about Ehrengard's transformation in the last scene to be much less tragic compared to the final version: 'She would not have believed, had anybody told her so, that to part with Kurt von Blittersdorff could mean such a strange physical sadness'. This passage is subsequently changed to the much stronger: 'there was a terrible sadness as well' (Dinesen 1963: 275) as we know it from the final version. The tragic element of the Alpen-Glühen phenomenon in connection to Ehrengard's fall was also sharpened. The passage 'black night will follow' is missing from the Alpen-Glühen passage in the first version, but later added as the tragic contours of Ehrengard's character became clearer for Dinesen (Dinesen 1963: 234).

Conclusion: Seduction

Dinesen was annoyed with the total absence of female voices in Kierkegaard's production and the general one-sidedness with which women are depicted in relation to seduction.[10] Thus, as we have seen, she decided to implement some gender equality. In 'Carnival' she created a female seducer dressed as the young Søren Kierkegaard, a radical aesthete, who at the same time is 'gentleman' enough not to hold her object of seduction 'in the dark' with regard to her plans. She also created another type of female seducer, Polly, who in the tale experiences a fall when she develops from an unreflected to a reflected seducer and suffers from it. As she points out: it can be painful to lose your spiritual 'virginity' and there is no way back from the fall. Ehrengard also experiences her spiritual seduction of Cazotte as something tragic, and we also found the tragic to be the very bass that runs through 'The Dreamers' when Dinesen's Pellegrina, no matter what identity she takes on, is seducing the men around her without wanting it to the extent that it ends up killing her. The comical versions of the seducer are all reserved for the male characters: Baron Guildenstern in 'The Dreamers' (a Don Juan parody), Cazotte (parody of the biographical Kierkegaard/Goethe) and the Councilor (parody of Constantin

Constantius from *Gjentagelsen*, see Chapter 14). The conclusions we can draw from Dinesen's counter-stories to Kierkegaard concerning seduction and gender are: woman is seductive to man, because she is woman. Thus, man is seduced by woman, not the other way around. Then, that it takes two for a seduction to succeed as Lincoln Forsner rightly points out — and that applies to both women and men. Seduction should also be a noble affair meaning that the joys and risks should be evenly distributed. The discovery that one is a seducer for the female characters seems to be connected with pain, which is not the case for the male characters who enjoy the feeling of omnipotence and the prospects of annihilating their 'victims'.

Notes to Chapter 10

1. The third character is French writer and occultist, Jaques Cazotte, who was beheaded during the French Revolution in 1792 on the part of his counter-revolutionary letters. His most popular work *Le Diable amoureux* [The Devil in Love] from 1772 was highly appreciated by Dinesen. The role this work plays in connection to 'Ehrengard' has been thoroughly examined by Sørensen 2002 (143–45).

2. This evaluation that big game hunting is 'a fine and fascinating art, in the spirit of that masterpiece of my countryman Sören Kierkegaard, *The Seducer's Diary*', yet not 'the real thing' is in line with Dinesen's letter passage in Chapter 8 about seduction and Annelise's interpretation of seduction as an undertaking that must be carried out on equal terms. The terms are not equal, neither in *The Seducer's Diary* nor in big game hunting.

3. These two letters from Cordelia are the only examples in Kierkegaard's entire production where a female character is granted her own point of view.

4. Johann Wolfgang Goethe: *Faust. Tweiter Teil* (1832). The Gutenberg EBook of Faust. January 26. 2010 (updated May, 2012). Produced by Michael Pullen. <http://www.gutenberg.org/cache/epub/2230/pg2230-images.html> [Accessed 29 August 2016].

5. Johann Wolfgang Goethe: *Faust: Part Two*. Translated by A. S. Kline (2003). Available online: <http://www.poetryintranslation.com/PITBR/German/FaustIIActIIScenesItoIV.htm> [accessed 29 August 2016].

6. The earliest version of the manuscript at the Royal Library is not identical to the version that Dinesen sent to Erik Clemmesen and Ellen Dahl in the summer of 1952. In a letter to Dinesen dated 14 July 1952, Erik Clemmesen writes: 'Gartneren er vred — hvor er han dog vred! — Men hvor er det dog mærkeligt. Cazottes Forhold til de andre — han er baade indenfor og udenfor paa en Gang. Han har rigtig godt af, at han ikke kan faa Brug for de Miniaturemalerier senere hen — for han kan jo ikke sidde i Rom og male Prins Echo. Det er det bedste ved Prins Lothar, — at han kunne hitte paa det Navn!' [The gardener is angry — so angry! — But it is really curious. Cazotte's relationship to the others — he is both inside and outside at the same time. And he really deserves to not benefit from the miniatures later on — since he can't sit in Rome and paint Prince Echo. That is the best thing about Prince Lothar — that he could come up with such a name!]. Neither the gardener, the miniatures or Prince Echo (the suggested name for Lothar and Ludmilla's son), as Clemmesen mentions in the letter, appear in the earliest manuscript we have at The Royal Library in Copenhagen. The earliest manuscript at The Royal Library must consequently be a rewriting of the first draft Dinesen got back with comments from Clemmesen and Dahl in July 1952.

7. 'Karen Blixen satte kun yderst sjældent dato og årstal på udkastene' (Selborn 1974: 62) [Karen Blixen very rarely put date and year on the drafts].

8. Except for one small detail: Clara Selborn changed *Herr* Cazotte to *Geheimrat* Cazotte in her last revision in 1963 before the final print (manuscript in Capsule 133 in the Karen Blixen Archive at The Royal Library in Copenhagen).

9. This term is to be understood ironically here.

10. It is indeed also curious, as Brandes also notices in his critical Kierkegaard study, that

Kierkegaard's mother is not mentioned with one single word in his prolific diary: 'Moderen, hvem han først mistede i sit 22de Aar, nævner han mærkeligt nok aldrig med et Ord' (Brandes 1877: 7) [His mother, who did not pass away until he was twenty-two years of age, he, curiously, never mentions with a word].

CHAPTER 11

❖

Kierkegaard, Sexuality, and 'The Secret Note'

In this chapter, I will elaborate on Dinesen's notion of Kierkegaard as a 'macabre dandy' in connection to how she treats the theme of sexuality and abstinence in her Kierkegaard-tales. In a footnote in his Kierkegaard biography, Brandes suggests that Kierkegaard's painful break-up with Regine might have had something to do with 'det Sexuelle som det [...] der fremdeles særlig maatte komme i Betragtning ved Indgaaelsen af et Ægteskab' (Brandes 1877: 71) [the sexual (...) which must especially be considered when entering into a marriage]. In a convincing study published in a Danish medical journal in 2013, Staubrand and Weismann suggest that Kierkegaard suffered from the disease Pott's Paraplegia. It is a condition that can cause damages to the spinal cord and inability to control the bladder, which we know were symptoms that Kierkegaard suffered from. It has been documented in several medical papers that injuries to the spinal cord can also result in erectile dysfunction. If erectile dysfunction was indeed a condition Kierkegaard suffered from as indicated by Brandes (for example caused by Pott's Paraplegia), it would explain his lack of sexual relationships in general, but — more importantly — also why he had to break up with Regine Olsen, and why he (like Abraham) was unable to tell anyone about the real cause of his decision, even though people thought he was out of his mind.

Sexual Puns

The fact that Dinesen chose a female name ending in *gard* in 'Ehrengard' when dealing with a work by Kierke*gaard* is also not a coincidence. *Gard*, *gaard* and *guard* are homophones when pronounced in English and when we combine the Danish and English meanings of the two words *Kierke* and *gard* it means 'Guard of The Church' (Christianity). This stands out as a significant contrast to the connotation of Ehrengard's name 'The Guard of Honour' (referring to female sexuality). In the 1953 edition of the selected diary entries *Søren Kierkegaards dagbøger* by Peter P. Rohde (Rohde 1953: first page before 'Indledning') we find this quote from Kierkegaard's journal on the first page before the introduction:

> Efter min Død skal Ingen i mine Papirer (det er min Trøst) finde en eneste Oplysning om hvad der egentlig har udfyldt mit Liv; finde den Skrift i mit

Inderste, der forklarer Alt, og som ofte gjør hvad Verden vilde kalde Bagateller til uhyre vigtige Begivenheder for mig, og hvad jeg anseer for Ubetydelighed, naar jeg tager den hemmelige Note bort, der forklarer det. (Kierkegaard 1843e, JJ:95: 169)

[After my death no one will find in my papers (this is my consolation) the least information about what has really filled my life, find that script in my innermost being that explains everything, and which often, for me, makes what the world would call trifles into events of immense importance, and which I too consider of no significance once I take away the secret note that explains it.] (Kierkegaard 2008: 157)

This 1953 edition is to be found in the collection of books in Karen Blixen's Library (Bondesson 1982: 344) and it came into her possession while working on 'Ehrengard' (1952–1962). When counting in the secret note about Goethe as being a virgin up until his journey to Italy, the sexual content of the novella and the hidden homophonic meaning of Kierkegaard's name, it seems plausible that Dinesen on the level of the author in 'Ehrengard' also suggests that Kierkegaard was a virgin but — contrary to Goethe — stayed so for his whole life. There is nothing in Kierkegaard's diaries that indicates that Kierkegaard ever had a sexual relationship with a woman, and it seems likely, with Dinesen's insight into Goethe's late blooming physical sexuality and knowledge about artistic sublimation, that this was also Dinesen's interpretation of Kierkegaard's 'secret note'. In a letter to Aage Henriksen from 29 July 1953, while she was working on 'Ehrengard', she mentions that they have discussed Søren Kierkegaard's body and his secret:

Jeg vil gerne bemærke at jeg aldrig har sagt eller tænkt mig, at 'Hemmeligheden ved S.K. var hans ubehagelige Krop', — det er langt fra mig at paatage mig nogen Forklaring af S.K. eller hans Hemmelighed. Min Udtalelse skulde kun forklare, hvorfor det 'personlige Forhold til S.K.', som jeg gennem Deres Bog paa en Maade følte at være kommet til, altid maa forblive noget fjernt eller afmaalt. Jeg kunde jo falde Shakespeare om Halsen og kysse Heine,[1] — men jeg vilde, i denne Forstand, — allerhøjst i uhyggelig Grad falde S.K. for Brystet, — ja, undskyld et dumt Ordspil! (Blixen 1996b: 150)

[I would like to note that I have never said or thought that the 'The secret about S.K. was his unpleasant body', — it is not within my limits to take upon me any explanation of S.K. or his secret. My remark was only supposed to explain, why the 'personal relationship to S.K.', which I have felt in a way through your book, always will stay something distant or formal. I could throw myself in the arms of Shakespeare and kiss Heine, — but I would, in that sense, — at the very utmost be an offence to S.K., — to use a silly pun!]

In the letter Dinesen uses an indirect message to describe her relation to Kierkegaard, which is delivered in the shape of a pun: 'falde S.K. for Brystet'. This sentence literally means 'fall to his chest' but originally refers to an uncomfortable feeling of pressure on the chest caused by bad air or smoke. In a metaphorical sense, however, it means 'to be offended by' something or someone. Dinesen uses the pun on one level to describe her lack of erotic attraction to Kierkegaard as a contrast to the erotic loaded descriptions of her relationship to Shakespeare and Heine: 'throw myself in the arms of Shakespeare' and 'kiss Heine'. To add further proof of my suggestion that Kierkegaard — according to Dinesen — was a virgin and that that is how Dinesen understood his secret note: 'den Skrift i mit Inderste, der forklarer alt' (Kierkegaard in Rohde 1953, first page before 'Indledning'), I will present a couple of additional observations. In his famous, yet enigmatic, diary entry from 1846, a time when Kierkegaard is about to conclude his writing career and apply for a position as a priest, he describes a certain physical and/or psychological condition that has caused him infinite pain and hardship. The diary entry is titled 'Saaledes har jeg forstaaet mig selv i hele min Forfatter-Virksomhed' [How I have understood myself in my entire oeuvre]:

> Skjøndt ingen Ven af Medvidere, skjøndt absolut utilbøielig til at tale med Andre om mit Inderste; mener jeg dog og har jeg meent, at det er et Mskes Pligt ikke at overspringe den Instants som det er at beraadføre sig med et andet Msk; kun at dette ikke bliver en pianket Fortrolighed, men alvorlig og officiel Meddelelse. Jeg har derfor talt med min Læge, om han meente at hiint Misforhold i min Bygning mell. det Legemlige og det Psychiske lod sig hæve, saa jeg kunde realisere det Almene. Det har han betvivlet; jeg har spurgt ham, om han meente, at Aand var istand ved Villien at omskabe ell. omdanne et saadant Grund-Misforhold, han betvivlede; han vilde end ikke tilraade mig at sætte hele min Villies-Kraft i Bevægelse, om hvilken han har en Forestilling, da jeg kunde sprænge det Hele. Fra det Øieblik har jeg valgt. Hiint sørgelige Misforhold, med samt dets Lidelser (der upaatvivligt vilde have gjort de Fleste til Selvmordere af dem som havde igjen Aand nok til at fatte Qvalens hele Elendighed) har jeg anseet for min Pæl i Kjødet, min Grændse, mit Kors; jeg har meent, at dette var det dyre Kjøb hvorfor Gud i Himlene har solgt mig en Aands-Kraft, der blandt Medlevende søger sin Lige. Dette opblæser mig ikke, *thi jeg er dog knuset,* mit Ønske er dog bleven mig den daglig bittre Smerte og Ydmygelse. (Kierkegaard 1846b: 36)

> [Although no lover of confidants and absolutely averse to talking to others about my inmost self, I nevertheless think and have thought that it is a person's duty not to skip the opportunity of seeking the advice of another person, only it must not become a foolish confidence, but a serious and official communication. Therefore, I have consulted my doctor as to whether he thought that the discrepancy in my body between the psychical and the psychic could be resolved so that I might realize the universal. He doubted it. I asked him whether he thought that acting through my will my mind was capable of reforming and transforming such a fundamental discrepancy; he doubted it. He would not even advise me to set my whole will power in motion, of which he had some idea, for I could burst everything asunder. From that moment I made my choice. That sad discrepancy along with its suffering (which undoubtedly would have driven to suicide most people that still had enough sense to grasp the misery of anguish) I have viewed as my thorn in the flesh, my limit, my cross; I have thought that this was the expensive cost for God in Heaven having sold me an intellectual power, that has no equal among contemporaries. This does not swell me up, *for I am, though, shattered,* my wish has, however, become my daily bitter pain and humiliation.]

This particular diary entry is also to be found in Rohde's compilation of Kierkegaard's diary entries (Rohde 1953: 41–42). In his book about Kierkegaard, Brandes also elaborates on the nature of this enigmatic condition that has prevented Kierkegaard from 'at realisere det Almene' [realizing the universal], which in Kierkegaard's terminology means marriage. Brandes also cites the entire quote above, when he discusses the possible causes for Kierkegaard's painful and desperate condition (Brandes 1877: 70). The general explanation for what the scholarship believes Kierkegaard is hinting at in the diary entry, is that the nature of this disease, Kierkegaard's secret note, was his 'tungsind' (melancholia or depression), which Brandes also mentions (Brandes 1877: 67–71).[2] Brandes then, however, goes on to draw another, much more audacious conclusion, which is probably why he put it near the end of a footnote (!):

> Denne Modsigelse, sammenholdt med alle de foregaaende Udtalelser, peger hen i Retning af det Sexuelle som det i særlig Forstand Legemlig-Sjælelige, der fremdeles særlig maatte komme i Betragtning ved Indgaaelsen af et Ægteskab. (Brandes 1877: 71)

> [This contradiction, in relation to all previous statements, points in the direction of the sexual, as in the special sense of the physical-spiritual, which must especially be considered when entering into a marriage.]

Here Brandes strongly indicates that Kierkegaard might have been suffering from some kind of sexual dysfunction, which prevented him from consummating a marriage. This also explains the extremely strong words Kierkegaard uses in the long diary entry when he describes his sad condition 'which undoubtedly would have driven most people to suicide [...] for I am, though, shattered [...] my daily bitter pain and humiliation'. It also explains why Kierkegaard in no way could expect Regine to marry him if he told her about the true nature of his condition, and that she most likely would have been crushed if Kierkegaard had told her, as Brandes correctly points out:

> Han kunde ikke overvinde sig til at give den sande Forklaring af det kun tilsyneladende krænkende Skridt, han agtede at foretage. Han ansaa sig for saa høit elsket, at et saa pludseligt Brud vilde foraarsage hans Elskede den største maaskee dræbende Smerte. (Brandes 1877: 71–72)

> [He could not convince himself to provide the true explanation for the seemingly offensive step he intended to take. He considered himself so greatly loved that such a sudden break would cause his loved one the greatest, possibly fatal, pain.]

Injuries to the Spinal Cord and Erectile Dysfunction

In a co-written article from 2013 titled 'Søren Kierkegaards sygdom og død' (Staubrand & Weismann 2013) [Søren Kierkegaard's illness and death] Kierkegaard-scholar Jens Staubrand and medical doctor and Professor Kaare Weismann convincingly suggest that Kierkegaard suffered from Pott's Paraplegia also known as Tuberculous Spondylitis — a disease that attacks the spinal cord. The symptoms of the disease are partial destruction of the vertebral bones caused by a tuberculous infection often producing a curvature of the spine (sometimes visible as a humpback, which was a very significant trait of Kierkegaard's physiognomy) that eventually leads to paraplegia, which Kierkegaard suffered from the last part of his life when he was unable to control his legs and his bladder (Staubrand & Weismann 2013: 325). We find the same theory suggested in Staubrand's monograph *Søren Kierkegaard's Struggle to Live at Frederiks Hospital* (Staubrand 2014).[3] Kierkegaard himself thought the curvature of his spine was caused by a fall from a tree when he was in his early teens, resulting in a damaged and/or fractured vertebrae (Staubrand & Weismann 2013: 320). Whether the damage to Kierkegaard's spinal cord was caused by the fall from the tree or Pott's Paraplegia, or both, we don't know. But we do know that his spinal cord, one way or the other, was damaged (the curvature of his spine, his inability to control his legs and his bladder). It is a well-known fact that erectile dysfunction can be a side-effect of injuries to the spinal cord, which has been pointed out in many medical papers that deal with spinal cord injuries.[4] This means that Kierkegaard's 'thorn in the flesh' (Staubrand 2013: 72) could in fact very well has been *an actual physical condition* — erectile dysfunction — which there was very limited knowledge of and no remedy for in the nineteenth century, and would have made it impossible for him to consummate the marriage with Regine Olsen. Even though we will never know for sure, Brandes' suspicions suggesting some kind of sexual dysfunction seem to be supported by the latest medical investigations into Kierkegaard's illness and the knowledge we have today about spinal cord injuries and erectile dysfunction.

Erectile dysfunction, or another type of sexual dysfunction, might very well have been the secret condition that prevented Kierkegaard from having a sexual relationship, thus from marrying Regine. This also explains why Kierkegaard knows he is in the right, even though nobody from the outside understands the break-up and scorns him for it. Kierkegaard *is in the right*, but he is unable to communicate the real reason. In that regard his situation is similar to that of Abraham, who knows that he is in the right, but looks like a madman from the outside. The impossibility of having a sexual relationship was Kierkegaard's painful 'Pæl i Kjødet' [Thorn in the flesh], the secret note that explains everything, and Dinesen had figured out that he was a virgin (but she was — for good reasons — unable to tell why as she also mentions to Aage Henriksen in the letter passage). Sexual abstention leading to sublimation was an experience that Dinesen shared, thus it is logical that she would be the one to recognize the same condition in Goethe and Kierkegaard. It was not religion, but sublimation, it was not God, but sexual energy that led to Kierkegaard's prolific production is the conclusion Dinesen draws. To confuse God with sexual energy arguably puts Kierkegaard in the category of the comical.

Kierkegaard and Dinesen: Art and Sublimation

In a passage in the essay 'Daguerreotypier' ('Daguerreotypes')[5] Dinesen refers to Kierkegaard and the quote about 'Væren for Andet' (Kierkegaard 1843a: 417) [being-for-other] from 'Forførerens Dagbog' while elaborating on her notion about 'Heksen'[6] [The Witch]:

> Eva var blevet skabt af Adams ribben, det var for mandens skyld at kvinden var til, og Søren Kierkegaard definerer kvindens væsen som 'væren for andet'. Men der var en kvinde som, længe inden ordet 'kvindeemancipation' blev brugt, eksisterede uafhængig af manden og havde sit tyngdepunkt i sig selv. Det var heksen. Heksen har spillet en større eller mindre rolle i de forskellige tidsaldre, men hun er aldrig ganske forsvundet ud af tilværelsen. Man må tro at sagen for de fleste mænd står således, at en kvinde, som kan undvære manden, givetvis også kan undvære Gud, eller at en kvinde, som ikke vil besiddes af manden, ufravigelig måtte være besat af Djævlen. Heksen havde ingensomhelst skrupler ved at vise sine ben, hun satte sig aldeles ugenert overskrævs på kosteskaftet og stak tilvejrs. (Blixen 1951: 186–87)

> [Eve was created from Adam's rib; it was for man's sake that woman existed and Søren Kierkegaard defined woman's being as 'existence for something else'.[7] But there was a woman who, long before the words 'emancipation of woman' came into use, existed independently of a man and had her own center of gravity. She was the witch. The witch has played a greater or lesser role in various eras but she has never entirely disappeared. One may suppose that for most men the explanation is, that a woman who can exist without a man certainly can also exist without God, or that a woman who does not want to be possessed by a man necessarily must be possessed by the devil. The witch had absolutely no scruples about showing her legs; she sat quite unconstrained astride her broomstick and took off.] (Dinesen 1979: 33)

Here Dinesen juxtaposes 'manden' [man] and 'Gud' [God] and 'kvinden' [woman] and 'Djævlen' [the devil]. In a letter to Aage Henriksen from 29 July 1953, where she discusses Kierkegaard (two years after she wrote the essay), Dinesen elaborates on the above notion:

> Ogsaa et andet Citat, — til Forklaring af, hvad jeg har sagt til Dem, — har Deres Afhandling (eller Brandts Bog som jeg læste for dennes Skyld) givet mig. Goldschmidt skriver, at 'naar Møller gik itu ved Stødet med S. K., saa hidrørte det i sin inderste Grund fra, at K stod i et skønnere, renere, højere Forhold til Kvinden'. Jeg maa have Lov at bruge det til at forklare, at naar Kvinder kan le ad Mændene, 'hidrører det i sin inderste Grund, — (se Goethes Faust & Mephisto, og Thomas Mann's Dr. Faustus og hans Djævel) fra, at de staar i et elskværdigere, og værdigere, Forhold til Djævlen'. (I det hele taget: Hvor Lysets og Mørkets højeste Repræsentant gaar ind i Bevidstheden som *han*, dér giver selve Kvindeligheden Adgang til særligt inderlige Forhold, og vi faar Jomfru Maria, og Heksen. (Blixen 1996b: 150–51)

> [Your treatise (or Brandt's book, which I read because of that) has also given me another quote — to clarify what I have said to you. Goldschmidt writes that 'when Møller fell apart in his encounter with S.K., it originated in its innermost

core from the fact that K. had a more beautiful, purer, higher relationship to woman'. I must be allowed to use that to explain that when women can laugh at men, 'it originates in its innermost core (see Goethe Faust & Mephisto, and Thomas Mann's Dr. Faustus and his Devil) from the fact that they have a more amiable, and more honourable, relationship to the Devil'. (On the whole: Where the Light and the Dark's highest representative enters the consciousness as *he,* then womanhood becomes the entrance to matters of a particular inward nature — and so we get the Virgin Mary and the Witch.]

Dinesen here ironically uses Kierkegaard and his lack of sexual relationships with women — 'K stod i et skønnere, renere, højere Forhold til Kvinden' [K. had a more beautiful, purer, higher relationship to woman'] — to point out how he, as a sexually abstinent man,[8] came to be an ally of God (just like a catholic priest), while she, as a woman, who similar to Kierkegaard did not have sexual relationships with men upon her return to Denmark, or let herself be defined by them after the break up with Finch Hatton, came to be an ally of the Devil as 'Heksen' [The Witch]. A woman who has internalized the male agency does not need a man, since she has a relationship with the entire male sex (just like Kierkegaard had it the other way around) and the sexual energy is transformed through sublimation into artistic and spiritual creativity and we get either 'The Witch' (the female artist as the concrete equivalent) or 'Jomfru Maria' (the nun as the concrete equivalent). Lucifer was a revolutionary when he questioned the established (God), and in the eyes of atheist Georg Brandes also the one who brought light and truth. This notion of Brandes Dinesen took over, but, as we understand from the above quote, she also perceived Lucifer as the female male muse, the equivalent to the male female muse of the Madonna.

Notes to Chapter 11

1. Shakespeare and Heine were Dinesen's favorite writers. Dinesen identified with their wit, esprit, audacious humour (equal to Dinesen's Lucifer view), profound irony (this was their narrative strategy as well) and deep insights into human life and art.
2. This is also the explanation that Dinesen's sister Ellen Dahl delivers in her Kierkegaard essay (Dahl 1932).
3. The text in this book is both in Danish and English.
4. Here references to just a few of the many articles on the topic: Francois Giuliano et al., 'Randomized trial of sildenafil for the treatment of erectile dysfunction in spinal cord injury', *Annals of Neurology*, 46 (1999), 15–21; Manoj Monga et al., 'Male infertility and erectile dysfunction in spinal cord injury: A review', *Archives of Physical Medicine and Rehabilitation*, 80 (1999), 1331–39, and Barbara T. Benevento & Marca L. Sipski, 'Neurogenic Bladder, Neurogenigc Bowel, and Sexual Dysfunction in People With Spinal Cord Injury', *Psysical Therapy. Journal of the American Physical Therapy Association*, 82 (2002), 601–12.
5. 'Daguerreotypier' was first given as two radio talks on Danish National Radio. The talks were written during the fall of 1950 (only half a year after the publication of 'Babette's Feast' in *Ladies' Home Journal*, June 1950), recorded at Rungstedlund on 19 December 1950 (Blixen 1996b: 9) and broadcasted in the first week of January 1951. Gyldendal published the radio talks in their original oral form in 1951.
6. Again Dinesen ascribes the idea to the biographical Kierkegaard instead of his character narrator Johannes Forføreren.

7. I will stick to Hongs translation of the phrase 'Væren for Andet' as 'being-for-other' (Kierkegaard 1987a: 268–70).
8. Contrary to P. L. Møller, who indulged in several extra-marital sexual relationships (Bruun Andersen 1950: 37–38).

PART IV

❖

Gender

CHAPTER 12

Women at the Symposium: 'Carnival' and 'in vino veritas'

In this chapter I am returning to 'Carnival' with special attention to 'in vino veritas' and Dinesen's view on gender. The tale is set up as a Symposium, but in 'Carnival' we find the same number of male and female speakers, in contrast to Kierkegaard's 'in vino veritas' (and the Greek symposium) where only men were allowed to participate. The costumes and the names in 'Carnival' are furthermore created to obfuscate the gender of the speaker, so the reader is confused with regard to which gender the character who is speaking actually belongs to. The ideal behind this narrative strategy is that people should interact and listen to each other first and foremost as human beings, instead of one gender or another. This was, however, a position Dinesen very quickly departed from in favour of a complete different view on gender where she perceived the two genders as fundamentally different — and their mutual attraction as the fundamental energy that makes the world go round. This position we already find in *Seven Gothic Tales* (from which 'Carnival' was eventually left out), and most pointedly formulated in 'Oration at a Bonfire, 14 Years Late' (1953) (Dinesen 1979).

'Carnival' and 'in vino veritas'

Aside from being a tale about seduction with special attention to 'Forførerens Dagbog' and Kierkegaard as a 'macabre dandy' (as I have already mentioned in Chapter 8), 'Carnival' is also a counter-story to 'in vino veritas'. All in all, the structure of 'Carnival' is that of a Symposium and the frame is very similar to 'in vino veritas' from *Stadier paa Livets Vei*. *The Symposium* is a philosophical text by Plato dated c. 385–380 BCE. It concerns itself with the genesis, purpose and nature of love. In this work love is examined in a sequence of speeches given by the men attending the symposium. The major similarities with regard to setting, composition and theme between Kierkegaard's 'in vino veritas' and Dinesen's 'Carnival' are that they both take place at a location north of Copenhagen and the wine flows abundantly while the participants discuss erotic love. Especially the significance of wine plays an important role in both works. Here from 'Carnival': 'it is wonderful to have had so much to drink that you can speak as easily as you think' (Dinesen 1977: 64, said by Mimi), 'Hot from wine and dancing the guests arrived' (66), 'Flushed by wine under the powder of his mask' (68, about Julius), 'Deeply moved by drink and love' (69, about Charlie), 'he had drunk much tonight to get an inspiration' and 'Under the influence of these various moods and wines' (85–86, both about Tido), 'He refilled his glass and drunk it down' (92, about Rosendaal) and towards the end the narrator states that: 'The wine seemed somehow alive on its own now' (102).

In 'Carnival' we see how the wine influences and moves the characters in various ways and inspire them to the profound discussion 'upon life and death' and to 'speak as easily as you think' (to speak the truth, so to speak). Dinesen here seems to adopt the narrator's point of view that is apparent in 'in vino veritas': that fine wine is a metaphor for art and in the end synonymous with truth (veritas) but at the same time she can't help also poking fun at it: 'Charlie tried to run his mental eye over the situation, but he had drunk too much for that' (89). In both 'Carnival' and 'in vino veritas' we also find the majority of the participants to be unhappy lovers, with a couple of exceptions in each piece: Johannes 'in vino veritas' and Camelia in 'Carnival'. We also find one character in both works that has never been in love: 'det unge Menneske' [the young man] in 'in vino veritas' and Polly (Arlecchino) in 'Carnival'. We also find the depraved and demonic character of 'Modehandleren' [the fashion designer] from 'in vino veritas' (indeed a 'macabre dandy' type) mimicked in the artist Rosendaal, who is dressed as an old Chinese eunuch. Both are older, demonic, yet effeminate men, who do not seem to engage in any sexual relationships with women, but are utterly fascinated by them in a spiritual sense only.

But here the similarities stop. The bachelors in 'in vino veritas' all talk about women and love from a theoretical perspective but have themselves no practical experience (only exception being Johannes). This is very different from most of the characters in Dinesen's 'Carnival' (Rosendaal and Polly being the exceptions) since all of them are indulging in sexual relation- and partnerships. They are in the flesh, so to speak, what they discuss, and this is another example of how Dinesen chose to make concrete characters from the abstract ideas represented by the four bachelor theorists in 'in vino veritas' (Vigilius Haufniensis, Constantin Constantius, det unge Menneske and Modehandleren) since the discussions about love in 'Carnival' are based on real and practical experiences. Another major difference between 'Carnival' and 'in vino veritas' (and Plato's *Symposium* for that matter) is that Dinesen in 'Carnival' breaks the rule that only men are allowed to participate and speak at a Symposium. In 'Carnival' the party consists of 'the company of four lovely women, and the conversation, upon life and death, of four men' (102).

From Gender to 'Human Beings'

But Dinesen goes further. In 'Carnival' we not only find an equal number of women and men participating, but we also find men dressed as women, women dressed as men, a man dressed as a eunuch (a sort of non-gender) thus making it very difficult to grasp who is speaking and to what gender they actually belong. Here is the line-up:

Tido / Harlequin (futuristic Harlequin): A man wearing a man's costume

Camelia / Camelia: A woman wearing a woman's costume
Mimi / Pierrot: A woman wearing a man's costume
Polly / Arlecchino (traditional Harlequin): A woman wearing a man's costume
Annelise / Young Soren Kierkegaard: A woman wearing a man's costume
Julius / Venetian Lady: A man wearing a woman's costume
Charlie / Magenta Domino: A man wearing a woman's (or man's) costume
Rosendaal / Eunuch: A man wearing a non-gender costume

The purpose of this narration strategy is not only to represent the rapidly changing gender roles of the 1920s and the (homo)-sexual revolution (see Bunch 2012) but also an attempt to free the words spoken and the opinions expressed by the participants, by masking the person's gender, so the (first-time) reader is unsure whether it is a man or in fact a woman who is expressing the opinion. The main consequence of this gender obfuscation is to see the characters first and foremost as *human beings* and only secondly as gendered in line with the view Dinesen expressed in a letter to Mary Bess Westenholz from 23 May 1926, while she was working on 'Carnival':

> Er det i hvert Fald ikke at ønske, at under saadanne Forhold, hvor Mennesker mødes for at komme til Klarhed og bestemme over store Spørgsmaal, som angaar hele Menneskeheden, de kunde komme til at mødes som Mennesker og ikke, som før i Tiden, som først og fremmest Medlemmer af en Stamme eller et Lav eller, som nu, som Medlemmer af en Nation, et politisk Parti, eller af det ene eller andet køn. (Blixen 2013: 985–86).

> [Isn't it at least desirable that under such circumstances in which people meet to reach certainty and to decide on great matters regarding humanity that they could meet as human beings and not as in the past, first and foremost as members of a tribe or an association, or as now, as members of a nation, political party, or one gender or the other.]

As has been pointed out by many scholars over the years, most recently by Braad Thomsen (2010: 87) and Stecher (2014: 27–90), Dinesen would quickly leave her 1920s utopian idea of dissolving and merging the two gender categories under the umbrella of 'human beings' that we find expressed both in 'Carnival' and the essay 'Moderne ægteskab og andre betragtninger' (Blixen 1923–24) (*On Modern Marriage and Other Observations*, Dinesen 1986b). Instead, she developed another point of view on the two genders as being fundamentally and ontologically different (but often in new surprising ways) as she also expressed it in the essay 'En Baaltale med 14 Aars Forsinkelse' (Radio talk, delivered 11 January 1953) ('Oration at a Bonfire, 14 Years Late') (1979). But it is worth noting that she already from *Seven Gothic Tales* and onwards departed radically from her idea of the genderless human being that she promulgates in 'Carnival' and in 'Moderne ægteskab og andre betragtninger', which might very well be one of the reasons why Dinesen decided *not* to publish these works during her lifetime. In the following I will show how Dinesen made some interesting observations about gender, and women in particular (that are very different from the aforementioned earlier works) in her tales, which also have clear ties to Kierkegaard's works and Johannes' idea in 'Forførerens Dagbog' of woman as 'Væren for Andet' [being-for-other] in particular.

CHAPTER 13

❖

Woman. God(dess) of Man:
'The Deluge at Norderney', 'The Diver',
and *Enten — Eller. Anden Deel.*

In 'The Deluge at Norderney' Dinesen for the first time presents the idea of mutual attraction between the two genders, and the power of woman in that relation. The starting point is the subversion of a crucial headline paragraph from *Enten — Eller. Anden Deel*: 'Det Opbyggelige, der ligger i den Tanke, at mod Gud have vi altid Uret' (Kierkegaard 1843b: 326) [The Upbuilding That Lies in the Thought in Relation to God We Are Always in the Wrong] (Kierkegaard 1987b: 339) to this sentence uttered by Jonathan Mærsk in the tale: 'I feel how edifying is the thought that toward women we are always in the wrong' (Dinesen 1934: 51). Here Dinesen clearly, and very provocatively, substitutes God with Woman. In a significant scene, Calypso discovers her powers as a (beautiful) woman; she recognizes that men want women and will do whatever it takes to get them. This is not only a dismissal of God as the central power, it is also a subversion of nineteenth-century gender roles, where man is seen as primary and woman as the weaker sex, described in Kierkegaard's terminology as man being equal to 'Mennesket' (a human being) whereas woman is reduced to 'being-for-other'. The tale goes even further when it suggests that what men think they do for the sake of God or an ideal, they actually, and for the most part unknowingly, do for the sake of woman. This gender subversion of the power roles also has similarities with the notion of seduction and gender presented in 'The Dreamers' (see Chapter 9). Dinesen's major critique of Christianity, gender, and Kierkegaard is that 'Nature', 'Sensuousness', and 'Woman' have been looked down upon and suppressed as 'being-for-other' in the Christian tradition — even associated with sin and the Devil, when these categories in fact belong to the (organic) phenomena from which life, thought, arts and religion derive. The chapter concludes with a summary of the subversions of Kierkegaard's male characters in Dinesen's oeuvre and their views on woman.

'The Deluge at Norderney'

In Dinesen's materialistic parody of the genesis flood narrative of Noah 'The Deluge at Norderney' from *Seven Gothic Tales,* Miss Malin tells a story about her beautiful young friend Calypso, who is a part of the small group in the hayloft in the final scene. In her youth Calypso never perceived herself as beautiful but as a hideous, awkward being because she was brought up as a boy at 'Angelshorn'[1] where 'man' and the arts and sciences were the ideals for her (presumably homosexual, or at least asexual) misogynist uncle 'Grev Serafina':

> He taught the little girl Greek and Latin. He tried to convey to her the idea of the beauty of higher mathematics. But when he lectured to her upon the infinite loveliness of the circle, she asked him: if it were really so fair, what color was it — was it not blue? Ah, no, he said, it had no color at all. From that moment he began to fear that she would not become a boy. (Dinesen 1934: 43–44)[2]

Again we detect the irony with regard to Grev Serafina's fruitless attempts to trump gender with social environment (the men at Angelshorn) and culture (science and academics). He only succeeds in ruining Calypso's self-esteem as a female human being:

> In this dark castle the annihilated girl would walk about. She was the loveliest thing in the place, and would have adorned the court Queen of Venus, who would very likely have made her keeper of her doves, dove as she is herself. But here she knew that she did not exist, for nobody ever looked at her [...] In the end as you, Timon, [Jonathan] could not stand your existence, but meant to jump into the water from Langebro, she could no longer stand her nonexistence at Angelshorn. (Dinesen 1934: 45–46)[3]

After Miss Malin has finished her story about Calypso's sufferings at Angelshorn, the young Dane Jonathan Mærsk makes a startling conclusion:

> 'Madame, indeed,' said Jonathan, 'I do not know if you will think it strange, but I have never in my life, until you told me so now, thought that fair women could suffer. I held them to be precious flowers, which must be looked after carefully.' 'And what do you feel now that I have told you so?' Miss Malin asked him. 'Madame,' said the young man after having thought it over, 'I feel how edifying is the thought that toward women we are always in the wrong.' 'You are an honest young man,' said Miss Malin. 'Your side hurts now, where your rib was once taken out of you'. (Dinesen 1934: 50–51)

> ['Gud i Himlen, Deres Naade,' sagde Jonathan, 'det ville maaske forundre Dem, men aldrig i mine Dage, før De nu fortæller mig det, er det faldet mig ind, at skønne Kvinder kunde lide eller have det ondt. Jeg tænkte mig, at de var Jordens dejligste Blomster, som hele verden maatte værne om. 'Og nu, da jeg har fortalt Dem det, hvad føler De nu?' spurgte Frøken Malin. 'Deres Naade,' sagde den unge Mand efter at tænkt sig lidt om, 'jeg føler det opbyggelige, som ligger i den Tanke, at overfor Kvinderne har vi altid Uret.' 'De er en honnet ung Mand,' sagde Frøken Malin, 'nu gør det ondt i Siden paa Dem, der hvor man har taget Deres Ribben ud'.] (Dinesen 1935: 184)

The line from Jonathan's passage: 'jeg føler det opbyggelige, som ligger i den Tanke, at overfor Kvinderne har vi altid Uret' (Dinesen 1935: 184) [I feel how edifying is the thought that toward women we are always in the wrong] (Dinesen 1934: 50–51) is, as has been pointed out by Glienke (Glienke 1986: 111), a poignant allusion to the motto of Judge William's concluding paragraph in the third part 'Ultimatum' [Final Word] in Kierkegaard's *Enten — Eller. Anden Deel*: 'Det Opbyggelige, der ligger i den Tanke, at mod Gud have vi altid Uret' (Kierkegaard 1843b: 326) [The Upbuilding That Lies in the Thought in Relation to God We Are Always in the Wrong] (Kierkegaard 1987b: 339). The big question here is of course what Jonathan Mærsk's enigmatic conclusion means in relation to Kierkegaard and what implications it has for our understanding of Dinesen's notion of gender. This I will try to answer below.

Initially Jonathan's reversal of Judge William's claim means that man basically does not know the ways of women, just like man does not know the ways of God (the story of Job being the illustration), which means that man 'overfor Kvinderne' [toward women] is always in the wrong. 'Det Opbyggelige' [the edifying] that Jonathan finds in this recognition ironically alludes to this passage from *Enten — Eller. Anden Deel* when we, following the reversal of the quotation, substitute God with Woman in the passage below:

> Naar det hedder, Du skal ikke gaae i Rette med Gud, da vil det sige, Du maa ikke ville have Ret mod Gud, kun saaledes maa Du gaae i Rette med ham, at du lærer, at Du har Uret. Ja, det er, hvad Du selv bør ville. Naar det da forbydes Dig at gaae i Rette med Gud, da betegnes derved Din Fuldkommenhed, og ingenlunde siges der, at Du er et ringe Væsen, der ingen Betydning har for ham [...] Denne Betragtning er saa naturlig, saa indlysende for Enhver. Der ligger da noget Opbyggeligt i at have Uret, forsaavidt vi nemlig, idet vi tilstaae det, opbygge os ved Udsigterne til, at det sjeldnere og sjeldnere skal blive Tilfældet. (Kierkegaard 1843b: 324, 326)

> [When it says that you are not to argue with God, it means that you must not insist on being in the right in relation to God; you may argue with him only in such a way that you learn that you are in the wrong. Indeed, that is what you yourself should want. To be forbidden to argue with God indicates your perfection and in no way says that you are an inferior being who has no significance for him [...] The point of view is very natural and very obvious to everyone. Thus there is something upbuilding in being in the wrong, provided that we, in admitting it, build ourselves up by the prospect that it will more and more rarely be the case.] (Kierkegaard 1987b: 344, 347)

When Calypso in 'The Deluge at Norderney' finally discovers the painting at Angelshorn where woman is adorned and worshipped (as a God), we discover that Jonathan's recognition has far bigger implications:

> a scene out of the life of the nymphs, fauns, and satyrs, with the centaurs, playing in groves and on the flowery plains [...] But what surprised and overwhelmed her was the fact that these strong and lovely beings were obviously concentrating their attention upon following, adoring, and embracing young girls of her own age, and of her own figure and face, that the whole thing was done in their honor and inspired by their charms. (Dinesen 1934: 47–48)[4]

In this significant scene Calypso discovers her powers as a (beautiful) woman;[5] she recognizes that men want women and will do whatever it takes to get them and that her uncle and the other young men at Angelshorn are *the exception*. She discovers that it is she, woman, who is the central figure in life, not God. This also ties into the notion from 'The Dreamers' that women always seduce (the very beautiful ones in particular). Man, on the other hand, has to do everything in order to seduce women (like the Fauns and Satyrs in the painting — not to mention Don Juan, see Chapter 9). He is, as Dinesen says in 'En Baaltale med 14 Aars Forsinkelse' [Oration at a Bonfire, 14 Years Late], 'inspireret' [inspired] (see quote on pp. 130-31) by woman to do all sorts of things: create brilliant careers, fight wars, build houses, talk sweet, show admiration and dedication in order to get her. What men think they do for the sake of God or an ideal (science, arts, career, money, honour), they actually, and for the most part unknowingly, do for the sake of woman, or rather: in order to get women, which means that man 'overfor Kvinderne altid har uret' [toward women we are always in the wrong] (until he complies and does the right thing). Again we can illustrate this with a passage from Judge William's concluding chapter of *Enten — Eller. Anden Deel* when substituting 'Mennesket' with 'Man' and 'Gud' with 'Woman':

> Du har vel ofte hørt, en Viisdom, der nemt nok veed at forklare Alt, uden hverken at gjøre Gud eller Mennesket Uret: Mennesket er et skrøbeligt Væsen, siger den, det vilde være urimeligt af Gud at forlange det Umulige af ham, man gjør hvad man kan, og er man en enkelt Gang noget efterladende, saa vil Gud aldrig glemme, at vi ere svage og ufuldkomne Væsner. Skal jeg mest beundre de ophøiede Forestillinger om Guddommens Væsen, denne Kløgt forraader, eller det dybe Indblik i det menneskelige Hjerte, den prøvende Bevidsthed, der randsager sig selv, og nu kommer til den magelige og beqvemme Erkjendelse: man gjør hvad man kan? Var det saa let en Sag for Dig, min Tilhører, at afgjøre, hvor Meget det er: hvad man kan? Var Du aldrig i Fare, hvor Du næsten til Fortvivlelse anstrængede Dine Kræfter og dog saa uendelig gjerne ønskede at kunne Mere, og en Anden maaske med tvivlende og bedende Blikke saae paa Dig, om det ikke var muligt, at Du kunde gjøre Mere? (Kierkegaard 1843b: 324)

> [I would remind you of a wisdom you certainly have frequently heard, a wisdom that knows how to explain everything easily enough without doing an injustice either to God or to human beings. A human being is a frail creature, it says; it would be unreasonable of God to require the impossible of him. One does what one can, and if one is ever somewhat negligent, God will never forget that we are weak and imperfect creatures. Shall I admire more the sublime concepts of the nature of the Godhead that this ingenuity makes manifest or the profound insight into the human heart, the probing consciousness that scrutinizes itself and now comes to the easy, cozy conclusion: One does what one can? Was it such an easy matter for you, my listener, to determine how much that is: what one can? Were you never in such danger that you almost desperately exerted yourself and yet so infinitely wished to be able to do more, and perhaps someone else looked at you with a skeptical and imploring look, whether it was not possible that you could do more?] (Kierkegaard 1987b: 344–45)

But after Calypso has discovered her own worth as a female sexual being through the painting, the narrator also goes on to state that a woman's beauty is one of her biggest assets, which also implies that a woman must do everything to achieve beauty in order to attract the male gaze, humorously described in this passage:

Where, My Lord, is music bred? — upon the instrument or within the ear that
listens? The loveliness of woman is created in the eye of man. You talk, Timon
[Jonathan], of Lucifer offending God by looking at him to see what he was like.
That shows that you worship a male deity. A goddess would ask her worshiper
first of all: 'How am I looking?' (Dinesen 1934: 45)[6]

All in all we can conclude from these analyses of Dinesen's tales that the two
genders create each other in their ideal image, since each gender caters to the ideal
of the other gender to a degree so it is almost impossible to separate what is what. As
Dinesen points out, again hinting at Kierkegaard, it makes no sense to argue about
who is the stronger or weaker sex. They are strong and weak each in their own way.
In 'En Baaltale med 14 Aars Forsinkelse' from 1953 she concludes:

Og Søren Kierkegaard[7] siger, at det kunne have sin interesse at lade et eller
andet litterært udgangsøg udarbejde et regnskab over, hvorvidt, i digtningen
ned gennem tiderne, manden oftest har svigtet kvinden eller kvinden manden.
Hun er svagere, og hun er stærkere, hun står de høje ånder fjernere, hun er
nærmere englene. (Blixen 1953: 220)

[And Søren Kierkegaard says that it would be interesting to have some literary
hack calculate how frequently in the course of time the man has betrayed the
woman, or the woman the man, in world literature. She is weaker and she is
stronger; she is farther removed from elevated spirits, she is nearer the angels.]
(Dinesen 1979: 72–73)

The basic dynamic between the two genders is, however, sexual attraction, which
is also what, according to Dinesen, drives the world and what she, tongue in cheek,
means by 'den gensidige inspiration' [mutual inspiration] in the following quote
from 'En Baaltale':

Jeg selv anser *inspiration* for at være den højeste menneskelige lykke. Og
inspiration kræver altid to elementer. Jeg tror at den gensidige inspiration mand
og kvinde imellem har været den mægtigste drivkraft i vor slægts historie, og
fremfor andre har skabt, hvad der kendetegner vor adel: bedrift, poesi, kunst og
smag. Jeg tænker mig, at et af de forhold, hvorved menneskene har hævet sig
over dyrene, er dette: at menneskene har parringstid hele året, — et samfund,
hvor de to køns tiltrækning for hinanden var indskrænket til en bestemt kort
periode, måtte blive besynderlig afstumpet. Ja, jeg tror, at jo mægtigere denne
gensidige inspiration virker, jo mere levende vil et samfund udvikle sig [...] Skal
jeg fra mit eget personlige synspunkt definere denne dybe forskelligartethed
hos menneskehedens to køn, da udtrykker jeg min opfattelse bedst, idet jeg
siger: 'Mandens tyngdepunkt, hans væsens gehalt, ligger i, hvad han i livet
udretter, kvindens i, hvad hun er'. (Blixen 1953: 217–18, 220)

[I myself look upon *inspiration* as the greatest human blessing. And inspiration
always requires two elements. I think that the mutual inspiration of man and
woman has been the most powerful force in the history of the race, and above
all has created what is characteristic of our aristocracy: courageous exploits,
poetry, the arts, and the refinement of taste. I think that one of the ways in
which human beings have elevated themselves above animals is this: human
beings mate the year around — a society in which the attraction of the two
sexes to one another was limited to a distinct, brief period, must become

notably blunted. Yes, I think that the more strongly the mutual inspiration functions, the richer and more animated a society will develop. [...] If, from my own personal point of view, I have to define this profoundly inspirational difference between the two sexes of mankind, then I can phrase my opinion best by saying, 'A man's center of gravity, the substance of his being, consists in what he has executed and performed in life; the woman's, in what she is'.]
(Dinesen 1979: 70, 73)

The ideals of men and women created by the opposite gender are, however, different from culture to culture and are constantly altered as history progresses, which means that the contrast outlined in Dinesen's tales and in her essay above has many modifications and degrees. In 'Tales of two Old Gentlemen' from *Last Tales* Mateo, however, develops the above notion of woman as 'being' with a closer relationship to her fate, sense of purpose and own worth — as more 'earth-bound', so to speak:

And as to the shedding of blood, this to our shepherdess — as to any lady — is a high privilege and is inseparably united with the sublimest [sic] moments of existence, with promotion and beatification. What little girl will not joyously shed her blood in order to become a virgin, what bride not hers in order to become a wife, what young wife not hers to become a mother? Man, troubled and perplexed about the relation between divinity and humanity, is ever striving to find a foothold in the matter by drawing on his own normal experience. He will view it in the light of relations between tutor and pupil, or of commander and soldier, and he will lose breath — and heart — in search and investigation. The ladies, whose nature is nearer to the nature of the deity, take no such trouble; they see the relation between Cosmos and Creator quite plainly as a love affair. And in a love affair search and investigation is an absurdity, and unseemly. (Dinesen 1957: 65)

[Og hvad Blodsudgydelse angaar, da er denne, i vor Hyrdindes — som i enhver Dames — Øjne et ophøjet Privilegium og uadskilleligt forbundet med Tilværelsens mest sublime Øjeblikke, og med Forfremmelse og Fuldkommengørelse. Hvilken lille Pige udgyder ikke gladelig sit Blod for at blive Jomfru? Hvilken Brud ikke sit Blod for at blive Hustru? Og hvilken ung Hustru ikke sit for at blive Moder? Mennesket, Manden, søger, dybt foruroliget og forvirret overfor Forholdet mellem Guddom og Menneske, bestandig — og bestandig forgæves — et Fodfæste i Erfaringer fra sit eget Menneskeliv. Han anlægger paa dette ophøjede Forhold en Maalestok hentet fra Forholdet mellem Lærer og Elev, eller mellem Befalingsmand og Soldat, og jo dybere han i sin Grublen trænger ned i Sagen, jo mere pinefuld bliver hans Uro. Vore Damer, hvis Natur, ligger Guddommens Natur nærmere, græmmer sig ikke over saadanne Uoverensstemmelser, men ser og erkender, ganske enkelt og som om det var en given Sag, Forholdet mellem Skaberen og Kosmos som et Kærlighedsforhold, — og i et Kærlighedsforhold er Forskning ørkesløs og Analyse usømmelig.] (Blixen 1957, 61–62)

Here we find the juxtaposition 'Mennesket, Manden' in Dinesen's Danish version (lost in the English version) to be an ironic comment to Kierkegaard, who throughout his oeuvre refers to 'Manden' as 'Mennesket' with meticulous consistency, even though 'menneske' in Danish is not gendered and just means 'human being'.[8] The young poet is called 'det unge *Menneske*' seventeen times in *Gjentagelsen* (Kierkegaard 1843c) and we even have a character with that generic name in 'in vino veritas' (Kierkegaard 1845). We find numerous other examples in Kierkegaard's works, so I will just mention a couple to stress the point that 'Menneske' is synonymous with 'Manden' [the man]. Here from the essay 'Vexel-Driften' [Rotation of Crops] in *Enten — Eller. Første Deel*: 'Og hvilke Følger havde ikke denne Kjedsommelighed. Mennesket stod høit og faldt dybt, først ved Eva, saa fra det babyloniske Taarn' (Kierkegaard 1843a: 276) [And what consequences this boredom had: humankind stood tall and fell far, first through Eve, then from the Babylonian tower] (Kierkegaard 1987a: 286) and from 'Ligevægten': 'Netop ved at arbeide frigjør Mennesket sig, ved at arbeide bliver han Herre over Naturen, ved at arbeide viser han, at han er høiere end Naturen' (Kierkegaard 1843b: 268). [It is precisely by working that a person liberates himself; by working, he becomes master over nature; by working, he shows that he is higher than nature] (Kierkegaard 1987b: 282). This clearly implies that a woman is not a 'Menneske' [Human Being] but something else, 'Væren for Andet', [being-for-other] as Johannes suggests in this passage from 'Forførerens Dagbog':

> Deraf lader det sig ogsaa forklare, hvorfor Gud, da han skabte Eva, lod en dyb Søvn falde paa Adam; thi Qvinden er Mandens Drøm. Ogsaa paa en anden Maade læres af hiin Fortælling, at Qvinden er Væren for Andet. Der siges nemlig, at Jehova tog et af Mandens Sidebeen. Havde han f. Ex. taget af Mandens Hjerne, saa var Qvinden vel vedbleven at være Væren for Andet, men Bestemmelsen var ikke, at hun skulde være et Hjernespind, men noget ganske Andet. Hun blev Kjød og Blod, men falder netop derved ind under Bestemmelsen af Natur, der væsentlig er Væren for Andet. (Kierkegaard 1843a: 417–18)

> [This explains why God, when he created Eve, had a deep sleep fall upon Adam, for woman is man's dream. The story teaches us in another way that woman is being-for-other. That is, it says that Jehovah took one of man's ribs. If he had, for example, taken from man's brain, woman would certainly have continued to be being-for-other, but the purpose was not that she should be a figment of the brain but something quite different. She became flesh and blood, but precisely thereby she falls within the category of nature, which essentially is being-for-other.] (Kierkegaard 1987a: 268)

As we have seen above, Dinesen, contrary to Johannes, clearly suggests that both genders are 'being-for-other' and that woman is (of course) a human being on equal terms with the man. One could even go further and suggest that Dinesen actually suggests the opposite: that it is the man who is 'being-for-other', since Dinesen, as she already showed us in *Sandhedens Hævn*, perceives 'nature' as the primary and culture and Christianity, the symbolic world of ideas (to where man belongs) as the secondary that derives from the primary: 'nature'. These two spheres do, however, interact, which is eventually what drives the world forward. Dinesen's major critique is that 'nature', 'sensuousness' and 'women' within the notion of Christianity have been looked down upon as 'being-for-other' and suppressed, even associated with the Devil, when these categories in fact belong to the (organic) phenomena from where all life, thinking, arts and religion derive. This notion runs through her oeuvre from *Sandhedens Hævn* (1926) to *Anecdotes of Destiny* (1958) and here Kierkegaard as a male precursor and philosopher within the frame of Christianity became a natural target.

'The Diver'

As a continuation of these ideas expressed in 'The Deluge at Norderney', Dinesen develops the idea in 'The Diver' from *Anecdotes of Destiny* that female beauty and sexuality is man's paradise on earth.[9] With usual affinity for ironic, materialistic embodiments of religious ideas and gender reversals (this time from the Koran), the tale suggests that man's notion of angels in heaven derive from certain, materialistic flesh and blood embodiments on earth: extremely beautiful women. In 'The Diver' (which is told by Mira Jama from 'The Dreamers'), the young Softa Saufe is fooled into believing that he has met a real angel from Heaven, when Mirza Aghai sends the flaming hot dancer Thusmu to distract him from trying to build wings so he can fly and meet the angels in Heaven. She, instead, manages to keep him grounded, so to speak:

> 'We angels,' she said, 'do not really need wings to move between heaven and earth, but our own limbs suffice. If you and I become real friends it will be the same with you, and you may destroy the wings on which you are working.' All trembling with ecstasy he asked her how such flight could possibly be performed against all laws of science. She laughed at him, with a laughter like a little clear bell. 'You men,' she said, 'love laws and argument, and have great faith in the words that come out through your beards. But I am going to convince you that we have a mouth for sweeter debates, and a sweeter mouth for debates. I am going to teach you how angels and men arrive at perfect understanding without argument, in the heavenly manner.' And this she did. For a month the Softa's happiness was so great that his heart gave way beneath it. He forgot all about his work, as time after time he gave himself up to the celestial understanding. (Dinesen 1958: 7)[10]

Again, we detect the irony with regard to young Saufe and his delusional ideas about angels and the origin of Thusmu. When she finally reveals her true nature to him, they are forced to depart and Saufe eventually gives up his project. Within Christian mythology angels are mostly perceived as asexual creatures (which is also Vigilius Haufniensis' interpretation in *Begrebet Angest* as we saw in the analysis of 'The Pearls') not belonging to either gender (which fits the personality of Grev Serafina at Angelshorn).[11] All of their names are, however, masculine (for example Michael, Gabriel and Sataniel) and they are for the most part depicted in paintings and sculpture as male human beings. In iconoclastic Islam, we find no depictions of angels, but they too all have male names. There are many references in 'The Diver' to the Koran and its notion of angels, but one of them seems of particular interest, which is that it is the angels that guard hellfire (Malik being one of them). When Saufe discovers that it is Mirza Aghai, who has sent Thusmu (who he first believed to be an angel) and that he is going to lose his beloved, he concludes 'God has appointed none but angels to preside over hell-fire' (Dinesen 1958: 9)[12] and in the last part of the story concludes: 'a young woman will make her lover taste the pain of burning' (Dinesen 1958: 17)[13]. Here we find the male angel of Islam substituted with a beautiful female dancer of flesh and blood as the guard of hellfire, which in this case is *unhappy love as the earthly and materialistic version of Islam and Christianity's lofty, theoretical notions of Hell*. We also detect the authorial irony when Saufe states that: 'And you cannot expect a dancing-girl to be an angel' (Dinesen 1958: 9)[14] and Thusmu did, subsequently, marry a rich merchant just a year after her love affair with Saufe ended. Saufe, on the other hand, never had a relationship with a woman again but instead became a hermit and pearl diver.

Subverting the Male Gaze of Kierkegaard's Characters

There is also no question that Dinesen was annoyed with the one-sided depiction of women in Kierkegaard's works. Aside from two short letters from Cordelia in the foreword to 'Forførerens Dagbog' (Kierkegaard 1843a) all female characters are described and focalized through male characters and have otherwise no names. The notion of women as innocent, spiritually underdeveloped creatures with no knowledge about men that most of Kierkegaard's male characters from his aesthetic-pseudonymous authorship seem to propagate, is ironically described in this passage from 'Copenhagen Season' from *Last Tales*:

> With the conquest of town by country, femininity, the world of woman, rose like a tide and inundated Copenhagen. Normally the spiritual atmosphere of the city was masculine, and had been so for fifty years. The capital of Denmark held the one university of the country and the primary See of its Church, and around these venerable institutions learned and brilliant philosophers, divines and aesthetes gathered, to solve profound problems and hold sparkling discussions. Less than twenty years before the circle had had the opportunity of sharpening its wit on the edge of the wit of Magister Soren [sic] Kirkegaard [sic]; adversaries of his were still arguing. From the time when the country had got its free constitution, Parliament had resided in Copenhagen. The upholding of intellectual values fell to Adam's sons. Eve was to be found at her lace pillow or her household accounts or watering the flowerpots in her windows. She was the pure and demure guardian angel of the hearth; her mental color was white and her principal virtues more passive than active — innocence and patience and total ignorance of those demons of doubt and ambition which were supposed to harass the heart of her husband. (Dinesen 1957: 249)[15]

Dinesen proves this notion wrong with her female seducers Annelise and Ehrengard, who, on the contrary, are very knowledgeable about men and have no problems posing nude and engaging in sexual activity, contrary to their male counterparts The Councilor and Cazotte, who can be seen as ironic parodies of Kierkegaard's male seducer-aesthetes Johannes Forføreren and Constantin Constantius. Kierkegaard's 'unge Menneske' is also subjected to parodic inversions in both 'Carnival' and 'The Poet' as well as in 'The Dreamers'. Dinesen turns A's notion of the male seducer Don Juan from Mozart's opera upside down, so he becomes a comical, spiritless 'Pralhans' [braggart]. In his place she instead puts the real embodiment of music:

the stunningly talented and beautiful prima donna Pellegrina Leoni, who, on the other hand, as a naïve female seducer, is perceived as a tragic figure. Already in her first work *Sandhedens Hævn* we find the Pagan female witch Amiane in the role as the omnipotent Christian God and Abraham from Kierkegaard's *Frygt og Bæven*, the founder of faith, as a simple murderer and villain. In 'The Pearls' Christian ethics are subverted and deemed demonic, which we find embodied in the female character Jensine, whereas the male character Alexander, who gambles and owes money, is the innocent ideal of a human being before the fall, which is a subversion of the ideas propagated by Vigilius Haufniensis in *Begrebet Angest*. In 'The Deluge at Norderney' Dinesen inverts Judge William's claim: 'Det Opbyggelige, der ligger i den Tanke, at mod Gud have vi altid Uret' (Kierkegaard 1843b: 326) [The Upbuilding That Lies in the Thought in Relation to God We Are Always in the Wrong] (Kierkegaard 1987b: 339) and places 'Kvinderne' [women] in the position of 'Gud' [God] as the real, earthly and materialistic center that the world evolves around and life is created from (literally, one could say).

Notes to Chapter 13

1. Note the irony of the phallic name of the castle 'Angelshorn' (Dinesen 1935: 180) as a sort of homosexual/misogynist fortress for the arts and sciences. In 'Ehrengard', on the other hand, Schloss Rosenbad is described as a 'Venusberg', which is the frame of a passionate and audacious love affair between Ludmilla and Prince Lothar that has resulted in a child consummated three months before their official marriage.
2. Dinesen 1935: 178
3. Dinesen 1935: 179–80.
4. Dinesen 1935: 181.
5. Her name alludes to Kalypso, the nymph from Greek mythology, who lived on the island of Ogygia where she enchanted and attracted the sailors with her irresistible singing, most famously described in Homer's *Odyssey* where she lures Odysseus to her island and detains him for several years.
6. Dinesen 1935: 179.
7. Notice how Dinesen in this passage again ascribes this notion to the biographical Kierkegaard even though it is an opinion put forward by the character narrator Johannes Forføreren in 'Forførerens Dagbog' (Kierkegaard 1843a: 368).
8. Ironically hinted at too in 'Syndfloden over Norderney' ('The Deluge at Norderney'): 'Men de havde det nemmere, De higede blot efter at forsvinde, men hun, hun skulde skabe et Menneske, sig selv, og er det ikke meget forlangt af en ung Pige, at hun skal gøre det helt paa egen Haand?' (Dinesen 1935: 180) [But your task was easier. You wanted only to disappear, while she had to create herself] (Dinesen 1934: 46). Note how the last part about 'Menneske' and 'ung pige' has been added by Dinesen in the Danish version to strengthen the connection to Kierkegaard's use of 'Menneske'.
9. This is a materialistic subversion of Islam's notion of Heaven as being inhabited by fifteen-year-old female virgins.
10. Blixen 1958: 14.
11. For example in Matthew 22:30: 'For in the resurrection they neither marry, nor are given in marriage, but are as the angels of God in heaven' (King James version).
12. Blixen 1958: 16.
13. Blixen 1958: 26.
14. Blixen 1958: 16.
15. Blixen 1957: 220.

PART V

❖

Repetition

CHAPTER 14

❖

The Demonic Bachelor-Aesthete: 'The Poet' and *Gjentagelsen*

In this chapter, I will show how Dinesen in 'The Poet' develops the plot and the characters from *Gjentagelsen* in new directions, with the unhappy love triangle from *Gjentagelsen* as the starting point. The tale is also inspired by Victor Eremita's statement in *Stadier paa Livets Vei* that a man did not become a poet because of the woman he got, but because of the woman he did not get.

The tale is also a good example of Dinesen's irony toward the elderly Bachelor-Aesthete that we find as a recurring character in both Kierkegaard's and Dinesen's productions. In 'The Poet' Dinesen makes this character, the Councillor, even more radical and demonic than Constantin Constantius from *Gjentagelsen*, but unlike Kierkegaard's bachelor aesthetes who get away with their manipulations and machinations, Dinesen lets nemesis strike when she, in the final scene, sends the Councillor straight to hell. In the tale Dinesen also reverses the levels of fiction and reality when the Councillor tries to carry out in real life what a poet only does in fiction. The title thus refers to a man who is not a poet in terms of writing, but in terms of his attempts to stage life, to create poetry in the flesh by scrupulously manipulating the people around him.

It is, however, important to state that both Kierkegaard and Dinesen see right through this archetypal character. In Kierkegaard's works he is a haunted elderly bachelor caught in the demonic (Constantin Constantius, Victor Eremita, and The Fashion Designer) who is unable to enter actuality through the ethical or to 'make a religious movement' (Kierkegaard 1983a: 129). In Dinesen's version, he is a powerful eunuch-like elderly bachelor (Rosendaal, the Councillor, Prince Potenziani, Mr. Clay, and Cazotte) who in various ways tries to assert omnipotence in life by manipulating the people who are close to him and whose pain and annihilation he secretly and sadistically enjoys. Physically he is an impotent man, lonely, desperate — and in the eyes of Dinesen — comical.

The tale also deals with the concept of repetition and agrees with the young man in *Gjentagelsen* that repetition is only possible in spirit — and, according to Dinesen, in literature.

The Chinese Puzzle

On the surface 'The Poet' — like 'Ehrengard' — initially presents itself as a narrative concerned with Goethe, since in the tale we primarily find allusions to Johann Wolfgang Goethe, whom the Councilor[1] in the story-world of the tale has met in Weimar. But this is a strategy that we saw Dinesen repeat twenty-eight years later in the novella 'Ehrengard' where we also found the main character Johann W. Cazotte to be modeled on Johann Wolfgang Goethe, and the tale to have numerous direct allusions to Goethe's works, despite the fact that Kierkegaard's 'Forførerens Dagbog' is actually the main literary target. The title 'Forførerens Dagbog' or the name Kierkegaard are never mentioned directly in 'Ehrengard', thus the connections are only established through allusions to passages in 'Forførerens Dagbog' and through character- and plot reversal and name similarity (Johann/Johannes) (Langbaum 1964, Bunch 2013b, et al.).

In this chapter I will argue that Dinesen in 'The Poet' uses the same allusive strategy and that we, behind the surface allusions to Goethe, find a counter-story to Kierkegaard's *Gjentagelsen* that deals with one of Kierkegaard's reoccurring characters 'the demonic bachelor-aesthete' (Constantin Constantius), the idea of how to become a poet and the notion of repetition. Thus, in both 'The Poet' and in 'Ehrengard', Dinesen uses her own version of the Chinese puzzle composition system that Victor Eremita describes in the foreword to *Enten — Eller. Første Deel* as the main composition structure of 'Forførerens Dagbog': 'idet den ene Forfatter kommer til at ligge inden i den anden som Æsker i et chinesisk Æskespil' (Kierkegaard 1843a: 16) [since one author becomes enclosed within the other like the boxes of a Chinese puzzle] (Kierkegaard 1987a: 20). Thus, when we open the second box in Dinesen's Chinese puzzle, behind Goethe, we find Kierkegaard.

Firstly, I will show how Dinesen in 'The Poet' unfolds ideas coined, but never carried out, by the first person narrator Constantin Constantius in *Gjentagelsen*, secondly I will show how Dinesen reverses the plot from *Gjentagelsen* and develops the characters in new ways, and thirdly how she, on a meta-level, deals with the notions of poetry and repetition from 'in vino veritas' and *Gjentagelsen* in 'The Poet'.

Structure and Composition: *Gjentagelsen* and 'The Poet'

In a passage in *Gjentagelsen* Constantin Constantius expresses the following about 'det unge Menneske' [the young man] and the nature of his own narrative:

> Hvis jeg udførligt vilde forfølge Stemningerne i det unge Menneske, saaledes som jeg lærte dem at kjende, endsige hvis jeg paa Digterviis vilde tage en Mængde uvedkommende Ting med: Dagligstuer og Gangklæder, skjønne Egne, Paarørende og Venner, saa kunde denne Historie blive en alenlang Novelle. Det gider jeg imidlertid ikke. (Kierkegaard 1843c: 18)

> [If I were to elaborate on the young man's moods as I learned to know them, to say nothing of anecdotally including a host of irrelevant things — living rooms and wearing apparel, lovely localities, relatives and friends — this

narrative could become an interminable story. That, however, I do not want.]
(Kierkegaard 1983a: 104)

Dinesen's response to Constantin not caring about developing his narrative is to do
the opposite. In the Danish version of 'The Poet' ('Digteren') she closely follows
the moods of 'det unge Menneske' [the young man] as August von Schimmelmann
in the tale calls the melancholy young poet Anders Kube (Dinesen 1935: 364).[2]
Dinesen does so by developing the passage in *Gjentagelsen* and 'paa Digterviis' (as a
poet, lost in the English translation) create a narrative that include 'uvedkommende
ting' [irrelevant things] and where 'Dagligstuer' [living rooms], 'Gangklæder'
[wearing apparel], 'skjønne Egne' [lovely localities], 'Paarørende' [relatives] and
'Venner' [friends] are indeed elaborately depicted. Even the title of the main
character, the Councilor, and his behaviour in Hirschholm seems to allude to a
passage in *Gjentagelsen*:

> Den, der vil Gjentagelsen, han er modnet i Alvor. Dette er mit Separat-Votum,
> der tillige mener, at det ingenlunde er Livets Alvor, at sidde i sin Sopha
> og stange Tænder — og være Noget f. Ex Justitsraad; eller at gaae adstadig
> gjennem Gaderne — og være Noget, f. Ex Velærværdighed; ligesaalidet som
> det er Livets Alvor at være kongelig Beridder. Alt Sligt er mine Øjne kun Spøg,
> og som stundom daarlig nok. (Kierkegaard 1843c: 11)

> [The person who wills repetition is mature in earnestness. This is my private
> opinion, and this also means that it is not the earnestness of life to sit on the
> sofa and grind one's teeth — and to be somebody, for example a councilor —
> or to walk the streets sedately — and to be somebody, His Reverence — any
> more than it is the earnestness of life to be a riding master. In my opinion, all
> such things are but jests, and sometimes rather poor ones at that.] (Kierkegaard
> 1983a: 100)

The protagonist in 'The Poet', the Councilor, is in Dinesen's Danish version
'Digteren' called Justitsraad Mathiesen,[3] who is 'Noget' [someone] and considered
a 'Velærværdighed' [His Reverence] but who also turns out to behave in the
completely opposite way of what we would normally expect from a man with such
a title, which is a humorous reversal of the character Constantin contemplates in
the above passage. Another significant starting point for Dinesen's plot development
in 'The Poet' is the idea that Constantin Constantius evolves in *Gjentagelsen*, when
he is thinking about how to solve the young man's desperate situation: 'Dersom
jeg ikke selv var saa gammel, skulde jeg gjøre mig en Fornøielse af at tage hende,
alene for at hjælpe Mennesket' (Kierkegaard 1843c: 83) [If I myself were not so old,
I would give myself the pleasure of taking her simply to help the man] (Kierkegaard
1983a: 149). Constantin contemplates this bold move as a means to put an end to
the young man's ethical scruples and melancholy, which stem from the fact that he
is betrothed to a girl he loves but at the same time feels psychologically incapable
of marrying her, since she has ignited in him an unstoppable and prolific poetic
creativity. Constantin never acts upon this audacious idea in *Gjentagelsen* and the
girl eventually marries another man after the young man has fled to Sweden.
It is, however, this unrealized love triangle, pregnant with piquant possibilities

that Dinesen stages in 'The Poet', but with the opposite outcome in mind: the Councilor's goal is *to create an unhappy love, not to solve one*, so he can sustain and feed the poetic creativity of his young man; the poet to be Anders Kube. During a morning walk in the woods, the Councilor at first evolves the idea of marrying Anders off to the newly arrived young widow Fransine, but when he recalls her lightness and grace, he fears that the idea is no good — that Anders might instead give up poetry and decide to take on the world with Fransine and move from Hirschholm. Suddenly, in a moment of epiphany, he discovers that he in fact has to do the opposite and a devilish plan emerges:

> His thoughts went a little further while the sun rose up higher. An unhappy love is an inspiring feeling. It has created the greatest works of history. A hopeless passion for his benefactor's wife might make a young poet immortal; it was a dramatic thing to have in the house. The two young people would remain loyal to him, however much they suffer. (Dinesen 1934: 377)

> [Hans Tanker steg, alt som Solen steg højere paa Himlen. Ulykkelig Kærlighed er en *mægtig beaandende Følelse*, den har før inspireret unge Mænd til Historiens største *Digterværker*. En haabløs Lidenskab for hans Velynders letfodede Hustru kunde meget vel komme til at udødeliggøre den unge Digter. *Det kunde ogsaa blive et stort Drama at iagttage og følge med i*. De to Unge vilde bevare deres Troskab imod ham, hvor gruligt de end blev pint.] (Dinesen 1935: 355–56)[4]

By marrying Fransine, with whom Anders is in love, the Councilor's plan is to make Anders a great poet, since his unhappy and unfulfilled love will be transformed into sublime poetic creativity as the above passage describes,[5] while the Councilor at the same time will be able to keep both of them in Hirschholm. Another passage from 'in vino veritas' articulated by Victor Eremita also informs this passage in 'The Poet'. Here Eremita states that a man only becomes a poet because of the girl he did *not* get:

> Der er mangen Mand bleven Geni ved en Pige, mangen Mand bleven Helt ved en Pige, mangen Mand bleven Digter ved en Pige, mangen Mand bleven Helgen ved en Pige; — men han blev ikke Geni ved den Pige, han fik; thi med hende blev han kun Etatsraad; han blev ikke Helt ved den Pige, han fik, thi ved hende blev han kun General; han blev ikke Digter ved den Pige, han fik, thi ved hende blev han kun Fader; han blev ikke Helgen ved den Pige, han fik, thi han fik slet ingen og vilde kun have en eneste, som han ikke fik, ligesom Enhver af de Andre blev Geni, blev Helt, blev Digter ved den Piges Hjælp, de ikke fik. (Kierkegaard 1845: 60)

> [Many a man became a genius because of a girl, many a man became a hero because of a girl, many a man became a poet because of a girl, many a man became a saint because of a girl — but he did not become a genius because of the girl he got, for with her he became only a cabinet official; he did not become a hero because of the girl he got, for because of her he became only a general; he did not become a poet because of the girl he got, for because of her he became only a father; he did not become a saint because of the girl he got, for he got none at all and wanted only to have the one and only whom he did not get, just as each of the others became a genius, a hero, a poet with the aid of the girl he did not get.] (Kierkegaard 1988: 50)

Young Peter Mathiesen did not become a poet, but instead married Madam Mathiesen and became Councilor Mathiesen of the town of Hirschholm (even though he never loved her and later did away with her). Now he wants to make a poet out of Anders instead, so that he can write poetry by proxy and at the same time achieve immortality as his Maecenas.

In the following I will show how Anders' love for Fransine, his melancholy, outburst of poetic creativity and the disintegrating friendship with the Councilor, closely follow the development of the young man in *Gjentagelsen* up until the part where the Councilor decides to marry Fransine. Here 'The Poet' develops in new directions in order to realize other potentials in the characters from *Gjentagelsen* and create a different outcome of the love triangle. In the final scene Dinesen also suggests a different interpretation of the psychology of a poet, which is a reversal of Constantin's conclusion in the closing pages of *Gjentagelsen*.

The Melancholy Young Man: 'Det unge Menneske' and Anders Kube

As previously mentioned, Dinesen made the allusion to Constantin Constantius' character 'det unge Menneske' [the young man] from *Gjentagelsen* more obvious in her Danish version by calling Anders Kube 'det unge Menneske' in this passage, where August von Schimmelmann evaluates his future prospects of becoming a successful poet:

> Count Augustus praised the beauty of the poem and thought the beauty of the little fairy queen charmingly put into words. *The boy*, he thought, had in him a very strong streak of primitive sensuality which would have to be watched if the tastefulness of his production were not to suffer. (Dinesen 1934: 387)[6]

> [Grev Augustus roste Digtets Skønhed og mente, at den unge Digter havde fundet indsmigrende Ord i sin Skildring af den lille Elledronnings Skønhed. Han tænkte ved sig selv, at det unge Menneske i sin Natur havde et stærkt Drag af Sanselighed, hvormed der burde holdes Øje, hvis ikke den sikre Smag i hans Produktion skulde lide derunder.] (Dinesen 1935: 364–65)

Like the young man in *Gjentagelsen*: 'Han havde allerede i nogen Tid været forelsket, men skjult det endog for mig' (Kierkegaard 1843c: 12) [He had been in love for some time now, concealing it even from me] (Kierkegaard 1983a: 100), Anders also hides his newfound love from the Councilor:

> All through the service the Councilor's mind was playing about with his recent impression. It had come to him at a seasonable moment, for he had lately been uneasy about his poet. This young slave of his had been singularly absent-minded, and even absent bodily from one or two of their Saturday suppers. There was in his whole manner an unconscious restlessness, and underneath it the sign of a melancholy about which the Councilor was anxious, for he knew well that he could find no remedy for it. (Dinesen 1934: 370)

What the Councilor does not yet realize is that Anders has discovered Fransine at 'La Liberté', watched her nightly dance-sessions, and has fallen in love with her. Contrary to the young man, who confides his love to Constantin, Anders keeps his love for Fransine a secret all through the tale, even though the Councilor figures it out and starts to exploit it. Anders's melancholy condition upon falling in love is however similar to the one that strikes 'det unge Menneske' in *Gjentagelsen*: 'Store Gud! Tænkte jeg, en saadan Melancholi er endnu aldrig forekommen i min Praxis. At han var melancholsk vidste jeg nok, men at Forelskelse kunde virke saaledes paa ham!' (Kierkegaard 1843c: 13) [Good God, I thought, never in my practice had I seen such melancholy as this. That he was melancholy, I knew very well — but that falling in love could affect him in this way!] (Kierkegaard 1983a: 102). In both young men, their melancholy stems from the unhappy love affair, but the reasons are very different: the young man is melancholy because he is caught in the paradox that he is able to get the girl he loves, but feels psychologically incapable of marrying her. Anders, on the contrary, is melancholy because he is in love with a girl he in no possible way is able to get. At the same time, the unrealized love affair makes both of the young men extremely creative poetically. Constantin notes about the young man: 'En digterisk Productivitet vaagnede i ham efter en Maalestok, som jeg aldrig havde troet mulig' (Kierkegaard 1843c: 15) [A poetic creativity awakened in him on a scale I had never believed possible] (Kierkegaard 1983a: 103) and Anders experiences a similar outburst of poetic creativity when he creates several significant long poems during the months he is in love with Fransine (Dinesen 1935: 364, 374).

The big difference between the young man in *Gjentagelsen* and Anders is that the young man could very well have married the girl he was in love with. His love was requited and nothing stood between them, except for the young man's own psychological indisposition and ethical scruples. Anders finds himself in the complete opposite situation: he can't have Fransine since she is betrothed to the Councilor, and this is the material from which tragedies are created (*Romeo and Juliet*: the young lovers who can't have each other). Instead of fleeing from the unhappy love affair, as the young man eventually does in *Gjentagelsen*, Anders decides to stay. Contrary to the young man who hopes to receive his former life back free from guilt towards the young girl, Anders has instead made up his mind to take it on the very same day that Fransine is to marry the Councilor. When he can't have Fransine he prefers to die instead of returning to his former life, or go on living as a poet in the sphere of ideas, which in the end becomes the fate of the young man in *Gjentagelsen*. In relation to woman this makes Anders the tragic hero in Dinesen's tale.

Repetition of the Archetypal Mentor-Protégé Relationship

In *Gjentagelsen* there are passages where Constantin Constantius's descriptions of his relationship with 'det unge Menneske' resemble a description of a love relationship. At the same time, Constantin does everything he can to manipulate 'det unge Menneske' and stir up his melancholy for the sake of his own pleasure and enjoyment:

> Det er omtrent 1 Aar siden, at jeg ret for Alvor blev opmærksom paa et ungt Menneske, hvem jeg tilforn allerede oftere havde berørt, fordi hans skjønne

Udvortes, det sjælfulde Udtryk i hans Øie næsten fristede mig [...] Ved Hjelp af disse skjødesløse, tilnærmende Conditor-Inclinationer havde jeg allerede draget ham til mig, og lært ham i mig at see en Fortrolig, hvis Tale paa mange Maader fristede det Melancholske i ham frem under Brydningens Form, idet jeg ligesom en Farinelli lokkede den sindssvage Konge ud af hans mørke Gjemme.[7] (Kierkegaard 1843c: 11)

[About a year ago, I became very much aware of a young man (with whom I had already often been in contact), because his handsome appearance, the soulful expression of his eyes, had an almost alluring effect upon me [...] Through casual coffee-shop associations, I had already attracted him to me and taught him to regard me as a confidant whose conversation in many ways lured forth his melancholy in refracted form, since I, like a Farinelli, enticed the deranged king out of his dark hiding place.] (Kierkegaard 1983a: 100)

When the two of them are waiting in Constantin's home for a carriage that will take them north of Copenhagen to explore the forests, Constantin can't help glancing at 'det unge Menneske' with a special affection: 'Jeg kunde ikke lade være af og til at skotte næsten forelsket til ham; thi en saadan Yngling er nok saa forførerisk at see paa som en ung Pige' (Kierkegaard 1843c: 13) [I could not resist stealing an almost enamored glance at him now and then, for a young man like that is just as enchanting to the eye as a young girl] (Kierkegaard 1983a: 101). But Constantin's role as a father figure, his manipulation and cynicism, also become a burden for 'det unge Menneske', who wishes he could finally show him off: 'Gid jeg stod hos Dem, gid jeg med mit sidste Nei kunde løsrive mig fra Dem, som Don Juan fra Commandanten' (Kierkegaard 1843c: 62) [Would that I stood beside you, that I could tear myself from you with the last 'no' as Don Giovanni did from the Commandatore] (Kierkegaard 1983a: 135). In a couple of crucial passages in 'The Poet' we also get to learn that the Councilor's relationship to Anders has the same affectionate nature as Constantin's:

Looking then, in the mild, glowing evening light, across the tea table at the two young people who were both so precious to him — although their order might have surprised them — the Councilor felt happy and in harmony with the universe. (Dinesen 1934: 395)[8]

When Anders finally discovers how the Councilor has manipulated him and Fransine, he shoots him as a last violent 'no' to 'the Commandatore' that the young man in *Gjentagelsen* does not have the courage to give Constantin: 'Anders half lifted his gun, and without taking aim fired it off straight into the body of the old man' (Dinesen 1934: 412)[9] and the deadly injured Councilor realizes: 'He was going to die. The young man, whom he loved, had meant him to die' (Dinesen 1934: 413).[10] Again we find this scene to be the staging of a fantasy Constantin Constantius has in *Gjentagelsen*, when he fantasizes about how the young man killing him would prove the sincerity of his love for the girl:

Dog maaskee forstaar jeg ham ikke ganske, maaskee skjuler han Noget, maaskee elsker han dog i Sandhed. Saa bliver vel Enden paa Historien, at han engang slaaer mig ihjel for at betroe mig det Allerhelligste. Man seer, at det at være Iagttager er en farefuld Stilling. (Kierkegaard 1843c: 56)

> [But perhaps I do not fully understand him, perhaps he is hiding something. Maybe he does in truth love after all. Then it will probably all end with his murdering me in order to confide to me the holiest of the holy. It is obvious that being an observer is a dangerous position.] (Kierkegaard 1983a: 131)

Being an observer, as Councilor Mathiesen is in the temple in the final scene, can indeed be a dangerous position; we see the irony here. But importantly, Anders, when murdering the Councilor, also proves his love, when he confides to him 'the holiest of holy': his love for Fransine. This is also how Fransine perceives it, according to the narrator, when she figures out that Anders has shot the Councilor: 'At last the girl understood. Her lover had shot this old man [...] After she had gone from him, Anders had proved that he loved her. And only she and the old man knew' (Dinesen 1934: 418–19).[11] With this violent action Anders does two things the young man in *Gjentagelsen* is not able to do in relation to Constantin and the young girl: he tells the Councilor no and so proves his love for Fransine.[12] Fransine requites it by finishing off the Councilor, which means that she will be swinging on the gallows with Anders and, thus, finally be united with him in death: 'Let Anders have done what he liked, he and she belonged to one another, were one' (Dinesen 1934: 418–19).[13]

Eunuchs Living by Proxy

As I mentioned in the previous section, Constantin compares himself to one of the most famous eunuchs in world history, the castrate singer Farinelli, when he describes his relation to the young man: 'idet jeg ligesom en Farinelli lokkede den sindssvage Konge ud af hans mørke Gjemme' (Kierkegaard 1843c: 11) [since I, like a Farinelli, enticed the deranged king out of his dark hiding place] (Kierkegaard 1983a: 100). We find a similar comparison to a eunuch in 'The Poet' when the Councilor's relationship to Anders is compared by the narrator to that of a Kislar Aga: 'At any rate its effect was that the old man kept an untiring eye on the youth, like a sort of unselfish lover, like a mighty and dignified Kislar Aga[14] toward a budding beauty of the seraglio for whom he has planned great things' (Dinesen 1934: 364).[15] Constantin describes his relation to women in this way:

> Hvad det andet Kjøn angaaer, har jeg min egen Mening, eller rettere, jeg har slet ingen, da jeg kun saare sjelden har seet en Pige, hvis Liv lod sig opfatte i en Kategori. Hun mangler som oftest den Consequents, der er fornøden for at man skal beundre eller foragte et Menneske. En Qvinde er først bedragen af sig selv, før hun bedrager en Anden, og derfor har man slet ingen Maalestok. (Kierkegaard 1843c: 85)[16]

> [As far as the other sex is concerned, I have my own opinion, or, more correctly, I have none at all, for I have rarely seen a girl whose life could be comprehended in a category. She usually lacks the consistency required for admiring or scorning a person. Before a woman deceives another, she first deceives herself, and therefore there is no criterion at all.] (Kierkegaard 1983a: 150)

Neither Constantin Constantius nor the Councilor has any physical interest in women, but only enjoys them when observing or manipulating them, making them eunuchs in relation to women, albeit not technically. The scene where the Councilor during his nightly carriage trip back to Hirschholm spies on Fransine in awe when she dances at La Liberté, is similar to the pleasure and exhilaration Constantin gets from spying on the young girl in the early morning after one of his many nightly carriage-trips due to his insomnia (Kierkegaard 1843c: 42). Constantin is also excited when he watches the young girl at the Königsberg Theater and gets pleasure out of fantasizing about her, but his worst nightmare would be if she found out about it: 'Havde hun blot anet min stumme halvforelskte Glæde, da var Alt fordærvet og ikke til at erstatte, ikke ved hele hendes Kjærlighed' (Kierkegaard 1843c: 42) [If she had even suspected my mute, half-infatuated delight, everything would have been spoiled beyond repair, even with all her love] (Kierkegaard 1983a: 120) and he could never dream of approaching or interact with her. The young man describes Constantin's personality like this:

> er det ikke en Art Sindssvaghed, i den Grad at have underlagt enhver liden-skab, enhver Hjertets Rørelse, enhver Stemning under Reflexionens kolde Regimente. Er det ikke Sindssvaghed saaledes at være normal, blot Idee, ikke Menneske, ikke som vi Andre. (Kierkegaard 1843c: 59)

> [Is it not, in fact, a kind of mental disorder to have subjugated to such a degree every passion, every emotion, every mood under the cold regimentation of reflection! Is it not mental disorder to be normal in this way — pure idea, not a human being like the rest of us.] (Kierkegaard 1983a: 132)

The Councilor and Constantin are all head and reflection and that is the reason why they are neither able to write poetry, nor to love a woman. It also explains why they are so fond of their young men and need them in their lives: Constantin's relationship to the young man is an attempt to experience love and affection by proxy (since Constantin himself is unable to love in the way we normally understand the word) just as the Councilor has made his astute set-up in Hirschholm in order to use Anders for making love to his young bride and write poetry by proxy:

> He discussed it much with the poet, and even advised him upon it, so that not a few of the Councilor's own ideas and reflections were, in one way or another, echoed within the epos, and he was, during these summer months, in a way making love, and writing poetry, to his bride by proxy — a piquant situation, which would last until his wedding day. (Dinesen 1934: 399)[17]

Who is 'The Poet'?

It is thought-provoking that the main character in 'The Poet' is in fact not the poet in the story, which is, as we know, the young man Anders. Nevertheless, the Councilor is labeled 'Poet' by Fransine in the dramatic final scene, right before she gives him his deathblow: '"You!" she cried at him. "You poet!"' (Dinesen 1934: 420).[18] The explanation for this paradox is that the Councilor belongs to a very special type of poets, who do not produce, but instead *practice* poetry. Instead of writing poetry he turns life into poetry through diabolic manipulation, since his biggest enjoyment in life is the exhilaration and pleasure he feels when he can be the spectator of an unhappy love story. He is a collector of fine 'fleurs du mal'[19] as erotic and piquant (or evil) situations he creates in life that he can later recollect with enjoyment. This passage sums up this special type of behavior and how it relates to the overall flower metaphor:

> The Councilor walked on, pleased. He thought of Count Schimmelmann's quotation: 'He is a fool who knows not the half to be more than the whole.' This long-forgotten incident [his boyhood love, Nanna] was a little flower in his life, in the garland of his life, a field flower, a wild forget-me-not. There were not a few flowers, violets, pansies, in his life. Would this night put a rose into the garland? (Dinesen 1934: 408)[20]

These 'flowers' are erotic situations with women that the Councilor infuses with dread and destruction: he terrorizes his mentally unstable wife using a pansy so that she falls back into insanity and eventually dies; and the rose he hopes to put in his garland tonight is Fransine showing herself naked to the devastated Anders Kube in the small temple. When the Councilor thinks about how to repeat the situation from Karl Gutzkow's novel *Wally, die Zweiflerin* (1835) (*Wally, Tvivlersken*) where Sigune shows herself naked to her beloved Cæsar for the first — and last — time before marrying the ambassador of Sardinia (with Anders and Fransine cast in the roles of Wally and Cæsar), his conception of the idea is described like this: 'Let the critics say that such things do not happen; that does not really matter, for a new variety of flower has been forced in the frame of imagination' (Dinesen 1934: 401) [Lad kun Kritikerne sige, at den Slags Ting ikke sker i Verden. Det har ikke noget at sige, en ny Blomsterart er i alle Tilfælde drevet frem i Fantasiens Mistbænk] (Dinesen 1935: 377). Note how Dinesen here has sharpened the fleurs du mal metaphor by using the word 'Mistbænk' [hotbed] in the Danish version.

In that manner, the Councilor is very similar to Johannes in 'Forførerens Dagbog' (Kierkegaard 1843a), who is also living poetically, who through his intellectual and manipulative powers creates poetic situations in life (with a clear destructive element too; the seduction of Cordelia), but who himself is not a poet. The description of Gutzkow's novel in Dinesen's Danish version 'Digteren' (Dinesen 1935: 376–77) is an almost a word for word reproduction of Georg Brandes' description of the novel that we find in *Hovedstrømninger. Det unge Tyskland* (Brandes 1895: 336–37), which was given to Dinesen by Knud Dahl as a Christmas present in 1925 (see Chapter 2).

In *Gjentagelsen* we seem to encounter a similar paradox with regard to who is in fact the poet in the narrative — just the other way around. Towards the end of the narrative Constantin writes that the young man he has created is a poet, but that he himself is not:

> Det unge Menneske, som jeg har ladet blive til, han er Digter. Mere kan jeg ikke gjøre; thi jeg kan i det Højeste komme saavidt, at jeg kan tænke mig en Digter og ved min Tænken frembringe ham, selv kan jeg ikke blive Digter, som ogsaa min Interesse ligger paa et andet Sted. Min opgave har beskæftiget mig reent æsthetisk og psychologisk. (Kierkegaard 1843c: 94)

> [The young man I have brought into being is a poet. I can do no more, for the most I can do is to imagine a poet and to produce him by my thought. I myself

cannot become a poet, and in any case my interest lies elsewhere. My task has engaged me purely esthetically and psychologically.] (Kierkegaard 1983a: 155)

It is a paradox that the author of a narrative about a young man and his unhappy love affair denies that he himself is a 'Poet', but claims that only his imaginative (read: poetic) creation is. Constantin backs this claim by summing up certain differences in their personalities; the young man is emotional, bordering the religious, whereas Constantin is pure intellect and unable to make a religious movement, which in his own eyes disqualifies him as a poet. By labeling the Councilor 'The Poet' Dinesen seems to suggest the opposite of Constantin. In order to be a poet one needs the intellectual and manipulative skills and the ability to dedicate oneself completely to an idea, cost it what it may. This also includes the motto: 'He is a fool who knows not the half to be more than the whole' (August von Schimmelmann in Dinesen 1934: 408). These are qualities that both Constantin and the Councilor have, but what the young man and Anders lack. The reversal of this set-up in *Gjentagelsen* is carried out in this way: Constantin is a poet who has written a narrative in which he denies being a poet and instead claims his imaginative character to be one, whereas the Councilor, who is not a poet, tries to create a poet in real life (Anders) but in the end is himself labeled a poet! (by the author: Dinesen). In the closing lines in *Gjentagelsen* Constantin furthermore claims: 'Min kjære Læser! Du vil nu forstaae, at Interessen dreier sig om det unge Menneske, medens jeg er en forsvindende Person' (Kierkegaard 1843c: 96) [My dear reader, you will now understand that the interest focuses on the young man, whereas I am a vanishing person] (Kierkegaard 1983a: 157). Dinesen seems to see it differently. She rightly sees that Constantin is the central figure in *Gjentagelsen* and in 'The Poet' she creates a similar type (albeit way more radical — like the demonic bachelorette-aesthete Annelise in 'Carnival') and lets him play the main role in a narrative, but she does it by letting her main character make the exact opposite movement of Constantin. In 'The Poet', Dinesen creates a story in which everything a poet does only in spirit and in fiction (planning the plot, manipulate the characters and the events, living by proxy through the characters and getting pleasure out of the omnipotent position)[21] is carried out by the Councilor in the flesh, in actuality. Conversely, Constantin arranges the narrative so we believe the events have happened in real life, but in the end tells us that it has only been a sort of spiritual exercise; that his narrative is just fiction. This way of reversing the spiritual and the actual Dinesen repeated twenty-eight years later, when she made the opposite movement as a response 'Forførerens Dagbog': what Johannes carries out in the flesh in 'Forførerens Dagbog', when he seduces Cordelia physically, she lets Cazotte (try to) carry out in spirit only in 'Ehrengard', when he sets out to seduce Ehrengard avoiding any physical touch whatsoever.

Kierkegaard and Dinesen: The Demonic Bachelor-Aesthete

In the closing lines of his essay *Karen Blixen og marionetterne* [Karen Blixen and the Marionettes] from 1952, Aage Henriksen establishes the first substantial connection between Søren Kierkegaard and Dinesen.[22] Henriksen finishes his essay with this bold, yet cryptic, statement:

> og med det sidste ord føre tanken hen på Søren Kierkegaard, som skrev en bog, der hedder *Gjentagelsen*. I dette begreb kan Søren Kierkegaard og Karen Blixen mødes og i frygten for den dæmoniske æstetiker, men de mødes kun ved, fra denne skikkelse, at gå i modsatte retninger og følge to meget forskellige arter af fromhed. (Henriksen 1952: 32)

> [and that last word leads our thoughts to Søren Kierkegaard, who wrote a book called *Repetition*. Søren Kierkegaard and Karen Blixen converge in this idea — and in fear of the demonic aesthete — but they converge only to depart from this figure in opposite directions and to follow two very different types of piety.]

Henriksen is correct when he points out that both Kierkegaard and Dinesen are interested in the idea of repetition and the character of the demonic aesthete, but it seems to me that 'fear' is the wrong word to use here.[23] Neither Kierkegaard nor Dinesen fear the demonic aesthete; they see right through him. In Kierkegaard's work he is a haunted elderly bachelor caught in the demonic (Constantin Constantius, Victor Eremita and Modehandleren) who is unable to enter actuality through the ethical or to 'make a religious movement' (Kierkegaard 1983a: 129). In Dinesen's version, he is a powerful eunuch-like elderly bachelor (Rosendaal,[24] the Councilor, Prince Potenziani,[25] Mr. Clay and Cazotte[26]) who, in various ways, tries to assert omnipotence in life by manipulating the people who are close to him and whose pain and annihilation he secretly and sadistically enjoys. Dinesen submits these eunuch-like demonic aesthetes to the comical through nemesis; a nemesis that hits them when their omnipotence is out-powered by a source or a person they thought they could control. The comical lies in the discrepancy between their omnipotent natures and their sexual incapability, their will to power and how they, in the end, are out-powered by fate.[27] In 'The Poet' we find the Councilor subjected to the comical on his death-bed when he firmly believes to be in the safe hands of Goethe and on his way to a Weimarian Elysium, when he in fact is in the hands of Dinesen who is sending him straight to hell: 'he was thrown down in three or four great leaps from one cataract to the other. And meanwhile, from all sides, like an echo in the engulfing darkness, winding and rolling in long caverns, her last word was repeated again and again' (Dinesen 1934: 420).[28]

To conclude: the major difference between Dinesen and Kierkegaard's demonic aesthetes is that Kierkegaard's characters gets away with their manipulative behavior without nemesis striking, but that is never the case for Dinesen's demonic aesthetes, who in the end must all face nemesis and the deep irony of life. Thus, to expound Henriksen's enigmatic closing line about the different nature of Kierkegaard and Dinesen's approaches to the demonic aesthete and their different paths of piety:

Dinesen took the path of irony and humour, whereas Kierkegaard took the path of the religious.

The Concept of Repetition in *Gjentagelsen* and in 'The Poet'

Most scholars agree that Kierkegaard's *Gjentagelsen* is one of his most difficult works and as such does not offer an overall definition of the concept of repetition, but instead unfolds as a polyphonic exploration of the concept with no final result.[29] It is outside the scope of this book to explore and explain all the different notions and variations on repetition put forward in *Gjentagelsen*, but here only deal with the concept of repetition as long as it enlightens and connects Dinesen's 'The Poet' to *Gjentagelsen*.

It is, however, striking that all of Constantin's attempts to orchestrate and experience a repetition fail: he is unable to *reset* the young man and get him out of his melancholy and spleen, and when he instead tries to find repetition by taking a second trip to Berlin, he finds that things have changed and that he is unable to recreate his feelings and impressions from the first trip. He then returns to Copenhagen in disappointment, only to find that his valet, on his own accord, has rearranged his apartment in order to conduct a major cleaning, which shatters Constantin's last hope of making a repetition in homely surroundings. After these three defeats Constantin finally concludes: 'Jeg indsaae, at der ingen Gjentagelse er til, og min tidligere Betragtning af Livet havde seiret' (Kierkegaard 1843c: 45) [I perceived that there is no repetition, and my earlier conception of life was victorious] (Kierkegaard 1983a: 122). In 'The Poet' the Councilor also makes various attempts to make a repetition. He uses Anders and Fransine as guinea pigs when he tries to make a great poet out of Anders, which is an attempt to repeat the love-story of some of the greatest poets from world literature for whom an unfulfilled love-relationship ignited their genius (Dante-Beatrice, Goethe-Lotte, and Kierkegaard-Regine). The Councilor also tries to create another type of repetition when he attempts to repeat a situation from literature — the piquant meeting from Gutzkow's novel — and stage it in real life with Anders and Fransine in the roles of Wally and Cæsar. In both cases he fails when his puppets revolt, and in the end he even gets himself killed. Based on Constantin and the Councilor's practical experiences with repetition we understand that certain types of repetition pertaining to actuality do not seem possible (or at last they seem to be impossible to *stage*). This leads us to believe that repetition is only possible in spirit, which is also what the young man suggests in *Gjentagelsen* towards the end of the narrative. After having received a handful of sad and desperate letters from the young man over a period of six months, Constantin finally gets a letter, where the young man triumphantly claims that he has experienced a repetition:

> Hun er gift [...] Jeg er atter mig selv; her har jeg Gjentagelsen; jeg forstaaer Alt, og Tilværelsen forekommer mig skjønnere end nogensinde [...] Er der da ikke en Gjentagelse? Fik jeg ikke Alt dobbelt? Fik jeg ikke mig selv igjen, netop saaledes, at jeg dobbelt maatte føle Betydningen deraf? Og hvad er en Gjentagelse af jordisk Gods, der er ligegyldigt mod Aandens Bestemmelse, i

Sammenligning med en saadan Gjentagelse? *Kun Børnene fik Job ikke dobbelt, fordi et Menneskeliv ikke saaledes lader sig fordoble. Her er kun Aandens Gjentagelse mulig,* om end den end i Timeligheden aldrig bliver saa fuldkommen som i Evigheden, der er den sande Gjentagelse. (Kierkegaard 1843c: 88)

[She is married [...] I am myself again. Here I have repetition; I understand everything, and life seems more beautiful to me than ever [...] Is there, not, then a repetition? Did I not get everything double? Did I not get myself again and precisely in such a way that I might have a double sense of its meaning? Compared with such a repetition, what is a repetition of worldly possessions, which is indifferent toward the qualification of the spirit? Only his children did Job not receive double again, for a human life cannot be redoubled that way. Here only repetition of the spirit is possible, even though it is never so perfect in time as in eternity, which is the true repetition.] (Kierkegaard 1983a: 151)

According to the young man, repetition is possible, but only in spirit. The young man got himself again in the sense that he is now free from guilt towards the girl, which is a repetition of his guilt-free mental condition from before he met the girl: 'Naar Ideen kalder, da forlader jeg Alt [...] jeg svigter Ingen, jeg bedrøver Ingen ved at være den tro, min Aand bedrøves ikke ved at jeg maa bedrøve en Anden' (Kierkegaard 1843c: 88) [When the idea calls, I abandon everything [...] I defraud no one, I sadden no one by being loyal to it; my spirit is not saddened by my having to make another one sad] (Kierkegaard 1983a: 152). We find a similar situation in 'The Poet', when the Councilor repeats the situation with the pansy that made his wife lose her mind some years ago, and — after she has gotten better again — now successfully manages to bring her back to her former state of insanity. This is a negative reversal of the young man's happy experience with 'Aandens Gjentagelse' [repetition of the spirit] and an ironic variation on how one can also get oneself again in spirit. The way the Councilor is able to recollect his erotic 'fleurs du mal' in spirit with pleasure and security also seems to be an ironic variation on the bold opening statement that Constantin put forward on the first pages in *Gjentagelsen*: 'Gjentagelsens Kjærlighed er i Sandhed den ene lykkelige. Den har ligesom Erindringens ikke Haabets Uro, ikke Opdagelsens ængstende Eventyrlighed, men heller ei Erindringens Vemod, den har Øieblikkets salige Sikkerhed' (Kierkegaard 1843c: 9) [Repetition's love is in truth the only happy love. Like recollection's love, it does not have the restlessness of hope, the uneasy adventurousness of discovery, but neither does it have the sadness of recollection — it has the blissful security of the moment] (Kierkegaard 1983a: 99).

In the sphere of spirit, literature is also able to repeat literature, since characters, plots and ideas are preserved in the immortal piece of art and can be repeated in the succeeding works an infinite amount of times (as well as by us readers) following the dialectic of repetition: 'Gjentagelsens Dialektik er let; thi det, der gjentages, har været, eller kunde det ikke gjentages, men netop det, at har været, gjør Gjentagelsen til det Nye' (Kierkegaard 1843c: 25). [The dialectic of repetition is easy, for that which is repeated has been — otherwise it could not be repeated — but the very fact that it has been makes the repetition into something new] (Kierkegaard 1983a: 109).

'The Poet' can thus be regarded, not only as a repetition and restaging of the plot structure in *Gjentagelsen*, but also as a part of a longer chain of repetitions of the archetypal unhappy love triangle from world literature to which we find many allusions in 'The Poet'.[30] The allusions in 'The Poet' are (again) organized as a Kierkegaardian Chinese puzzle, in which one love triangle is enclosed in the other: Loke-Nanna-Balder (*Balders død* by Johannes Ewald, 1773), Albert-Lotte-Werther (*Die Leiden des jungen Werthers* by Johann Wolfgang Goethe, 1774), The Ambassador of Sardinia-Wally-Cæsar (*Wally die Zweiflerin* by Karl Gutzkow, 1835) and in last box Constantin Constantius-the young girl-the young man from Kierkegaard's *Gjentagelsen* (1843). This strategy of repetition is an integral part of Dinesen's poetics. As she said at the foot of the Acropolis, when she visited Greece with Knud W. and Benedicte Jensen in May 1951: 'al Poesi begynder ved Gentagelsen, og hvad særligt vilde een Søjle være — men disse Søjlerækker' (Jensen 1953: 278–79) [All poetry starts with repetition and what would one column be in itself — but these rows of columns]. Thus, we can regard 'The Poet' as one of the columns in the long line of love triangles that together make up the temple of world literature, and conclude by quoting Harold Bloom who uses Kierkegaard's *Repetition* in his influential essay 'Kenosis or Repetition and Discontinuity' in *The Anxiety of Influence* to describe the dialectic of poetry and tradition:

> The strong poet survives because he lives the discontinuity of an 'undoing'[31] and an 'isolating' repetition, but he would cease to be a poet unless he kept living the continuity of 'recollecting forwards', of breaking forth into a freshening that yet repeats his precursor's achievements'. (Bloom 1973: 83)

Notes to Chapter 14

1. Dinesen consistently spells 'Councilor' with only one l in the English version 'The Poet' (Dinesen 1934).
2. This direct allusion to Kierkegaard's character 'det unge Menneske' from *Gjentagelsen* is deliberately enhanced in Dinesen's Danish translation. I will elaborate more on this quote later.
3. In Dinesen's English original, Mathiesen's Danish title is 'Kammerraad, a chamber-councilor' (Dinesen 1934: 375), but this is changed to 'Justitsraad' in Dinesen's Danish translation. In *Gjentagelsen* Kierkegaard also mentions the name Mathiesen, even though it otherwise has no importance for the narrative: 'og hvor en Dansk kan faa Leilighed til at opfriske Mindet om Lars Mathiesen og Kehlet' (Kierkegaard 1843c: 30) [where a Dane has the opportunity to refresh his memory of Lars Mathiesen and Kehlet] (Kierkegaard 1983a: 112). Dinesen might have combined 'Justitsraad' and 'Mathiesen' into 'Justitsraad Mathiesen' in order to establish a clearer connection to *Gjentagelsen*. In the note section to *Syv fantastiske Fortællinger* (Dinesen 1934: 622) the character 'fuldmægtig Mathiesen' from Meïr Aron Goldschmidt's *Breve fra Choleratiden, indeholdende en lille Begivenhed* (1865) is mentioned as a possible source for the name 'Mathiesen', even though he, in Goldschmith's narrative, is just a subordinate 'fuldmægtig' [managing clerk], who himself is manipulated by his friend Frantz Holm. See Goldschmidt, *Breve fra Choleratiden, indeholdende en lille Begivenhed* (Copenhagen: Forlaget Christian Steen & Søn, 1865), pp 14–78, available at <http://adl.dk/adl_pub/pg/cv/ShowPgImg.xsql?p_udg_id=345&p_sidenr=14&hist=&nnoc=adl_pub> [accessed 10 October 2015].
4. Author's italics show elements in the passage Dinesen emphasized in her Danish version in order to give extra detail to certain points. This allusion to Kierkegaard is not mentioned in the note section to 'Digteren' in the latest Danish edition of *Syv fantastiske Fortællinger* (Copenhagen: Gyldendal, 2012), pp 617–55 (Dinesen 1935).

5. Christian Braad Thomsen briefly mentions this connection to Kierkegaard in 'Digteren' in his book *Boganis Gæstebud* but he does not elaborate further on it (Braad Thomsen 2010: 228).

6. Dinesen made an interesting choice in the English original calling Anders 'boy' in this passage and a couple of others. Otherwise she refers to Anders as 'the young man' seven other places in the tale, which is similar to the normal English translation of Kierkegaard's term 'det unge Menneske'. Important information (and the clear allusion to Kierkegaard) is however lost in the English version since 'menneske' is synonymous with 'man' in English. 'Human being' would be a more accurate translation, but it does not work properly in English.

7. Here Constantin identifies with the famous castrate singer Carlo Broschi Farinelli (1705–1782), who in 1737 was hired by the Spanish Queen Elisabetta Farnese to cure her husband the Spanish King Philip V of his depression. Farinelli stayed with the King of Spain and later his son Ferdinand VI for more than twenty years.

8. Dinesen 1935: 372.

9. Dinesen 1935: 389.

10. Dinesen 1935: 389–90.

11. Dinesen 1935: 395.

12. This interpretation of the two of them as being genuinely in love is supported by Aage Henriksen's analysis (Henriksen 1965: 17) even though I disagree with Henriksen's idea that Anders in the story knows that the Councilor is in the temple with them in the final scene (ibid.18).

13. Dinesen 1935: 395.

14. The Kislar Aga was the black eunuch leader of the seraglio (the harem) under the Ottoman Empire. Dinesen later used Farinelli as a model for the character Marelli in 'The Cardinal's First Tale' in *Last Tales* (Dinesen 1957).

15. Dinesen 1935: 343.

16. The Councilor expresses a similar idea when he elaborates on the special *code de femme* that he believes Fransine to subscribe to in order for her to perceive their marriage as a good thing (Dinesen 1934: 414).

17. Dinesen 1935: 376.

18. Dinesen 1935: 396.

19. This is a slight rephrasing of the title of Charles Baudelaire's poetry collection *Les Fleurs du Mal* (1857) (*Flowers of Evil*).

20. Dinesen 1935: 384.

21. Which is ultimately what literature and film offer us human beings: to experience horror, triumph, sex and tragedy by proxy through characters in a fictional story-world.

22. The essay was first given as two radio talks in May 1952 before Henriksen came to know Dinesen in person and later eagerly discussed Kierkegaard with her as we know from their prolific letter correspondence 1952–1954 (Henriksen 1985). Henriksen was in the process of writing a doctoral thesis about Kierkegaard during these years. Gyldendal published it in 1954 under the title *Kierkegaards Romaner* [Kierkegaard's Novels] (Henriksen 1954).

23. Henriksen later moderated this opinion (Poul Behrendt, pers. comment).

24. In 'Carnival' Rosendaal is dressed as a Chinese eunuch (Dinesen 1977: 60).

25. Who is impotent.

26. Who is a virgin.

27. Constantin can indeed be regarded as a comical character, even though scholars rarely perceive him that way. But everything Constantin sets out do, either fails or gets out of hand, even though he arrogantly believes he has it all figured out. He is in fact a bit of a Don Quixote, even though it can be difficult to see, since his opinions are put forward with such an authority (and Kierkegaard even grants him the authority to take everything back in the final scene), so we don't immediately see the comic.

28. Dinesen 1935: 396.

29. For example Henriksen 1954, Tøjner 1996 and Tjønneland 1996. In his Ph.D. thesis 'Tyvesprogets mester' Mads Sohl Jessen suggests that the concept of repetition should mainly be understood as a parody in relation to J. L. Heiberg (Jessen 2010).

30. Dinesen also repeats and explores this type of love triangle from 'The Poet' in other tales, for example 'Sorrow-Acre', 'The Immortal Story', 'Tempests', and 'Ehrengard' where an older man in various ways tries to manipulate two young lovers.

31. 'As defined by Fenichel: "in undoing, one more step is taken. Something positive is done which, actually or magically, is the opposite of something which, again actually or in imagination, was done before ..."' (Bloom 1973: 80).

CHAPTER 15

❖

Nemesis of the Aesthetic: 'Babette's Feast' and Kierkegaard's Three Stages

In this chapter, I will discuss how repetition also occurs in Dinesen's tales as an internal narrative structure formed by a second meeting between two characters where in between, in the words of Pipistrello from the tale 'Second Meeting': 'the story lies' (Dinesen 1977: 335). The example here is 'Babette's Feast' and the second meeting between Loewenhielm and Martine, and how it leads Loewenhielm to a critical evaluation of the life he has lived, since he left Martine and Berlevaag as an unhappy lover thirty years ago. He expects that the second meeting with the Pietist Berlevaagians will reassure him that he made the right choice thirty years ago. Instead he is treated to the most exclusive and lavish dinner, which causes him to reproach himself for having left the love of his life and his creative powers behind thirty years ago, in favor of a Christian-Bourgeois lifestyle, a loveless marriage and a career as a General (the sphere of the ethical). The Berlevaagians, who belong to the sphere of the religious, are fooled to believe that they, during the lavish dinner, have 'been given an hour of the millennium' (Dinesen 1958: 54) by God, when it is in fact just the material and bodily effect from drinking the finest wine and champagne in the world that have brought them into ecstasy. These radical shifts are provoked by the machinations of the female artist, the master chef Babette, who belongs to the sphere of the aesthetic.

Thus, in 'Babette's Feast', Kierkegaard's three stages, or modes of existence and how they are valued, are reversed in this materialist counter-story, where the religious, embodied by the Pietist, joy-denying and bitter Berlevaagians, is the lowest stage. Loewenhielm, who lives his life in the ethical, accounts for the middle stage, but his loveless, career-oriented life is grounded in 'affectation' as P. M. Møller defines it (see Chapter 6, pp. 50–51) and is thus false. Babette and her culinary art represents the aesthetic, and the set-up of the evening is a perfect example: she decides to spend 10,000 francs, all that she owns, on a dinner which will only last a few hours, and where the majority, had they been able to choose, would have preferred water and bread. Babette, however, manages to create an evening of ecstasy and beauty, where body and spirit are united and people get insights and forgive each other. In the tale it is the aesthetic that brings peace and grace not religion. Thus, the aesthetic, even though fundamentally a materialistic phenomenon according to Dinesen, both holds finite (lavish dinners and other bodily ecstasies) and infinite qualities (spiritual repetitions, immortal works of art) and has, in Dinesen's view, wrongly, been confused with the religious, also by Kierkegaard. 'Babette's Feast' is an ironical counter-story where Christianity and Kierkegaard's classification of the religious is taken off the serious theoretical pedestal and brought down into the comical reality.

Dynamics of Repetition in Dinesen

As I have shown in my analyses of *Sandhedens Hævn*, 'The Pearls', 'Carnival', 'The Dreamers', 'Ehrengard', 'The Deluge at Norderney' and 'The Poet' with particular attention to Kierkegaard, Dinesen's repetitions on the level of the work of her precursor are always subversive and polemical when dealing with ideas, plots and characters. However, repetition also plays a role as a rhetorical structure in Dinesen's oeuvre, especially from *Winter's Tales* and onwards, as has been pointed out by Behrendt. In a passage in the article 'Juryens Veto' (Behrendt 2011) he unveils the two most important structuring principles in Dinesen's narratives: 'repetition' and 'the second meeting':

> 'Skibsdrengens Fortælling' er således det første sted, hvor forfatterskabets to strukturerende grundelementer: *gentagelsen* og *gensynet*, bringes systematisk og klart reflekteret i anvendelse som narrativ praksis. Gentagelsen ikke forstået som repetition, men som en udfoldelse ved det *andet* møde af noget, der lå skjult i det *første*, uden dog at kunne udledes heraf, før det uventet indfinder sig. Mellem det første og det andet møde ligger historien, og der ville, som det hedder i den efterladte fortælling 'Second Meeting', ingen historie have været, hvis ikke det havde været for det andet møde. (Behrendt 2011: 170)

> [Thus, 'The Sailor-Boy's Tale' is the first place in which the authorship's two basic structural elements, *repetition* and *second meeting*, are conveyed systematically and clearly reflected in application as narrative practice. Repetition understood not merely as repeating, but as developing from the *second* encounter of something that lay hidden in the *first*, without being able to be inferred from it before it appears unexpectedly. Between the first and second encounter lies the story and, as referred to in the abandoned tale 'Second Meeting', no story would have existed if not for the second encounter.]

The observation has similarities to the ideas presented in this quote from *Gjentagelsen* where Constantin Constantius lectures us about the dialectic of repetition:

> Gjentagelsens Dialektik er let; thi det, der gjentages, har været, ellers kunde det ikke gjentages, men netop det, at det har været, gjør Gjentagelsen til det Nye. Naar Grækerne sagde, at al Erkjenden er Erindren, saa sagde de, hele Tilværelsen, som er til, har været til, naar man siger, at Livet er en Gjentagelse, saa siger man: Tilværelsen, som har været til, bliver nu til. Naar man ikke har Erindringens eller Gjentagelsens Kategori, saa opløser hele livet sig i en tom og indholdsløs Larmen. (Kierkegaard 1843c: 25)

> [The dialectic of repetition is easy, for that which is repeated has been — otherwise it could not be repeated — but the very fact that it has been makes the repetition into something new. When the Greeks said that all knowing

> is recollecting, they said that all existence, which is, has been; when one says
> that life is a repetition, one says: actuality, which has been, now comes into
> existence. If one does not have the category of recollection or of repetition, all
> life dissolves into an empty, meaningless noise.] (Kierkegaard 1983a: 109)

One passage in the quote fits especially well with Dinesen's idea of the second
meeting and the story: 'naar man siger, at Livet er en Gjentagelse, saa siger man:
Tilværelsen, som har været til, bliver nu til' [when one says that life is a repetition,
one says: actuality, which has been, now comes into existence]. Dinesen lets
Pipistrello articulate this poetics of repetition in the tale 'Second Meeting'[1] when he
lectures Lord Byron using the story of Ali Baba as an example: 'between this first
and second meeting the story lies, and if the second meeting had not been there,
there would have been no story' (Dinesen 1977: 335). It is between the first and
the second meeting the story lies, which means that the second meeting triggers
a retrospective view infused with interpretation and evaluation of the events that
have unfolded since the first meeting that carries a transformative potential for the
characters: A retrospective view that would not have emerged, had there been no
second meeting, but when the second meeting occurs 'recollecting forward' begins
(the story) and so the possible transformations.

'Babette's Feast'

In the following I will conduct an analysis of 'Babette's Feast'[2] as a prime example of
how Dinesen uses the rhetorical strategy of 'gentagelsen' [repetition] and 'gensynet'
[second meeting] that Behrendt outlined in the previous paragraph.[3] The tale is also
a very poignant example of Dinesen's subversive repetitions on an overall level with
regard to Kierkegaard, since we find significant repetitions of plots and/or ideas put
forward by Constantin Constantius in *Gjentagelsen*, subversions of ideas about the
choice and the ethical put forward by Judge William in *Enten — Eller. Anden Deel*,
and the ideas about the three stages: the religious (highest), the ethical (middle) and
the aesthetic (lowest). Once again, we also find 'in vino veritas' to be a target for
Dinesen's ironical subversions.

Lorens Loewenhielm

On the level of the structure, Loewenhielm's trip to Berlevaag can be regarded as a
repetition of Constantin Constantius' experiment in *Gjentagelsen*, when he decides
to go on a second journey to Berlin in order to experience repetition. After his
rejection of the love of his life, Martine, in Berlevaag, Loewenhielm instead chooses
to marry a woman from a very wealthy family (out of duty and convenience —
not love) and make a career in the military (choices belonging to the ethical).
Loewenhielm, who is now in his early fifties, has, however, recently been plagued
by discontent and doubts with regard to the choice he made thirty years ago and
the way his life has unfolded as a result of this choice:

> General Loewenhielm[4] had obtained everything that he had striven for in life
> and was admired and envied by everyone. Only he himself knew of a queer

fact, which jarred with his prosperous existence: that he was not perfectly happy. Something was wrong somewhere, and he carefully felt his mental self all over, as one feels a finger over to determine the place of a deep-seated, invisible thorn. [...] he would find himself worrying about his immortal soul. Did he have any reason for doing so? He was a moral person, loyal to his king, his wife and his friends, an example to everybody. (Dinesen 1958: 45)[5]

Loewenhielm wants to use the second meeting in Berlevaag to get rid of the doubt and once and for all convince himself that he made *the right choice* thirty years ago when he abandoned the love of his life, Martine, and the poor Pietist Berlevaag. This is the repetition he is hoping to get, so he can to prove to himself that he has indeed lived a happy, splendid life and has nothing to regret:

He would, he resolved, tonight make up his account with young Lorens Loewenhielm, who had felt himself to be a shy and sorry figure in the house of the Dean, and who in the end had shaken its dust off his riding boots. He would let the youth prove to him, once and for all, that thirty-one years ago he had made the right choice. The low rooms, the haddock and the glass of water on the table before him should all be called in to bear evidence that in their milieu the existence of Lorens Loewenhielm would very soon have become sheer misery. (Dinesen 1958: 46–47)[6]

This quest appears to be a concrete staging of an idea put forward by Judge William in *Enten — Eller. Anden Deel*:

Jeg tænker paa de mange mindre vigtige men for mig ikke ligegyldige Tilfælde i Livet, hvor det gjaldt om at vælge; thi om der end kun er eet Forhold, hvor dette Ord har sin absolute Betydning, hver Gang der nemlig paa den ene Side viser sig Sandhed, Retfærdighed og Hellighed; paa den anden Side Lyst og Tilbøieligheder, og dunkle Lidenskaber og Fortabelse, saa er det dog altid af Vigtighed ogsaa i Ting, hvor det i og for sig er uskyldigt, hvilket man vælger, at vælge rigtigt, at prøve sig selv, at man ikke engang med Smerte skal begynde et Tilbagetog til det Punkt, man gik ud fra. (Kierkegaard 1843b: 155)

[I think of the many less important but for me not trivial incidents in my life when it was a matter of choosing, for even if there is only one situation in which these words have absolute meaning — namely, every time truth, justice, and sanctity appear on one side and lust and natural inclinations, dark passions and perdition on the other side. Nevertheless, even in matters that in and by themselves are innocent, what a person chooses is always important. It is important that he choose properly, test himself, so that eventually he does not have to begin a painful retreat to the point where he started.] (Kierkegaard 1987b: 157)

Thirty years ago Loewenhielm rejected his 'Lyst og Tilbøieligheder' [dark passions] when he fled Berlevaag, and also for many years successfully managed to put a lid on them (his imaginative powers and his gift as a foreteller). Instead he chose a Bourgeois life that according to Judge William is connected to 'truth, justice, and sanctity' (which equals marriage, public career, etc.). 'The increasing 'pain' he has recently experienced has, however, forced him to 'to begin a painful retreat to the point where he started' in order to eliminate the idea that has been eating him up lately: that he made the wrong choice thirty years ago. And so the story unfolds, when the second meeting with Martine occurs during Babette's lavish dinner, and Loewenhielm's choice is put to the test.

Unexpected Repetitions

Had Babette not been in Berlevaag and won in the lottery, Loewenhielm would indeed have gotten his repetition — 'the haddock and the glass of water on the table before him' (Dinesen 1958: 48) — since religious life is ritualized repetition. But on this particular night Loewenhielm is fooled into believing otherwise because he is served an abundant, lavish and very expensive dinner. As the reader knows, the inhabitants of Berlevaag, out of support for Martine and Philippa, have sworn that they would just eat and drink whatever is served for them by Babette and not comment on it. Loewenhielm misunderstands their behavior during the lavish dinner and is in absolute shock: 'He looked round at his fellow-diners. They were all quietly eating their Blinis Demidoff without any sign of either surprise or approval, as if they had been doing so every day for thirty years' (Dinesen 1958: 49).[7] The extravagant dinner, his intoxication caused by the finest wines in the world and the behavior of the Berlevaagians[8] fool him into believing that he made the wrong choice thirty years ago (since it seems that life in Berlevaag has been one long hedonist party since he left) and the preserved beauty of Martine adds to his initial impression: 'The golden hair was now streaked with silver; the flowerlike face had slowly been turning into alabaster. But how serene was the forehead, how quietly trustful the eyes, how pure and sweet the mouth, as if no hasty word had ever passed its lips' (Dinesen 1958: 48).[9] In his excited and intoxicated[10] state of mind, he delivers a speech:

> We tremble before making our choice in life, and after having made it again tremble in fear of having chosen wrong. But the moment comes when our eyes are opened, and we see and realize that grace is infinite. Grace, my friends, demands nothing from us but that we shall await it with confidence and acknowledge it in gratitude. Grace, brothers, makes no conditions and singles out none of us in particular; grace takes us all to its bosom and proclaims general amnesty. See! that which we have chosen is given us, and that which we have refused is, also and at the same time, granted us. Ay, that which we have rejected is poured upon us abundantly. (Dinesen 1958: 52)[11]

Loewenhielm did not get the repetition he had hoped for on a material level (haddock and water) and the desired result: that he once and for all would stop loving Martine and finally give her up. Instead, he is given the opposite: a repetition of the extravagant and lavish dinner that he experienced at Café Anglais in Paris many years ago (also made by Babette!) and a repetition of his love for Martine that he now, in his exalted state of mind, is determined to repeat every day in spirit for the rest of his life:

> 'I have been with you every day of my life. You know, do you not, that it has been so?' 'Yes,' said Martine, 'I know that it has been so.' 'And,' he continued, 'I shall be with you every day that is left to me. Every evening I shall sit

down, if not in the flesh, which means nothing, in spirit, which is all, to dine with you, just like tonight. For tonight I have learned, dear sister, that in this world anything is possible.' 'Yes, it is so, dear brother,' said Martine. 'In this world anything is possible.' Upon this they departed. (Dinesen 1958: 54)[12]

Loewenhielm's newfound method closely follows the strategy of 'recollection's love' in spirit that Constantin Constantius outlines in *Gjentagelsen*:

> Erindringens Kjærlighed er den ene lykkelige, har en Forfatter sagt [Johannes Forføreren in 'Forførerens Dagbog']. Deri har han ogsaa fuldkommen Ret, naar man blot erindrer, at den først gjør et Menneske ulykkeligt. Gjentagelsens Kjærlighed er i Sandhed den ene lykkelige. Den har ligesom Erindringens ikke Haabets Uro, ikke Opdagelsens ængstende Eventyrlighed, men heller ei Erindringens Vemod, den har Øieblikkets salige Sikkerhed. (Kierkegaard 1843c: 9)

> [Recollection's love [*Kjærlighed*], an author has said, is the only happy love. He is perfectly right in that, of course, provided one recollects that initially it makes a person unhappy. Repetition's love is in truth the only happy love. Like recollection's love, it does not have the restlessness of hope, the uneasy adventurousness of discovery, but neither does it have the sadness of recollection — it has the blissful security of the moment.] (Kierkegaard 1983a: 99)

The way that Loewenhielm approaches Martine to confirm his love and the way she responds, indicate that his love might very well not be requited, and that she is just sweet-talking him in order to get him out of the house quickly. And they might very well also have very different interpretations of what the sentence 'In this world anything is possible', which they both refer to, actually means (Martine most likely understands it religiously and Loewenhielm — now — aesthetically). After Loewenhielm's departure, Martine seems more occupied with evaluating the congregations' success with regard to keeping up appearances during the luxurious dinner than thinking about Loewenhielm (note the irony in the passage, especially with regard to the turtle):

> Their hearts suddenly filled with gratitude. They realized that none of their guests had said a single word about the food. Indeed, try as they might, they could not themselves remember any of the dishes which had been served. Martine bethought herself of the turtle. It had not appeared at all, and now seemed very vague and far away; it was quite possible that it had been nothing but a nightmare. (Dinesen 1958: 55–56)[13]

This behavior strongly indicates that Loewenhielm is the only one of them who is determined to employ his newfound strategy of love's repetition belonging to the sphere of the aesthetic (also practiced by Johannes Forføreren and Constantin Constantius). As a strictly brought up Pietist who has lived all her life in chastity, doing charity work and worrying about her congregation and her immortal soul, Martine does not seem capable of (or interested in) this type of love's repetition.

'in vino veritas'

As Selboe has correctly observed, the meal can also be regarded as parodic repetition of 'in vino veritas' (Selboe 1996: 110) since it is the wine and champagne that make the Berlevaagians speak the truth and subsequently forgive each other, which is a real ethical effect of the wine compared to the lofty, theoretical ideas of love presented by the five wine-influenced male speakers and unhappy lovers in 'in vino veritas'. Neither Martine nor the Berlevaagians have, however, ironically any idea that they are drinking alcohol:

> All the same when Martine saw a barrow load of bottles wheeled into the kitchen, she stood still [...] 'What is there in this bottle Babette?' she asked in a low voice. 'Not wine?' 'Wine, Madame!' Babette answered. 'No, Madame. It is a Clos Vougeot 1846!' After a moment she added: 'From Philippe, in Rue Montorgueil!' Martine had never suspected that wines could have names to them, and was put to silence. (Dinesen 1958: 39–40)[14]

And:

> Usually in Berlevaag people did not speak much while they were eating. But somehow this evening tongues had been loosened [...] The boy once more filled the glasses. This time the Brothers and Sisters knew that what they were given to drink was not wine, for it sparkled. It must be some kind of lemonade. The lemonade agreed with their exalted state of mind and seemed to lift them off the ground, into a higher and purer sphere. (Dinesen 1958: 49–50)[15]

They wrongly believe that they are experiencing a divine intervention: 'The vain illusions of this earth had dissolved before their eyes like smoke, and they had seen the universe as it really is. They had been given an hour of the millennium' (Dinesen 1958: 54).[16] In 'Babette's Feast' 'in vino veritas' (in wine there is truth) is here taken literally, since the Berlevaagians are finally speaking the truth to each other (about their resentments and old feuds) — and, of course, deeply ironically, since the Berlevaagians believe that they are lifted off the ground and 'into a higher and purer sphere' by God, when it is in fact the purely material and bodily effect of drinking the finest wine and champagne in the world. They wrongly believe that their love and forgiveness has to do with 'an hour of the millennium' (God) when it is in fact the fine wine and food (material) that has made them see 'the universe as it really is' and brought laughter, love and forgiveness into their otherwise ascetic, anxiety-plagued and gloomy lives. As the narrator ironically concludes: 'The old Dean's flock were [sic] humble people. When later in life they thought of this evening it never occurred to any of them that they might have been exalted by their own merit' (Dinesen 1958: 53).[17]

But it is also a subversive reversal of the goal of Kierkegaard's narrative strategy that we find presented in *Synspunktet for min Forfatter-Virksomhed*, which was in Dinesen's library at Rungstedlund when she died:

> Men fra den hele Forfatter-Virksomheds totale Synspunkt er den æsthetiske Produktivitet et Bedrag, og heri 'Pseudonymitetens' dybere Betydning. Dog et Bedrag, det er jo noget stygt Noget. Hertil vilde jeg svare: man lade sig ikke

bedrage af det Ord 'Bedrag'. Man kan bedrage et Menneske for det Sande, og man kan, for at erindre om gamle Socrates, bedrage et Menneske ind i det Sande. [...] Hvad vil saa det sige at 'bedrage'? Det vil sige, at man ikke begynder *ligefrem* med det man vil meddele [...] Man begynder altsaa (for at blive ved hvad der væsentlig er dette Skrifts Gjenstand) ikke saaledes: Jeg er Christen, Du er ikke en Christen; men saaledes: Du er en Christen, jeg er ingen Christen. Eller man begynder ikke saaledes: Det er Christendom, jeg forkynder, og Du lever i blot æsthetiske Bestemmelser, nei, man begynder saaledes: lad os tale om det Æsthetiske; Bedraget ligger i, at man taler saaledes, just for at komme til det Religieuse. (Kierkegaard 1859: 35–36)

[But from the total point of view of my whole work as an author, the esthetic writing is a deception, and herein is the deeper significance of the *pseudonymity*. But a deception, that is indeed something rather ugly. To that I would answer: Do not be deceived by the word *deception*. One can deceive a person of what is true, and — to recall old Socrates — one can deceive a person into what is true. [...] What, then, does it mean 'to deceive'? It means that one does not begin directly with what one wishes to communicate [...] Thus one does not begin (to hold what essentially is the theme of this book) in this way: I am a Christian, you are not Christian — but this way: You are a Christian, I am not a Christian. Or one does not begin this way: It is Christianity I am proclaiming, and you are living in purely esthetic categories. No, one begins this way: Let us talk about the esthetic. The deception consists in one's speaking this way precisely in order to arrive at the religious.] (Kierkegaard 1998: 53–54)

Dinesen's tales are, like the narratives from Kierkegaard's aesthetic-pseudonymous authorship, indirect messages: 'It means that one does not begin directly with what one wishes to communicate', which account for most works of fiction in general, but in particular for both Kierkegaard's and Dinesen's very complex narratives. Dinesen's tales have the same goal as Kierkegaard, which is to 'deceive a person into what is true', but the final outcome is the opposite of Kierkegaard's, which was 'to arrive at the religious'. Both the Berlevaagians and Loewenhielm are 'deceived into what is true' by Babette, but 'the religious' and spiritual is substituted by 'the aesthetic' and material by Dinesen.

Nemesis: Revenge of the Refused

The tale ultimately understands refusal as the nemesis of the choice, since we ultimately are also granted what we have refused (whether we want it or not): 'that which we have refused is, also and at the same time, granted us. Ay, that which we have rejected is poured upon us abundantly' (Dinesen 1958: 58). The profound and original recognition of the tale is that what we have rejected in life has just as much influence on our lives as the (positive) choices we have made and these two sides of the coin together form our life (the whole coin). This is a significant correlative to Judge William and his ideas about choices and the ethical in *Enten — Eller. Anden Deel*.

Loewenhielm is of course the prime example in Dinesen's tale. He is still haunted by his rejection of Martine thirty years after he fled to Stockholm (same city as 'det unge Menneske' in *Gjentagelsen*) to a degree that makes him set out for Berlevaag to try to confirm his choice. But the Berlevaagians too suffer from the thorn in the flesh of having made the wrong choices many years ago:

> There were in the congregation two old women who before their conversation had spread slander upon each other, and thereby to each other ruined a marriage and an inheritance. Today they could not remember happenings of yesterday or a week ago, but they remembered this forty-year-old wrong and kept going through the ancient accounts; they scowled at eachother (Dinesen 1958: 34–35)[18]

This dialectical way of thinking we also find in *Sandhedens Hævn* where the nemesis of the lie is the truth if we substitute 'lie' with 'refusal'. In 'Babette's Feast' the nemesis of what we have gotten and achieved in life (our choices) is what we have refused. Martine and Philippa's fundamentalist, pietistic and ascetic father, 'the Dean', also ends up getting, on his hundredth birthday, what he had rejected in his earthly life: a lavish, luxurious and super-abundant dinner, spent and consumed in just one evening (he would for sure have turned in his grave, had he known): the ultimate nemesis. In a more general way, Dinesen also seems to suggest that the more we try to control our own and other people's lives (like 'the Dean'), the more it will backfire. To paraphrase Elishama from 'The Immortal Story' (*Anecdotes of Destiny*): '"Yes," said Elishama. "Reversed. In this pattern the road runs the other way. And runs on"' (Dinesen 1958: 166). The Dean wants the congregation to surrender to him and his ideas, but in the end himself becomes the subject of higher powers. The marionettes always revolt one way or the other — or history (both understood as history and as a story) will eventually paint another, less flattering picture.

Reversal of the Three Stages

And the road for sure runs the other way that evening in 'Babette's Feast' when Kierkegaard's stages: the religious, the ethical, and the aesthetic are reversed. In the tale, the religious (the Berlevaagians) is regarded as the lowest stage. The Berlevaagians live in an illusion where they believe that their refusal of bodily pleasures and their ascetic lifestyle will grant them access to Heaven: a place that in Dinesen's world is nothing but an illusion. It simply does not exist, which makes the ascetic lifestyle and sufferings of the Berlevaagians an act of profound irony (whether this is comical or tragic depends on the point of view). The ethical is the middle stage and Loewenhielm its representative. He is, however, not satisfied even though he has achieved everything when measured from a common Christian-Bourgeois perspective: marriage, money, career and status. He is also liked by everyone and has close ties to the King and the Court. By the machinations of Babette, Loewenhielm is, however, lifted from the ethical sphere (where he is secretly unhappy living a life in 'affectation') to the aesthetic sphere when he, during the dinner, experiences an epiphany that reactivates his imagination ('second sight') and makes him surrender to love's repetition in spirit. A spiritual exercise that has nothing to do with the religious but is connected to art, love and spiritual creativity. Loewenhielm is finally granted peace (grace), but in another way than he had thought. Not through a repetition of the first rejection, but through surrender to love and his creative imagination that now enables him to blissfully repeat his love to Martine every day in spirit. Loewenhielm becomes an example of an individual that has 'courage enough to let himself be esthetically transformed' and after the dinner has achieved 'the highest in esthetics' as described by Judge William:

> Og i Sandhed, den, der har Ydmyghed og Mod nok til her at lade sig æsthetisk forklare, den, der føler sig med som en Person i det Skuespil, Guddommen digter [Babette], hvor Digteren og Souffleuren ikke ere forskjellige Personer, hvor Individet [Loewenhielm], som den øvede Skuespiller, der har levet sig ind i sin Charakteer og sin Replik, ikke forstyrres af Souffleuren, men føler, at det, der tilhvidskes ham, er det, han selv vil sige, saa det næsten bliver tvivlsomt, om han lægger Souffleuren Ordene i Munden, eller Souffleuren ham, den, der i dybeste Forstand føler sig paa eengang digtende og digtet, der i det Øieblik, han føler sig digtende [towards Martine], har Replikkens oprindelige Pathos, i det Øieblik, han føler sig digtet, det erotiske Øre, der opfanger enhver Lyd [love's repetition], han og først han har realiseret det Høieste i Æsthetiken. (Kierkegaard 1843b: 136)

> [And in truth, he who has humility and courage enough to let himself be esthetically transformed, he who feels himself present as a character in a drama the deity is writing, in which the poet and the prompter are not different persons, in which the individual, as the experienced actor who has lived into his character and his lines is not disturbed by the prompter but feels that he himself wants to say what is being whispered to him, so that it almost becomes a question whether he is putting the words in the prompter's mouth or the prompter in his, he who in the most profound sense feels himself creating and created, who in the moment he feels himself creating has the original pathos af the lines, and in the moment he feels himself created has the erotic ear that picks up every sound — he and he alone has brought into actual existence the highest in esthetics.] (Kierkegaard 1987b: 137)

Even though Loewenhielm enters the sphere of the aesthetic and employs the same strategy with regard to love's repetition as Johannes Forføreren and Constantin Constantius the big difference is that he lets himself be 'digtet' [created] unlike Dinesen's counter-characters to Johannes and Constantin, Cazotte and The Councilor, who tries to control and manipulate and 'create' the world around them instead of surrender to it. This is why Loewenhielm is the hero of the story — and Babette the heroine. Babette — as a celebrated chef — is the embodiment of the aesthetic as action, as lived life, meaning that she too, according to Judge William, has achieved 'det Høieste i det Æsthetiske' [the summit of the esthetic]:

> Det Æsthetiske altsaa, der bliver incommensurabelt endog for Poesiens Fremstilling, hvorledes lader det sig fremstille? Svar: derved at det leves. Det faaer derved en Lighed med Musik, der blot er, fordi den bestandig gjentages, blot er i Udførelsens Øieblik. Derfor gjorde jeg i det Foregaaende opmærksom paa den fordærvelige Forvexling af det Æsthetiske og det, som æsthetisk lader sig fremstille i digterisk Reproduktion. Alt, hvad jeg nemlig her taler om, lader sig visselig æsthetisk fremstille, men ikke i digterisk Reproduktion, men derved, at man lever det, i Virkelighedens Liv realiserer det. Saaledes hæver

Æsthetiken sig selv og forsoner sig med Livet; thi som i een Forstand Poesi og Kunst netop er en Forsoning med Livet, saa ere de i en anden Forstand Fjendskab til Livet, fordi de kun forsone een Side af Sjælen. Her er jeg ved det Høieste i det Æsthetiske. (Kierkegaard 1843b: 135–36)

[How, then, can the esthetic, which is incommensurable even for portrayal in poetry, be represented? Answer: by being lived. It thereby has a similarity to music, which is only because it is continually repeated, is only in the moment of being performed. That is why in the foregoing I called attention to the ruinous confusing of the aesthetic and that which can be esthetically portrayed in poetic reproduction. Everything I am talking about here certainly can be portrayed esthetically, but not in poetic reproduction, but only by living it, by realizing it in the life of actuality. In this way the aesthetic elevates itself and reconciles itself with life, for just as poetry and art in one sense are precisely a reconciliation with life, yet in another sense they are enmity to life, because they reconcile only one side of the soul. Here I am at the summit of the esthetic.] (Kierkegaard 1987b: 137)

In 'Babette's Feast' the religious and the aesthetic stages have shifted rank. All in all, the tale is a subversive rewriting of this passage from *Enten — Eller. Anden Deel*:

Dette Høiere er nu det Religiøse [det æstetiske], i hvilket Forstands-Reflexionen ender, og som for Gud [digteren — Babette] Intet er umuligt, saaledes er for det religiøse [det æstetiske] Individ heller Intet umuligt. I det Religiøse [æstetiske] finder Kjærligheden atter den Uendelighed, som den i den reflekterende forgjeves søgte. Men dersom det Religiøse [det æstetiske], saa vist som det er et Høiere end alt Jordisk, tillige ikke er et i Forhold til den umiddelbare Kjærlighed Excentrisk men med den Concentrisk, saa lod jo Eenheden sig tilveiebringe, uden at den Smerte, som det Religiøse [det æstetiske] vel kan helbrede, men som dog altid er en dyb Smerte, blev nødvendig. Det er meget sjeldent, at man seer denne Sag gjort til Gjenstand for Overveielse. (Kierkegaard 1843b: 38, author's insertions in square brackets)

[This something higher is the religious [aesthetic], in which the reflection of the understanding ends, and just as nothing is impossible for God [The poet — Babette], so also nothing is impossible for the religious [aesthetic] individual either. In the religious [the aesthetic], love again finds the infinity that it sought in vain in reflective love. But if the religious [aesthetic], as surely as it is something higher than everything earthly, is also not something eccentric in relation to the immediate love but concentric with it, then the unity can indeed be brought about, except that the pain, which the religious [aesthetic] certainly can heal but which nevertheless is a deep pain, would not become necessary. It is very seldom that one sees this issue made the subject of deliberation.] (Kierkegaard 1987b: 30)

Again we see how Dinesen realizes theoretical potentials in Kierkegaard's works and gives life to the abstract ideas through concrete characters and images. As the story also tells us: it is indeed possible to live aesthetically and still have both repetition and the ethical, contrary to what Judge William preaches in *Enten — Eller. Anden Deel*. In the story, the religious Berlevaagians are envious, unforgiving and petty (lowest stage). Loewenhielm is a good-hearted man, but he has rejected love and his true self to 'gain the whole world'. He is too occupied with his outer life; how people view him, his status (middle stage) until Babette lifts him (and he lets himself be lifted) into the aesthetic. Babette transcends the qualities belonging to spheres of the religious and ethical (as we find them depicted in the tale). She is true to herself as an artist, she is not petty but caring and respectful, and she has the ability to truly transform people's lives, so that it becomes 'a love affair of the noble and romantic category in which one no longer distinguishes between bodily and spiritual appetite or satiety!' (Dinesen 1958: 50–51).[19] Thus, a unity between body and spirit, which in Dinesen's world is the ideal — the unity we should all strive for, even though Christian dualist tradition has told us otherwise.[20] The dinner guests are granted this unity between body and spirit when they are consuming Babette's gastronomic masterpieces, and Babette, the master chef and artist, are granted this unity from the ecstatic inspiration and creativity that emerge in the process of producing them. In that regard the aesthetic and the religious strive to achieve the same closeness and unity with life, but, as we have seen, they each have completely different departure points: the material, respectively the transcendental, which, according to the tale, equals reality vs. delusion.

Kierkegaard, Regine, and Repetition

'Babette's Feast' is a Chinese puzzle of repetitions, and inside the last box we find Kierkegaard's relationship to Regine, whom he, as we know, rejected just as Loewenhielm rejected Martine (note the same ending of the names –ine). Kierkegaard too experienced on a daily basis 'that which we have rejected is poured upon us abundantly' with regard to his unrealized marriage with Regine: 'Jeg reiste til Berlin. Jeg leed saare meget. Hende mindedes jeg hver Dag. Jeg har ubetinget indtil Dato holdt det: hver Dag i det mindste een Gang at bede for hende, ofte to Gange, foruden hvad jeg ellers har tænkt paa hende' (here quoted from Rohde 1953: 31). [I went to Berlin. I suffered very, very much. I thought of her every day. Until now I have kept up without fail: to pray for her every day at least once, often twice, besides thinking about her in other ways] (Rohde 1960: 41–42). As previously mentioned Kierkegaard produced three narratives that deal with his rejection of Regine, which is such an important event in his life that he in an almost neurotic-compulsory way repeats it over and over again in different variations in 'Forførerens Dagbog' from *Enten — Eller. Første Deel, Gjentagelsen,* and 'Skyldig' — 'Ikke-Skyldig?' from *Stadier paa Livets Vei.* These narratives can be understood as spiritual second meetings of what he rejected in the flesh (or, rather, most likely was forced to reject, see Chapter 11). Kierkegaard's nemesis was that he thought that Regine would never marry and that the two of them would have a spiritual love relationship for the rest of their lives. Instead she married rather quickly after Kierkegaard's second journey to Berlin (which also made him alter his *Gjentagelsen* manuscript), whereas Martine in 'Babette's Feast' never married, contrary to what Loewenhielm thought she would do when he left her.

The Second Meeting: Life must be Understood Backwards

Dinesen's rhetorical strategy of 'repetition' and 'second meeting' that we find very clearly demonstrated in 'Babette's Feast' also seems to have ties to a — now very famous — observation Kierkegaard made in his journal in 1843:

> Det er ganske sandt, hvad Philosophien siger, at Livet maa forstaaes baglænds. Men derover glemmer man den anden Sætning, at det maa *leves forlænds*. Hvilken Sætning, jo meer den gjennemtænkes, netop ender med, at Livet i Timeligheden aldrig ret bliver forstaaeligt, netop fordi jeg intet Øieblik kan faae fuldelig Ro til at indtage Stillingen: baglænds. (Kierkegaard 1843e, JJ:167: 194)

> [It is quite true what Philosophy says, that life must be understood backwards. But people also forget the other sentence, that it must *be lived forwards*. That sentence, the more it is contemplated, leads precisely to temporal life never being fully understood, exactly because in no moment can I find complete peace to assume the position: backwards.]

Dinesen would have become familiar with this quote in 1923 from reading Høffding's article about Pascal and Kierkegaard: 'Han [Kierkegaard] lægger særlig vægt paa, at vi lever i Tiden. Vi lever forlænds, men vi forstaar baglænds. En Afslutning kan derfor ikke naas' (Høffding 1923: 422). [He [Kierkegaard] puts special emphasis on the fact that we live in time. We live in a forward movement, but understand it backward. Thus, a conclusion cannot be reached.][21] In 'Babette's Feast' the second meeting makes Loewenhielm understand his life 'backwards' by 'recollecting it forward', and that is a retrospective view that transforms him when the young passionate lover and foreteller is resurrected. The story about the stork that Dinesen re-tells in the paragraph 'Livets Veje' in *Den afrikanske Farm* (Blixen 1937: 208–10) is another way of illustrating this and can be regarded as a paraphrase of Kierkegaard's famous quote.[22] As the quote points out, it is not possible to get the whole picture when a person is still alive (even though second meetings do help) since life is moving forward, thus constantly changing the whole picture until the person is finally dead. That is, however, a condition that art is not subjected to. When an artist is creating a story, he or she is able to develop the characters and look back on the plot in 'complete peace' and get the whole picture so it can be 'fully understood'. This is the important advantage stories have over lived life.

Notes to Chapter 15

1. Written 1961, published posthumously in Danish in 1975, and the original English version in 1977 (Selborn 1974: 189).
2. The tale in English, 'Babette's Feast', was first published in *The Ladies' Home Journal* in June 1950. Selborn points out that Dinesen made an effort to redevelop the Danish version that had been translated by Jørgen Claudi to the version we know from *Skæbne-Anekdoter* (1958): 'Efter at *Babettes Gæstebud* først havde været oversat til radioen af Jørgen Claudi, nyoversatte Karen Blixen den til dens optagelse i samlingen, og hun udvidede beskrivelsen af rusens virkninger på de fromme brødre og søstre. Hun sagde, det skulle være 'noget vildere' (Selborn 1974: 130) [After *Babette's Feast* had first been translated for radio by Jørgen Claudi, Karen Blixen re-translated it

for its inclusion in the collection, and she expanded the description of the intoxication's effects on the pious brothers and sisters. She said that it should be 'somewhat wilder'].

3. This has also been pointed out by Selboe (Selboe 1996: 112–14).

4. The spelling of the name is different from the Danish version: Löwenhielm.

5. Blixen 1958: 58–59.

6. Blixen 1958: 60.

7. Blixen 1958: 63.

8. This behavior is also depicted in the following passages when 1) Loewenhielm mentions 'Cliquot 1860' and 'His neighbor looked at him kindly, smiled at him and made a remark about the weather' (Dinesen 1958: 50) and 2) when he mentions *cailles en sarcophage* and his fellow Berlevaagian diner replies: '"Yes, Yes, certainly. What else would it be?"' (Dinesen 1958: 51).

9. Blixen 1958: 61.

10. The Berlevaagians are unable to recognize Loewenhielms intoxication: 'They were used to seeing sailors and vagabonds dead drunk with the crass gin of the country, but they did not recognize in a warrior and courtier the intoxication brought about by the noblest wine of the world' (Dinesen 1958: 51).

11. Blixen 1958: 66–67.

12. Blixen 1958: 68.

13. Blixen 1958: 70.

14. Blixen 1958: 52.

15. Blixen 1958: 63–64.

16. Blixen 1958: 68.

17. Blixen 1958: 68.

18. Blixen 1958: 46–47.

19. Blixen 1958: 65.

20. We find this sentence echoed in the conversation that Ole Wivel had with Dinesen on her birthday 17 April 1950 right after she had finished the English version of 'Babette's Feast' that came out in *Ladies' Home Journal* in June 1950. See the quote in Chapter 7, pp. 66–67.

21. Author's translation.

22. This is a story she already mentions in a letter from Africa in 1917 (Blixen 2013: 182–83) and most likely knew from childhood.

CHAPTER 16

❖

Conclusion:
Isak Dinesen and Søren Kierkegaard

An Ethical Aesthete

In 1951 the Danish scholar Ernst Frandsen categorizes Dinesen as an author belonging to the sphere of the aesthetic:

> 'saadan finder den stolte Mand sin Lykke i Fuldbyrdelsen af sin Skæbne.' Ordene angaar hende selv, men de virker, som var de skrevet om Nis Petersen og Kaj Munk. Ikke mindst Kaj Munk! De tilhører alle tre disse stoltes Kompagni. Med Blikket vendt mod Bestemmelsen og de evige Magter, som raader for Bestemmelsen, har disse tre hvælvet en Regnbue af Fantasi over Tredivernes graa Jævnhed. De har tildelt Perioden Storhed, Nis Petersen og Kaj Munk fra et religiøst Stadium, Karen Blixen fra et æstetisk. Det etiske som i Søren Kierkegaards Enten-Eller er det omstændeligste for ikke at sige det kedeligste, har de overladt til Samtiden og især den nærmeste Eftertid. (Frandsen and Johansen 1951: 22)

> ['this is how the proud man finds his happiness in the fulfillment of his destiny.' The words refer directly to her, but they seem as if they were written about Nis Petersen and Kaj Munk. Especially Kaj Munk! All three belong to this proud company. With their gaze turned toward destiny and the eternal powers that offer counsel for destiny, these three have vaulted a rainbow of fantasy over the grey uniformity of the thirties. They have bestowed greatness on the period, Nis Petersen and Kaj Munk from a religious stage; Karen Blixen from an aesthetic. They have left the ethical, which in Søren Kierkegaard's *Either/Or* is the most tedious as well as the most boring, to the present and especially to the immediate future.]

In a letter to Aage Henriksen about her father from 1 April 1956 Dinesen classifies her father and herself as 'Æstetikere' [aesthetes] but not in the negative Kierkegaardian sense of the word:[1]

> Den Egenskab, som tiest anerkendes hos ham er *esprit*, en anden er Lethed, — han er en Feinschmecker, en *élégant* i selve sit Væsen en Æstetiker. Det kan være, at noget af min Interesse for Emnet skyldes dette, at jeg mener, Faders Skæbne kuriøst nok i nogen Grad er blevet gentaget i min egen. Jeg tror ikke at Fader var 'Æstetiker' mere, end jeg selv er det. Jeg mener, at selv om han ikke var Alvorsmand, var der Ting som for ham, mulig paa en anden Maade end for andre Mennesker, var Alvor. (Blixen 1996b: 320–21)

[The quality most often recognized in him is *esprit,* another is lightness — he is a connoisseur, an *élégant,* in his very being, an aesthete. Perhaps some of my interest in the subject is that I think father's destiny, curiously enough, has to some extent been repeated in my own. I do not think father was an 'aesthete', any more than I am. I mean that even though he was not a serious man, there were things that, for him, perhaps in a way different than for other people, were serious.]

Dinesen's life-view is in its core Pagan and Greek. It is 'ateistisk-heroisk' [atheist-heroic] as Ole Wivel describes it (see quotation in Chapter 7, pp. 66–67), and it also includes seriousness, but not in the Christian sense of the word. It celebrates the laws of virtue, pride, honour and glory. This also fits the British gentleman ideals of her father (and her brother), which acknowledges fearlessness, sensuousness, audacity, creativity and humour as the virtues that a human being should be judged by. We also find the atheist-heroic life-view in my reading of 'Babette's Feast' where Dinesen reorders Kierkegaard's three stages and places the aesthetic as the highest stage above the ethical and the religious, which, as she herself points out in the letter to Aage Henriksen, does not make her an 'Æstetiker' [aesthete] in the negative Kierkegaardian sense of the word, but in the atheist-heroic sense I have outlined above. Her materialist, concrete, and upbuilding approach to the aesthetic is, just like her approach to the concept of irony, far more nuanced and positive, compared to the view we find presented in Kierkegaard's works.

A Strong Poet

In a passage in 'Echoes'[2] from *Last Tales*, Pellegrina very clearly articulates Dinesen's rhetorical strategy with regard to repetition, which, as I have already pointed out, has clear ties to Høffding's notion of 'artistic irony', defined as: 'an artistic irony is provided that connects precisely to art's great task, to offer concrete and individual portraits of characters and destinies, not abstractions and utopias' (see Chapter 3, pp. 28–31):

> 'Alas, Niccolo,' she said. 'Life is hard, and sad things happen round us in the world. Yet I can tell you that the Lord likes a jest, and that a *da capo* — which means: taking the same thing over again — is a favorite jest of his. He may have wanted, now, a sailor stuck on the top of a mountain, such as was Noah, whose name begins with the same letter as yours.' (Dinesen 1957: 160)[3]

When we substitute God with Dinesen, we understand her rhetorical strategy with regard to repetition and Kierkegaard, as I have also shown in the analysis of 'Babette's Feast'. Her stories are concrete, materialistic counter-stories to biblical narratives and to Kierkegaard's theoretical-idealistic works, which she at the same time, when she as a poet takes on the role of God, subjects to irony and parody since we in the '*da capo*' (repetition) of Kierkegaard's works also find a (hidden) 'jest' behind the seemingly serious surface, which then again generates seriousness (Høffding's 'great irony'). Through inversion of characters, plots and major ideas from the great works of world literature, Dinesen wants to prove a point. She wants to show the Loewenhielms of this world (the connoisseurs of literature) that she has read and understood these authors of world literature and their works and has another — truly original — view on the topics and characters than what is suggested in them.

This strategy, the ironical counter-stories — with the audacious gender subversions as the most consistent and poignant element — became Dinesen's unique way of joining the pedigree of world literature as a female writer. But on a more general level, this way of dealing with most of her precursors, for example William Shakespeare, Johann Wolfgang Goethe,[4] Sigrid Undset, Thomas Mann,[5] and Søren Kierkegaard — also shows that Dinesen is a strong poet engaging in the creative dialectic of 'Anxiety of Influence' as I have previously mentioned. Dinesen 1) makes a 'swerve' away from her precursors that Bloom calls 'Clinamen' and 2) executes what he calls 'Tessera':

> which is completion and antithesis; I take the word not from mosaic-making, where it is still used, but from the ancient mystery cults, where it meant a token of recognition, the fragment say of a small pot which with the other fragments would re-constitute the vessel. A poet antithetically 'completes' his precursor, by so reading the parent-poem as to retain its terms but to mean them in another sense, as though the precursor had failed to go far enough. (Bloom 1973: 14)

With her self-proclaimed Luciferian right to poke fun at everything, Dinesen goes as far as she can with regard to Kierkegaard and 'tessera' (completion and antithesis). But as we have seen, it is not just to pervert and make a fool out of him, since she in her 'serious parodies' to use Genette's term — based on his works — delivers new, astute and profound insights into human nature that Kierkegaard as a Christian, and a man of the first part of the nineteenth century, was not able to arrive at. All in all, we can juxtapose Dinesen's view on Kierkegaard, Christianity, and gender in relation to Kierkegaard in these pairs of opposites:

Kierkegaard — Dinesen
Christianity — Atheism
Religious — Aesthetic
Philosopher — Artist
Theoretical — Pragmatic
Spiritual — Sensuousness
Man — Woman
God — Devil

Thus, Dinesen's oeuvre can be regarded as a subversion of what has traditionally been valued as the highest within Christian Western culture, which is the left component in the above list of pairs, belonging to the male sphere. She also shows how this sphere derives from the materialistic phenomena, from 'nature', which is the primary, not something that is secondary and has to be suppressed as 'being-for-other'. In Dinesen's world it is: 'Reversed. In this pattern the road runs the other way. And runs on' (Dinesen 1958: 166). Thus, Dinesen can be regarded as the female, subversive correlative to her great male precursor and fellow countryman Søren Kierkegaard — even his nemesis.

Dinesen is, however, not alone in world literature when using this polemical strategy of serious parody. We just have to think of Cervantes, Shakespeare, Laurence Sterne, Heinrich Heine, Thomas Mann, and James Joyce to mention a few.[6] One might even go as far as to claim that 'serious parody' as defined by Genette is in fact a significant trait for most writers belonging to the Western canon, and maybe a sort of inbuilt mechanism that only strong poets are able to muster: 'My concern is only with strong poets, major figures with the persistence to wrestle with their strong precursors, even to death. Weaker talents idealize' (Bloom 1973: 5). And as we have seen in this book, Dinesen's wrestling-match with one of the greatest philosophers in the world, her precursor Søren Kierkegaard, certainly places her in the category of 'strong poets'.

Notes to Chapter 16

1. Henriksen was thinking about writing a book about Dinesen's father at that time. An idea he quickly abandoned when Dinesen started meddling and tried to guide and control the project.
2. Notice the title and the relation it has to repetition.
3. Blixen 1957: 143.
4. Bjørnvig recalls Dinesen characterizing Goethe in this less flattering way compared to Heine: 'Da hun ønskede at høre digtet, som hun ikke kendte, spurgte jeg, hvor Goethes værker stod. Hun svarede, at dem havde hun ikke, fordi hun ikke forstod og ikke kunne læse tysk. Det passede ikke ganske, for hun kunne citere adskilleligt på tysk, f.eks. hele passager af Heine, som hun elskede og satte langt over Goethe, mens jeg havde det omvendt. "Deres Goethe", som hun drillede mig med at sige, "denne petit maitre"' (Bjørnvig 1974: 56) [When she wanted to hear the poem that she did not know, I asked her where she kept Goethe's works. She replied that she did not have them, because she did not understand and could not read German. That did not seem right, because she could quote several things in German, for example entire passages by Heine, whom she loved and placed far above Goethe, whereas I felt the opposite. "Your Goethe", she would tease me by saying, "that *petit maître*"'].
5. Aage Henriksen about Dinesen: 'hun kom nu ind på Goethes og Thomas Manns værker om Faust, som hun fandt sørgelige og uværdige. Goethe, sagde hun, og hun talte altid om Goethe som om en stor og besværlig nabo, med hvem hun evigt lå i grænsestridigheder: "Goethe var ikke fri. Shakespeare var det"' (Henriksen 1965: 87) [She started talking about Goethe and Thomas Mann's works about Faust, which she found deplorable and undignified. Goethe, she said, and she always spoke of him as a big problematic neighbour with whom she had an ongoing border dispute: "Goethe was not free. Shakespeare was"] (author's translation). In a letter from Africa she also writes that she hates Strindberg (Blixen 2013: 1209) and we find numerous passages where she outlines how she profoundly disagrees with Sigrid Undset (for the long list of page numbers mentioning Undset see Blixen 2013: 2015).
6. Both Joyce and Mann are placed in the category of 'serious parody' by Genette (Genette 1997: 26).

BIBLIOGRAPHY

❖

ANDERSEN, HANS CHRISTIAN. 1847. 'Skyggen', in *H. C. Andersen* (Copenhagen: Gyldendal; repr. 1970).

ANZ, HEINRICH. 1999. '"Seinerzeit eine Art makabre Modefigur". Aspekte der Wirkungs-geschichte Søren Kierkegaards in der skandinavischen Literatur', in *Kierkegaard Studies Yearbook 1999*, ed. by N. J. Cappelørn and Hermann Deuser (Berlin/New York: De Gruyter), pp. 204–19.

——2010. 'Erbauliche Geschichten. Zum Wirkungsgeschichtlichen Gespräch zwischen Karen Blixen und Søren Kierkegaard', in *At være sig selv nærværende. Festskrift til Niels Jørgen Cappelørn*, ed. by Joakim Garff, Ettore Rocca and Pia Søltoft (Copenhagen: Kristeligt Dagblads forlag), pp. 420–29.

BAUDELAIRE, CHARLES. 1857. *Les Fleurs du mal* (Paris: Poulet-Malassis et de Broise).

BEHRENDT, POUL. 2003. 'An Essay in the Art of Writing Posthumous Papers: the Great Earthquake Revisited', in *Kierkegaard Studies Yearbook 2003*, ed. by N. J. Cappelørn, H. Deuser, and J. Stewart (Berlin/New York: De Gruyter), pp. 48–109.

——2004. 'Det pseudonyme firma: om juridiske fiktioner — et dobbeltportræt', *Fønix*, 28 (3/4), 36–57.

——2007. *Den hemmelige note* (Copenhagen: Gyldendal).

——2010. 'Efterskrift. Dansk Genesis', in *Karen Blixen. Værker. Vinter-Eventyr* (Copenhagen: DSL/Gyldendal), pp. 403–81.

——2011. 'Juryens veto — en boghistorie om det skjulte paradigme under deklasseringen af 'Skibsdrengens Fortælling' i de amerikanske udgaver af Isak Dinesen: *Winter's Tales*', *Spring*, 30: 164–86.

——2014. 'Dobbelteksistensen. Firmaet Dinesen & Blixen i det 21. århundrede', *Kritik*, 210: 23–42.

BENEVENTO, BARBARA T. & SIPSKI, MARCA L. 2002. 'Neurogenic Bladder, Neurogenigc Bowel, and Sexual Dysfunction in People With Spinal Cord Injury', *Physical Therapy. Journal of the American Physical Therapy Association*, 82 (6): 601–12.

BJØRNVIG, THORKILD. 1974. *Pagten. Mit venskab med Karen Blixen* (Copenhagen: Gyldendal).

BLICHER, STEEN STEENSEN. 1828. 'Sildig Opvaagnen', in *Noveller* (Copenhagen: Dansklærer-forenings Forlag; repr. 1992).

BLIXEN. KAREN. 1923–24. 'Moderne ægteskab og andre betragtninger' in *Karen Blixen. Samlede essays* (Copenhagen: Gyldendal; repr. 1997), pp. 7–55.

——1926. *Sandhedens Hævn* (Copenhagen: Gyldendal; repr. 1998).

——1937. *Den afrikanske Farm* (Copenhagen: DSL/Gyldendal; repr. 2007).

——1942. *Vinter-Eventyr* (Copenhagen: DSL/Gyldendal; repr. 2010).

——1950. 'Daguerrotypier', in *Karen Blixen. Samlede essays* (Copenhagen: Gyldendal; repr. 1997), pp. 173–212.

——1951. 'Til fire Kultegninger', in *Karen Blixens tegninger*, published by Frans Lasson (Copenhagen: Forening for Boghaandværk; repr. 1969).

——1953. 'En Baaltale med 14 Aars Forsinkelse', in *Karen Blixen. Samlede essays* (Copen-hagen: Gyldendal; repr. 1997), pp. 213–31.

——1954. 'Fra lægmand til lægmand', in *Karen Blixen. Samlede essays* (Copenhagen: Gyldendal; repr. 1997), pp. 232–49.

——1957. *Sidste Fortællinger* (Copenhagen: Gyldendal).

——1958. *Skæbne-Anekdoter* (Copenhagen: Gyldendal).

——1960. *Skygger på Græsset* (Copenhagen: Gyldendal).

——1996A. *Karen Blixen i Danmark: Breve 1931–62*. Vol. I ed. by Frans Lasson and Tom Engelbrecht (Copenhagen: Gyldendal).

——1996B. *Karen Blixen i Danmark: Breve 1931–62*. Vol. II ed. by Frans Lasson and Tom Engelbrecht (Copenhagen: Gyldendal).

——2008. *Karneval og andre fortællinger*. Partly a reprint of 'Efterladte Fortællinger' 1975. Published by Frans Lasson (Copenhagen: Gyldendal).

——2013. *Karen Blixen i Afrika. En brevsamling. 1914–31*. Vols. I–IV, ed. by Marianne Juhl and Marianne Wirenfeldt Asmussen (Copenhagen: Gyldendal).

BLOOM, HAROLD. 1973. *The Anxiety of Influence*. 2nd edition 1997 (Oxford: Oxford University Press).

BONDESSON, PIA. 1982. *Karen Blixens bogsamling på Rungstedlund* (Copenhagen: Gyldendal).

BRAAD THOMSEN, CHRISTIAN. 2010. *Boganis Gæstebud. Fadersporet i Karen Blixens liv og Værk* (Copenhagen: Tiderne Skifter).

BRANDES, GEORG. 1877. *Søren Kierkegaard. En kritisk Fremstilling i Grundrids.* (Copenhagen: Gyldendalske Boghandels Forlag).

——1890. *Hovedstrømninger. Det 19de Aarhundredes Litteratur. Det unge Tyskland* (Copenhagen: Gyldendalske Boghandels Forlag; repr. 1898).

——1923–26. *Georg Brandes' dagbøger 1860–1927*. Volume containing the diaries 1923–26. The Royal Danish Library <http://www.kb.dk/da/kb/nb/ha/web_udstil/gb_dagbog.html> [accessed 29 August 2015].

BUK-SWIENTY, TOM. 2014. *Kaptajn Dinesen — Til døden os skiller* (Copenhagen: Gyldendal).

BUNCH, MADS. 2012. 'Flappers and Macabre Dandies. Karen Blixen's "Carnival" in the light of Søren Kierkegaard', *Scandinavica*, 50 (2): 74–109.

——2013A. *The Devil's Advocate. Reading Blixen in the Light of Kierkegaard*. Ph.D. Thesis. Department of Nordic Studies and Linguistics, University of Copenhagen.

——2013B. '"Ehrengard", Kierkegaard, and the Secret Note', *Scandinavian Studies*, 84 (4): 489–523.

——2014. 'Karen Blixen's "The Poet" and Søren Kierkegaard's *Gjentagelsen*', *European Journal of Scandinavian Studies*, 44 (2): 165–85.

BRAAD THOMSEN, CHRISTIAN. 2010. *Boganis' Gæstebud. Fadersporet i Karen Blixens liv og værk* (Copenhagen: Tiderne skifter).

BRUUN ANDERSEN, K. 1950. *Søren Kierkegaard og Kritikeren P. L. Møller* (Copenhagen: Munksgaard).

DAHL, ELLEN. 1932. *Introductioner*, published under the pseudonym Paracelsus (Copenhagen: C. A. Reitzels Forlag).

DINESEN, ISAK. 1934. *Seven Gothic Tales* (New York: Harrison Smith and Robert Haas).

——1935. *Syv fantastiske Fortællinger* (Copenhagen: DSL/Gyldendal; repr. 2012).

——1937. *Out of Africa* (London: Penguin; repr. 2001).

——1942. *Winter's Tales* (New York: Random House; reprint, First Vintage International Edition, 1993).

——1957. *Last Tales* (New York: Random House).

——1958. *Anecdotes of Destiny* (New York: Random House; repr. as *Anecdotes of Destiny and Ehrengard*, First Vintage International Edition, 1993).

——1963. 'Ehrengard' (New York: Random House; repr. as *Anecdotes of Destiny and Ehrengard*, First Vintage International Edition, 1993).

—— 1977. 'Carnival', in *Carnival: Entertainments and Posthumous Tales* (Chicago: University of Chicago Press; reprint, paperback edition 1979).

—— 1960. *Shadows on the Grass* (New York: Random House, 1961 edition).

—— 1979. 'Oration at a Bonfire, 14 Years Late'. In *Daguerreotypes and Other Essays*, trans. by P. M. Mitchell and W. D. Paden (Chicago: Chicago University Press).

—— 1981. *Isak Dinesen. Letters from Africa 1914–1931*, trans. by Anne Born (Chicago: University of Chicago Press).

—— 1986A. 'The Revenge of Truth: A Marionette Comedy', trans. by Donald Hannah, *Performing Arts Journal*, 10 (2): 107–27.

—— 1986B. *On Modern Marriage and Other Observations*, translated by Anne Born (New York: St. Martin's Press).

EISSLER, KURT ROBERT. 1963. *Goethe: a psychoanalytic study, 1775–1786* (Detroit: Wayne State University Press).

EWALD, JOHANNES. 1773. *Balders død* (Copenhagen: Dansk Selskab for Musikforskning, repr. 1980).

FRANDSEN, ERNST and NIELS KAAS JOHANSEN, eds. 1951. *Danske Digtere i det Tyvende Aarhundrede* (Copenhagen: G. E. C. Gads Forlag).

GENETTE, GÉRARD. 1997 (1982): *Palimpsests*, trans. by Channa Newman and Claude Doubinsky (Nebraska: University of Nebraska Press).

GIULIANO, FRANCOIS et al. 1999. 'Randomized trial of sildenafil for the treatment of erectile dysfunction in spinal cord injury', *Annals of Neurology*, 46 (1), 15–21.

GLICK, ELISA. 2009. *Materializing Queer Desire. Oscar Wilde to Andy Warhol* (New York: State University of New York Press).

GLIENKE, BERNHARD. 1986. *Fatale Präzedenz. Karen Blixens Mythologie* (Neumünster: Karl Wachholtz Verlag).

GOETHE, JOHANN WOLFGANG. 1774. *Die Leiden des jungen Werthers* (Leipzig: Weygandsche Buchhandlung).

—— 1832. *Faust. Zweiter Teil.* The Gutenberg EBook of Faust. January 26, 2010 (updated May, 2012). Produced by Michael Pullen. <http://www.gutenberg.org/cache/epub/2230/pg2230-images.html> [Accessed 29 August 2016].

—— 2003. *Faust: Part Two.* Translated by A. S. Kline (2003). Available online: <http://www.poetryintranslation.com/PITBR/German/FaustIIActIIScenesItoIV.htm> [Accessed 29 August 2016].

GOLDSCHMIDT, MEÏR ARON. 1865. *Breve fra Choleratiden, indeholdende en lille Begivenhed* (Copenhagen: Forlaget Christian Steen & Søn), pp. 14–78, available online: <http://adl.dk/adl_pub/pg/cv/ShowPgImg.xsql?p_udg_id=345&p_sidenr=14&hist=&nnoc=adl_pub> [accessed 10 October 2015].

GUTZKOW, KARL. 1835. *Wally, die Zweiflerin* (Mannheim: Löwenthal).

HEEDE, DAG. 2001. *Det umenneskelige. Analyser af seksualitet, køn og identitet hos Karen Blixen* (Odense: Odense Universitetsforlag).

HENRIKSEN, AAGE. 1954. *Søren Kierkegaards romaner* (Copenhagen: Gyldendal).

—— 1952. 'Karen Blixen og Marionetterne', in Det guddommelige barn og andre essays om Karen Blixen (Copenhagen: Gyldendal; repr. 1965), pp 9–32.

—— 1956. *Guder og galgenfugle* (Oslo: Gyldendal).

—— 1965. *Det guddommelige barn og andre essays om Karen Blixen* (Copenhagen: Gyldendal).

—— 1985. 'Karen Blixen. Aage Henriksen. En brevveksling 1952–1961', in Blixeniana (1985): 91–267.

—— 1998. *Litterært testamente* (Copenhagen: Gyldendal).

—— 2004. *Den eneste ene og andre essays* (Copenhagen: Gyldendal).

HØFFDING, HARALD. 1892. *Søren Kierkegaard som Filosof* (Ringkøbing: Det Danske Forlag; repr. 1989).

—— 1916. *Den store Humor.* 2nd edition 1923 (Copenhagen: Gyldendalske Boghandel).

—— 1923. 'Pascal og Kierkegaard', *Tilskueren*, 1923, (1. Halvbind): 412–34.

JENSEN, BENEDICTE. 1953. 'Med Karen Blixen i Grækenland og Rom. Et dagbogsbrev til Thorkild Bjørnvig fra sommeren 1951', *Blixeniana* (1985): 268–310.

JESSEN, MADS SOHL. 2010. *Tyvesprogets mester: Kierkegaards skjulte satire over Heiberg i Gjentagelsen.* Ph.D. Thesis. Faculty of Humanities, University of Copenhagen, Denmark.

KIERKEGAARD, SØREN. 1841. *Om Begrebet Ironie*, in *Søren Kierkegaards Skrifter* 1, 1997, ed. by Niels J. Cappelørn and others (Copenhagen: Gads forlag).

—— 1843A. *Enten — Eller Første Deel*, in *Søren Kierkegaards Skrifter* 2, 1997, ed. by Niels J. Cappelørn and others (Copenhagen: Gads forlag).

—— 1843B. *Enten — Eller. Anden Deel*, in *Søren Kierkegaards Skrifter* 3, 1997, ed. by Niels J. Cappelørn and others (Copenhagen: Gads forlag).

—— 1843C. *Gjentagelsen*, in *Søren Kierkegaards Skrifter* 4, 1998, ed. by Niels J. Cappelørn and others (Copenhagen: Gads forlag).

—— 1843D. *Frygt og Bæven*, in *Søren Kierkegaards Skrifter* 4, 1998, ed. by Niels J. Cappelørn and others (Copenhagen: Gads forlag).

—— 1843E. *Journalen,* in *Søren Kierkegaards Skrifter* 18, 2001, ed. by Niels J. Cappelørn and others (Copenhagen: Gads forlag).

—— 1844. *Begrebet Angest*, in *Søren Kierkegaards Skrifter* 4, 1998, ed. by Niels J. Cappelørn and others (Copenhagen: Gads forlag).

—— 1845. *Stadier paa Livets Vei*, in *Søren Kierkegaards Skrifter* 6, 1999, ed. by Niels J. Cappelørn and others (Copenhagen: Gads forlag).

—— 1846A. *En literair Anmeldelse*, in *Søren Kierkegaards Skrifter* 8, 2004, ed. by Niels J. Cappelørn and others (Copenhagen: Gads forlag).

—— 1846B. *Journalen. NB:34*, in *Søren Kierkegaards Skrifter* 20, 2002, ed. by Niels J. Cappelørn and others (Copenhagen: Gads forlag).

—— 1848. *Synspunktet for min Forfatter-Virksomhed*, in *Søren Kierkegaards Skrifter* 16, 2012, ed. by Niels J. Cappelørn and others (Copenhagen: Gads Forlag)

—— 1854. *Journalen. NB33: 24*, in *Søren Kierkegaards Skrifter* 26, 2009, ed. by Niels J. Cappelørn and others (Copenhagen: Gads forlag).

—— 1978. *Two Ages. The Age of Revolution and the Present Age. A Literary Review*, trans. by Howard V. & Edna H. Hong (Princeton: Princeton University Press; repr. 2009).

—— 1980. *Concept of Anxiety*, trans. by Reinar Thomte (Princeton: Princeton University Press; repr. 2013).

—— 1983A. *Repetition*, in *Repetition and Fear and Trembling*, trans. by Howard V. & Edna H. Hong (Princeton: Princeton University Press; repr. 2013).

—— 1983B. *Fear and Trembling*, in *Repetition and Fear and Trembling*, trans. by Howard V. & Edna H. Hong (Princeton: Princeton University Press; repr. 2013).

—— 1987A. *Either/Or. Part I*, trans. by Howard V. & Edna H. Hong (Princeton: Princeton University Press; repr. 2013).

—— 1987B. *Either/Or. Part II*, trans. by Howard V. & Edna H. Hong (Princeton: Princeton University Press; repr. 2013).

—— 1988. *Stages on Life's Way*, trans. by Howard V. & Edna H. Hong (Princeton: Princeton University Press; repr. 2013).

—— 1992. *The Concept of Irony*, trans. by Howard V. & Edna H. Hong (Princeton: Princeton University Press; repr. 2013).

—— 1998. *The point of view, on my work as an author, the point of view for my work as an author, armed neutrality*, trans. by Howard V. & Edna H. Hong (Princeton: Princeton University Press; repr. 2009).

—— 2008. *Kierkegaard's Journals and Notebooks.* Journals EE-KK. Vol. 2, 2008, ed. by Niels J. Cappelørn and others (Princeton and Oxford: Princeton University Press).

KNUDSEN, JØRGEN. 2004. *Georg Brandes. Uovervindelig taber. II Volume* (Copenhagen: Gyldendal).

KONDRUP, JOHNNY. 2011. 'Replik om forførelse. Karen Blixens "Ehrengard"', *Danske Studier* (2011): 89–110.

KRISTENSEN, SVEN MØLLER. 1981. 'Karen Blixen og Georg Brandes', *Blixeniana* (1981): 177–85.

LANGBAUM, ROBERT. 1964. *The Gayety of Vision: A Study of Isak Dinesen's Art* (London: Chatto & Windus).

LASSON, FRANS. 2008. 'Efterskrift'. In *Karneval og andre fortællinger*, by Karen Blixen, (Copenhagen: Gyldendal), pp. 475–82.

MAKARUSHKA, IRENA. 1992. 'Reflections on the 'Other' in Dinesen, Kierkegaard and

NIETZSCHE'. In *Kierkegaard on Art and Communication*, edited by George Pattison, pp. 150–59 (New York: St. Martin's Press).

MONGA, MANOJ et al. 1999. 'Male infertility and erectile dysfunction in spinal cord injury: A review', *Archives of Physical Medicine and Rehabilitation*, 80 (10): 1331–39.

MØLLER, P. M. 1843. *Skrifter i Udvalg 1–2*. Reprinted 1930. Published by Vilh. Andersen (Copenhagen: J. Jørgensen & Co. Ivar Jantzen). <http://adl.dk/adl_pub/pg/cv/ShowPgText.xsql?nnoc=adl_pub&p_udg_id=49&p_sidenr=291> [accessed 29 August 2016].

NILSSON, LARS. 2004. *Om Isak Dinesens "Drømmerne"* (Aarhus: Systime).

ØHRGAARD, PER. 1999. *Goethe. Et essay* (Copenhagen: Gyldendal).

ROHDE, PETER P. 1953. *Søren Kierkegaards dagbøger*, selected diary entries by Peter P. Rohde (Copenhagen: Dansklærerforeningens Forlag).

—— 1960. *The Diary of Søren Kierkegaard*, selected diary entries by Peter P. Rohde (New York: Citadel Press).

SELBOE, TONE. 1996. *Kunst og erfaring. En studie i Karen Blixens forfatterskab* (Odense: Syddansk Universitetsforlag).

—— 2008. 'The Infallible Rule of the Irregular. Time and Narrative in Blixen's Tales', in *Karen Blixen/Isak Dinesen/Tania Blixen. Eine international Erzählerin der Moderne*, Berliner Berträge zur Skandinavistik Band 12, edited by Heike Peetz, Stefanie von Schnurbein and Kirsten Wechsel (Berlin: Humboldt-Universität zu Berlin Nordeuropa Inst.), pp. 13–17.

SELBORN, CLARA. 1974. *Notater om Karen Blixen* (Copenhagen: Gyldendal; repr. 2008).

STAUBRAND, JENS and K. WEISMANN. 2013. 'Søren Kierkegaard's sygdom og død', *Bibliotek for Læger*, 205 (3): 314–26.

STAUBRAND, JENS. 2014. *Søren Kierkegaard's struggle to live at Frederiks Hospital in Copenhagen* (Copenhagen: SK Books).

STECHER, MARIANNE T. 2014. *The Creative Dialectic in Karen Blixen's Essays. On Gender, Nazi Germany, and Colonial Desire* (Copenhagen: Museum Tusculanum Press).

SØRENSEN, IVAN Ž. 2002. *'Gid De havde set mig dengang'. Et essay om Karens Blixens heltinder og Tizians gudinder* (Copenhagen: Gyldendal).

TJØNNELAND, EIVIND. 1996. 'Vanens virkelighet som gjentagelsens mulighet. Kierkegaard med menneskelig ansigt', in *Innøvelse i Kierkegaard. Fire essays*, edited by Joakim Garff et al. (Oslo: Cappelen Damm Akademisk), pp. 75–88.

TØJNER, POUL ERIK. 1996. 'Stilens tenker', in *Innøvelse i Kierkegaard. Fire essays*, edited by Joakim Garff et al. (Oslo: Cappelen Damm Akademisk), pp. 13–71.

WIVEL, OLE. 1972. *Romance for valdhorn. Erindringsmotiver* (Copenhagen: Gyldendal).

INDEX OF NAMES AND TEXTS

❖

SUBJECT INDEX

❖

Lightning Source UK Ltd.
Milton Keynes UK
UKOW07n2319060617

302805UK00008B/52/P